TEST YOUR C PROGRAMMING SKILLS

FOR

(All Indian Universities, Engineering and Technical Colleges and Institutions, IIT's and IT Organizations)

Ikvinderpal Singh

Khanna Book Publishing Co. (P) Ltd.
Delhi

TEST YOUR C PROGRAMMING SKILLS
Ikvinderpal Singh

ISBN: 978-93-80016-25-2

First Edition 2011

Published by:
Khanna Book Publishing Co. (P) Ltd.
4C/4344, Ansari Road, Darya Ganj, New Delhi-110 002
Phone: 011-23244448 Telefax: 011-23244447
E-mail: contact@khannabooks.com
Website: www.khannabooks.com

Regd. Off: 1694-95, 1st Floor, Nai Sarak, Delhi-110006 (India)
Phone: 011-23283211 Telefax: 011-23256658

Cover Design & Layout by
Limited Colors, Delhi

Printed in India by:
S.P.S. Printers & Binders, Delhi

Dedicated to
Jasjit Singh and Sarabjit Singh

"The C language is like a carving knife: simple, sharp, and extremely useful in skilled hands. Like any sharp tool, C can injure people who don't know how to handle it. This Book shows some of the ways C can injure the unwary, and how to avoid injury."

Preface

The C language and its typical implementations are designed to be used easily by experts. The language is terse and expressive. There are few restrictions to keep the user from blundering. A user who has blundered is often rewarded by an effect that is not obviously related to the cause. In this book, you will look at some of these unexpected rewards. Because they are unexpected, it may well be impossible to classify them completely. Nevertheless, we have made a rough effort to do so by looking at what has to happen in order to run a C program.

We assume the reader has at least a passing acquaintance with the C language.

Chapter 1, 2, 3 and 4 follows the program as the compiler groups its tokens into declarations, operators and expressions, and control statements.

Chapter 5 and 6 looks at the problems that occur in arrays and strings.

Chapter 7 recognizes that a C program is often made out of several parts that are compiled separately and bound together.

Chapter 8 shows the use of storage classes in C language.

Chapter 9 deals with misconceptions of meaning: things that happen while the program is actually running. How memory should be allocated to variables? Where the variables have to store in memory? Find the address of memory variable.

Chapter 10 describes the various tough nuts of structures and unions. It also covers declaration types of structure and pointers, structure and array, structure and function and use of bit fields.

Chapter 11 examines the relationship between our programs and the files they use for storage purpose

Chapter 12 we note that the program we write is not really the program we run; the pre-processor has gotten at it first.

At the last appendixes are given to summarize the complete Description of C programming techniques.

This book can be used by a wide reader audience, ranging from beginning programmers to practicing professionals. This book includes **code snippets, fill in the blanks, true or false and objective type questions** for each and every topic of C language.

Due to the growing influence of IT in several fields, C programming skills are highly sought after. All aptitude tests in the recruitment process include testing C skills. This book will be an excellent guide for aspiring IT professionals and a valuable resource bank, for IT companies, to frame entrance tests and technical interviews.

Suggestions for improvement of the book will be gratefully accepted for future editions.

Ikvinderpal Singh

Acknowledgement

I express our deep gratitude to Dr. Karanjit Singh Kahlon, Professor, Department of Computer Science & Engineering, G.N.D.U., Dr. Hardeep Singh, Professor, Department of Computer Science & Engineering, G.N.D.U., Dr. Gurvinder Singh, Reader, DCSE, GNDU, Amritsar, Mr. Avtar Singh Sandhu, Mr. Baljinder Singh, Mr. Jagbir Singh, Mr. Lovedeep Singh and Mr. Sukhwant Singh and our colleagues for their valuable co-operation and guidance. I am grateful to Mr. Puneet Khanna M/s Khanna Book Publishing Co. Pvt. Ltd. for his encouragement and motivation during this project.

Ikvinderpal Singh

Special Thanks

My special thanks go to Dr. Daljit Singh, Principal, Khalsa College, Amritsar for their valuable guidance and timely support during the compilation of this book.

Ikvinderpal Singh

Contents

CHAPTER 1

Getting Started

A. CODE SNIPPETS

Problem 1

Find the output of the following program?

```
#include<stdio.h>
#include<conio.h>
void main( )
{
printf ("%d%d%d%d", 72, 072,0x72,0X72);
getch();
}
```

Output:

```
72 58 114 114
```

Problem 2

Find the output of the following program?

```
#include<stdio.h>
#include<conio.h>
void main( )
{
```

```
printf ("%d % %x", 72,72,72);
getch();
}
```

Output:

```
72 110 48
```

Problem 3

Find the output of the following program?

```
#include<stdio.h>
#include<conio.h>
void main( )
{
printf ("%d %i%i", 72,072,0x72,0X72);
getch();
}
```

Output:

```
72 58 114 114
```

Problem 4

Find the output of the following program?

```
#include<stdio.h>
#include<conio.h>
void main( )
{
printf ("%05d,%5d,%-5d",32,32,32);
getch();
}
```

Output:

```
00032    32 32
```

Problem 5

Which of the operations are INCORRECT?

```
1. int i = 25; i = i % 5;
2. short int j = 255; j = j % 5;
3. long int k = 365L; k = k % 24;
4. float i = 3.14; i = i % 3;
5. double k = 6.24; k = k % 4;
```

Output:

4, 5

Problem 6

Write the statement to print the following values?

```
54.120000 8.480000 7.320000
float i = 54.12;
double j = 8.48;
long double k = 7.32;
```

Output:

```
printf ("%f %lf %Lf", i, j, k);
```

Problem 7

Write the correct representation for a long double constant?

```
1.1.24        2.1.24L
3.1.24f       4.1.24lf
5.1.24LF
```

Output:

2

Problem 8

Find the remainder after dividing 1.44 by 2.4?

```
1. rem = 1.44 % 2.4;
2. rem = modf (1.44, 2.4);
3. rem = fmod (1.44, 2.4);
4. rem = 1.44 mod 2.4;
5. We cannot obtain the remainder in floating point
   division
```

Output:

5

Problem 9

How would you round off a value 2.86 to 3.0 and truncate 5.75 to 5.0?

Output:

```
#include <stdio.h>
void main()
{
float i = 2.86;
float j = 5.75;
printf ("%f %f", ceil (i), floor (j));
getch();
}
```

Problem 10

Find the output of the following program?

```
#include <stdio.h>
#include <conio.h>
void main()
{
float f = 15.20;
printf ("%e", f);
printf ("%f", f);
```

```
printf ("%g", f);
getch();
}
```

Output:

```
1.520000e+01 15.200001 15.2
```

Problem 11

Find the output of the following program?

```
#include <stdio.h>
#include <conio.h>
void main()
{
double d = 1.25;
printf ("%e", d);
printf ("%f", d);
printf ("%g", d);
printf ("%f", d);
getch();
}
```

Output:

```
1.250000e+000 1.250000 1.25 1.250000
```

Problem 12

Find the output of the following program?

```
#include <stdio.h>
#include <conio.h>
void main()
{
float f = 0.2;
if (f < 0.2)
printf ("Avtar");
```

```
else
printf ("Sukhwant");
getch();
}
```

Output:

```
Avtar
```

Problem 13

Find the output of the following program?

```
#include<stdio.h>
#include<conio.h>
void main( )
{
printf
("%6.3f,%06.3f%09.3f,%09.3f,%60f,%6.0f",45.6,45.6,45.6,45.6,45.6,45.6);
getch();
}
```

Output:

```
45.600, 45.600, 00045.600, 45.600,    45,   46
```

Problem 14

Find the output of the following program?

```
#include<stdio.h>
#include<conio.h>
void main( )
{
int a=32768;
unsigned int b = 65536;
printf ("%d%d",a,b);
```

```
getch();
}
```

Output:

```
-32768 0
```

Problem 15

Find the output of the following program?

```
#include<stdio.h>
#include<conio.h>
void main( )
{
int i = 2, j = 3, k, l;
float a, b;
k = i / j * j;
l = j / i * i;
m = i / j * j;
n = j / i * i;
printf("%d %d %f %f", k, l, m, n) ;
getch();
}
```

Output:

```
0 2 0.000000 2.000000
```

Problem 16

Find the output of the following program?

```
#include<stdio.h>
#include<conio.h>
void main( )
{
int i, j;
```

```
i = -2 - - 2;
j = -2 - - (- 2);
printf ( "i = %d \n j = %d", i, j ) ;
getch();
}
```

Output:

```
i = 0
j = -4
```

Problem 17

Check the errors from the following program?

```
#include<stdio.h>
#include<conio.h>
void main( )
{
float i = 3, j = 2;
int k;
k = i % j;
printf ("%d", k );
getch();
}
```

Output:

```
Error.
```

NOTE: Modulus(%) operator cannot be used on floats

Problem 18

Find the output of the following program?

```
#include<stdio.h>
#include<conio.h>
int fun(int);
```

```
int fun1(int);
void main( )
{
int i, j, k = 2;
k *= 3;
j = fun(k);
i = fun1(k);
printf ( "\n%d %d %d", k, j, i);
getch();
}
int temp = 8;
fun(int m)
{
m += -5;
temp -= 4;
return ( m + temp );
}
fun1(int m)
{
m = 1;
temp += m;
return ( m + temp );
}
```

Output:

6 5 6

Problem 19

Find the output of the following program?

```
#include<stdio.h>
#include<conio.h>
```

```
void main( )
{
static int count = 8;
printf ( "\ncount = %d", count- ) ;
if ( count != 0 )
main( );
getch();
}
```

Output:

```
8 7 6 5 4 3 2 1
```

Problem 20

Find the output of the following program?

```
#include<stdio.h>
#include<conio.h>
int fun(int);
void main( )
{
int i, j;
for (i = 1; i < 5; i++)
{
j = fun(i);
printf ("\n%d", j);
}
getch();
}
int fun( int m )
{
static int n = 1;
```

```
int p = 3;
n += m;
return (n + m + p);
}
```

Output:

6 9 13 18

Problem 21

Find the output of the following program?

```
#include<stdio.h>
#include<conio.h>
void main( )
{
char a=128;
unsigned char b = 256;
printf ("%d%d\n",a,b);
getch();
}
```

Output:

-128 0

Problem 22

Check the errors from the following program?

```
#include<stdio.h>
#include<conio.h>
void main( )
{
float a = 3.5e38;
double b=3.5e309;
```

```
printf ("%f%f", a,b);
getch();
}
```

Output:

```
No error
```

Problem 23

Find the output of the following program?

```
#include<stdio.h>
#include<conio.h>
void main( )
{
printf ("%d%c", 'B', 'B');
getch();
}
```

Output:

```
66 B
```

Problem 24

Find the output of the following program?

```
#include<stdio.h>
#include<conio.h>
void main( )
{
printf("char occupies %d bytes\n", sizeof(char));
printf ("int occupies %d bytes \n", sizeof(int));
printf ("float occupies %d bytes", sizeof(float));
getch();
}
```

Output:

```
char occupies 1 bytes
int occupies 2 bytes
float occupies 4 bytes
```

Problem 25

Find the output of the following program?

```
#include<stdio.h>
#include<conio.h>
void main( )
{
printf ("Bytes occupied by '5'=%d\n", sizeof('7'));
printf ("Bytes occupied by 5=%d\n", sizeof(7));
printf ("Bytes occupied by 5.0=%d", sizeof(7.0));
getch();
}
```

Output:

```
Bytes occupied by '5'=1
Bytes occupied by 5=2
Bytes occupied by 5.0=8
```

Problem 26

Find the output of the following program?

```
#include<stdio.h>
#include<conio.h>
void main( )
{
printf ("%d",sizeof('\n'));
getch();
}
```

Output:

```
1
```

Problem 27

Find the output of the following program?

```
#include<stdio.h>
#include<conio.h>
void main( )
{
printf("%d%c");
getch();
}
```

Output:

```
Garbage value
```

Problem 28

Find the output of the following program?

```
#include<stdio.h>
#include<conio.h>
void main( )
{
printf("%d%d%d%d%d\n", sizeof(032), sizeof(0x32),
   sizeof(32), sizeof(32U), sizeof(32L));
getch();
}
```

Output:

```
2 2 2 2 4
8 4 4
```

Problem 29

Find the output of the following program?

```
#include<stdio.h>
#include<conio.h>
void main( )
{
printf ("\nab");
printf ("\bsi");
printf("\rha");
getch();
}
```

Output:

```
hai
```

Problem 30

Find the output of the following program?

```
#include<stdio.h>
#include<conio.h>
void main( )
{
printf("c: \tc\bin");
getch();
}
```

Output:

```
c: in
```

Problem 31

Find the output of the following program?

```
#include<stdio.h>
#include<conio.h>
void main( )
{
```

```
printf("c:\\tc\\bin");
getch();
}
```

Output:

```
c:\tc\bin
```

Problem 32

Find the output of the following program?

```
#include<stdio.h>
#include<conio.h>
float i = 4.5;
float fun(float);
void main( )
{
float y, float fun(float);
i *= 2.0;
j = fun(i);
printf ("\n%f %f", i, j);
getch();
}
float f ( float m )
{
m += 1.3;
i -= 4.5;
return ( m + i );
}
```

Output:

```
4.500000 5.800000
```

Problem 33

Find the output of the following program?

```
#include<stdio.h>
#include<conio.h>
void fun();
void main( )
{
fun( );
fun( );
getch();
}
void fun( )
{
auto int i = 0;
register int j = 0;
static int k = 0;
i++;
j++;
k++;
printf ("\n %d % d %d", i, j, k);
}
```

Output:

```
1 1 1
1 1 2
```

Problem 34

Find the output of the following program?

```
#include<stdio.h>
#include<conio.h>
```

```
int i = 10;
void main( )
{
int i = 30;
{
int i = 50;
printf ( "\n%d", i);
}
printf ("\n%d", i);
getch();
}
```

Output:

```
50
30
```

Problem 35

Check the errors from the following program?

```
#include<stdio.h>
#include<conio.h>
void main( )
{
long num;
num = 5;
printf ("\n%ld", num);
getch();
}
```

Output:

```
No error.
```

Problem 36

Check the errors from the following program?

```
#include<stdio.h>
#include<conio.h>
void main( )
{
char c = 100;
printf ( "\n%d", c);
getch();
}
```

Output:

No error.

Problem 37

Check the errors from the following program?

```
#include<stdio.h>
#include<conio.h>
void main( )
{
unsigned i = 25;
long unsigned j = 25l;
printf ( "\n%lu %u", i, j);
getch();
}
```

Output:

Error.

NOTE: format %lu should be used for j and %u should be used for i.

Problem 38

Check the errors from the following program?

```
#include<stdio.h>
```

```
#include<conio.h>
void main( )
{
long float i = 25.345e454;
unsigned double j = 25;
printf ( "\n%lf %d", i, j);
getch();
}
```

Output:

Error.

NOTE: Format %lf should be used for j.

Problem 39

Check the errors from the following program?

```
#include<stdio.h>
#include<conio.h>
void main( )
{
float i = 25.65;
float *j;
j = &i;
printf ( "\n%f %u", i, j);
getch();
}
```

Output:

No error.

Problem 40

Check the errors from the following program?

```
#include<stdio.h>
```

```
#include<conio.h>
static int j;
void main( )
{
static int k;
printf ("%d %d", j, k);
getch();
}
```

Output:

No error.

Problem 41

Is there any error, in the following code?

```
#include <stdio.h>
#include <conio.h>
void main( )
{
const int i;
i = 12;
printf ("%d", i);
getch();
}
```

Output:

No error

Problem 42

Find the output of the following program?

```
#include <stdio.h>
#include <conio.h>
void main( )
```

```
{
const i = -1;
const j = 2;
printf ("%d %d", i, j);
getch();
}
```

Output:

-1, 2

Problem 43

Find the output of the following program?

```
#include <stdio.h>
#include <conio.h>
void main( )
{
const char *s = "";
char str[] = "Hello";
s = str;
while (*s)
printf ("%c", *s++);
getch();
}
```

Output:

Hello

Problem 44

Find the output of the following program?

```
#include <stdio.h>
#include <conio.h>
int get( );
```

```
void main( )
{
const int i = set( );
printf ("%d", i);
getch();
}
set( )
{
return (15);
}
```

Output:

15

Problem 45

Is there any error, in the following code?

```
#include <stdio.h>
#include <conio.h>
#define I 12
void main( )
{
const int i = 12;
char array [i];
char string[I];
array [0] = string [0] = 'H';
printf ("%c %c", array [0], string[0]);
getch();
}
```

Output:

No error.

Problem 46

Find the output of the following program?

```
#include <stdio.h>
#include <conio.h>
void main( )
{
int i = 12;
const int j = i;
printf ("%d", j);
getch();
}
```

Output:

```
12
```

Problem 47

Check the errors from the following program?

```
#include <stdio.h>
#include <conio.h>
void main( )
{
const int i = 1;
printf ("%d", i++);
getch();
}
```

Output:

```
Error.
```

NOTE: Const value cannot modify.

Problem 48

Find the output of the following program?

```
#include <stdio.h>
#include <conio.h>
void main()
{
int a[5] = {2, 3};
printf ("\n%d %d %d", a[2], a[3], a[4]);
getch();
}
```

Output:

```
0 0 0.
```

NOTE: When an array is partially initialized, then remaining elements are initialized to 0.

Problem 49

Find the output of the following program?

```
#include <stdio.h>
#include <conio.h>
void main()
{
int x = 1, y = 2, z = 6, g;
g = x < y < z;
printf ("&d", i);
getch();
}
```

Output:

```
1
```

NOTE: First of all, we check the condition x < y if the condition is true result is 1 otherwise 0. Then result 1 of first true condition is compared with 6. Then again condition becomes truc gives result 1. This 1 is then assigned to g.

Problem 50

Find the output of the following program?

```
#include <stdio.h>
#include <conio.h>
void main()
{
enum status {high, low, medium};
enum status st1, st2, st3;
st1 = high;
st2 = medium;
st3 = low;
printf ("\n%d %d %d", st1, st2, st3);
getch();
}
```

Output:

```
0 2 1
```

NOTE: Enum elements always take values like 0, 1, 2, etc.

Problem 51

Find the incorrect declaration of structure?

```
1.
struct student
{
int rn;
float fees;
};

2.
struct student
```

```
{
int rn;
float fees;
struct student st;
};

3.
struct student
{
int rn;
float fees;
struct student *st;
};

4.
struct student
{
int rn;
float fees;
struct student **st;
};
```

Output:

2

Problem 52

Which of the following special symbol is allowed in a variable name?

1. $
2. |
3. -
4. _

Output:

4

Problem 53

Which of the following definition is correct?

1. int left;
2. char int;
3. int long;
4. float double;

Output:

1

Problem 54

Find the correct declaration of structure?

1.
```
struct book
{
char name[20];
float price;
int pages;
};
```
2.
```
struct
{
char name[20];
float price;
int pages;
}
```

```
3.
struct book
{
char name[20]
float price
int pages
};
4. All of the above
```

Output:

```
1
```

Problem 55

Which of the following is not a user-defined data type?

```
1.
struct book
{
char name[20];
float price;
int pages;
};
2. long int = 23.5;
3. enum month {Jan, Feb, march};
4. union u
{
int i;
char ch[2];
};
```

Output:

```
2
```

Problem 56

Find the declaration and definition from the following program?

```
#include <stdio.h>
#include <conio.h>
int i = 200;
void main()
{
extem int i;
printf ("%d", i);
getch();
}
```

Output:

Declaration: extem int i

Definition: int i = 200

Problem 57

Find the output of the following program?

```
#include <stdio.h>
#include <conio.h>
int i = 200;
void main()
{
extem int i;
printf ("\n%d", i);
getch();
}
```

Output:

200

Problem 58

The prototype of a function means we defining the function or declaring it?

Output:

We are declaring it. When the function, along with the statements belonging to it, is mentioned we are defining the function.

Problem 59

What's the difference between the following declarations?

```
extem int fun();
int fun();
```

Output:

There is no difference except for the fact that the first one gives a hint that the function fun() is probably in another source file.

Problem 60

Check the errors from the following program?

```
#include <stdio.h>
#include <conio.h>
void main()
{
display();
getch();
}
void display()
{
printf ("\n Khalsa College");
}
```

Output:

```
Error.
```

NOTE: display ( ) is called before it is defined.

Problem 61

Find the output of the following program?

```
#include <stdio.h>
#include <conio.h>
void main()
{
char *s1;
char far *s2;
char huge *s3;
printf ("%d %d %d", size of (s1), sizeof (s2), sizeof
    (s3));
getch();
}
```

Output:

In a 16-bit compiler like Turbo C/C++: 4 4 2.

In a 32-bit compiler like VC++: Error because there is no far and huge pointers. Every pointer is 4 byte wide.

Problem 62

Check the errors from the following program?

```
#include <stdio.h>
#include <conio.h>
void main()
{
char *iptr, i;
void *kptr, k;
i=10; k = 0;
iptr = &i;
kptr = &k;
getch();
}
```

Output:

Error:

NOTE: Size of variable k is unknown or zero. This is because k is declared as void. We can declare a void pointer but not a simple variable of type void.

Problem 63

Find the output of the following program?

```
#include <stdio.h>
#include <conio.h>
fun(struct student);
struct student
{
char name[20];
int age;
};
void main( )
{
struct student st = {"Ikvinder", 26};
fun(st);
getch();
}
fun(struct student st1)
{
printf ("\n%s%d"), st1.name, st1.age);
}
```

Output:

Declares the structure before the prototype of fun().

Problem 64

Find the output of the following program?

```
#include <stdio.h>
#include <conio.h>
void main()
{
struct student
{
char name[20];
int age;
float fees;
};
struct student st = {"Ikvinder"};
printf ("\n%d %f", st.age, st.fees);
getch();
}
```

Output:

```
0 0.000000
```

NOTE: When the first element of structure is initialized, then remaining elements of the structure are initialized to 0.

Problem 65

Is it possible?

```
int a[] = {2, 3, 4, 12, 32};
struct student st = {"Sunny", 23};
```

Output:

```
Different compilers give different results.
```

Problem 66

Find the output of the following program?

```
#include <stdio.h>
#include <conio.h>
```

```
void main()
{
float f = 0.2;
if (f < 0.2f)
printf ("Welcome");
else
printf ("How are you");
getch();
}
```

Output:

How are you

Problem 67

Find the output of the following program?

```
#include <stdio.h>
#include <conio.h>
#include <math.h>
void main()
{
printf ("%f", sqrt (25.0));
getch();
}
```

Output:

5.000000

Problem 68

Find the output of the following program?

```
#include <stdio.h>
#include <conio.h>
void main()
```

```
{
float f = 8.43;
printf ("%d", (int) f);
getch();
}
```

Output:

8

Problem 69

Find the output of the following program?

```
#include <stdio.h>
#include <conio.h>
void main()
{
float *p;
printf ("%d", sizeof (p));
getch();
}
```

Output:

2 in DOS and 4 in Windows

Problem 70

Check the errors from the following program?

```
#include <stdio.h>
#include <conio.h>
void main()
{
printf ("%f", log (25.0));
getch();
}
```

Output:

```
Error.
```

NOTE: include header file #include <math.h>

Problem 71

Check the errors from the following program?

```
#include <stdio.h>
#include <conio.h>
void main()
{
float f;
scanf ("%f", &f);
printf ("%f", f + f + f);
printf ("%f", 3 *f);
getch();
}
```

Output:

```
No error.
```

Problem 72

Which of the following is valid range of long double?

Output:

```
3.4E-4932 to 1.1E+4932
```

Problem 73

Find the output of the following program?

```
#include <stdio.h>
#include <conio.h>
#include <math.h>
void main()
```

```
{
float f = 1.54;
printf ("%f", ceil (f), floor (f));
getch();
}
```

Output:

```
2.000000 1.000000
```

Problem 74

Which are the three different types of real data types available in C, what are their sizes and what format specifiers are used for them?

Output:

Type	Size	Format Specifier
float	4 bytes	%f
double	8 bytes	%If
long double	10 bytes	%Lf

Problem 75

Which of the following is the correct datatype for the variable i in the statement given below?

```
i = 23.45;
```

Output:

float

Problem 76

What will you do to treat the constant 3.14 as a float?

Output:

3.14f

Problem 77

What will you do to treat the constant 3.14 as a long double?

Output:

```
Use 3.141
```

Problem 78

Find the output of the following program?

```
#include <stdio.h>
#include <conio.h>
void main()
{
printf ("%d %d %d", sizeof (3.14f), sizeof (3.14),
   sizeof (3.141));
getch();
}
```

Output:

```
4 8 10
```

Problem 79

The binary equivalent of 5.375 is

Output:

```
101.011
```

Problem 80

Find the output of the following program?

```
#include <stdio.h>
#include <conio.h>
void main()
{
float i = 0.2;
if (0.2 > i)
printf ("Welcome");
else
```

```
printf ("Hello");
}
```

Output:

```
Welcome
```

Problem 81

Check the errors from the following program?

```
#include<stdio.h>
#include<conio.h>
void main( )
{
printf("hello, world
");
getch();
}
```

Output:

```
Error
```

Problem 82

Find the output of the following program?

```
#include<stdio.h>
#include<conio.h>
void main( )
{
printf("hello, world\
");
getch();
}
```

Output:

```
hello world
```

Problem 83

Find the output of the following program?

```
#include<stdio.h>
#include<conio.h>
void main( )
{
char *p = “Welcome!..””to Khalsa College”;
printf(p);
getch();
}
```

Output:

```
Welcome!..to Khalsa College
```

Problem 84

Find the output of the following program?

```
#include<stdio.h>
#include<conio.h>
void main( )
{
printf ( “nn \n\n nn\n” );
printf ( “nn /n/n nn/n” );
printf (“\n n \n”);
getch();
}
```

Output:

```
nn
nn /n/n nn/n
n
```

Problem 85

Find the output of the following program?

```
#include<stdio.h>
#include<conio.h>
void main( )
{
int i, j;
printf ( “Enter values of i and j” );
scanf ( “ %d %d “, &i, &j );
printf ( “i = %d j = %d”, i, j );
getch();
}
```

Output:

Spaces that are given after and before double quotes in scanf() it waits even we can enter two values. We must have to enter one more variable to complete scan^() execution.

Problem 86

Find the output of the following program?

```
#include<stdio.h>
#include<conio.h>
void main( )
{
int i, j;
printf ( “Enter values of i and j”) ;
scanf ( “ %d %d “, i, j );
printf ( “i = %d j =%d”, i, j );
getch();
}
```

Output:

Address(&) operator is missing in scanf().

Problem 87

Find the output of the following program?

```
#include<stdio.h>
#include<conio.h>
void main( )
{
int i;
for ( i = 0 ; i <= 5000 ; i++ )
printf ("\n%d", i);
getch();
}
```

Output:

Infinite loop

Problem 88

Find the output of the following program?

```
#include<stdio.h>
#include<conio.h>
void main( )
{
float i = 1.5;
double j = 1.5;
printf ("\n%f %lf", i, j);
getch();
}
```

Output:

1.500000 1.500000

Problem 89

Find the output of the following program?

```
#include<stdio.h>
#include<conio.h>
int i = 0;
void incr();
void main( )
{
printf ("\nmain's i = %d", i);
i++;
incr( );
printf ("\nmain's i = %d", i);
incr( );
getch();
}
void incr( )
{
i = 100;
printf ("\nvalue of i = %d", i);
i++;
}
```

Output:

```
main's i=0
value of i=100
main's i=101
value of i=100
```

Problem 90

Find the output of the following program?

```
#include <stdio.h>
#include <conio.h>
```

```
int i = 100;
void main ()
{
int i = 200;
printf ("\n%d", i);
getch();
}
```

Output:

200.

NOTE: When there is a conflict between a local variable and a global variable, then the winner is local variable.

Problem 91

Find the output of the following program?

```
#include <stdio.h>
#include <conio.h>
void main()
{
int i = 100;
{
int i = 200;
printf ("\n%d", i);
}
printf ("%d", i);
getch();
}
```

Output:

200 100

NOTE: When there is a conflict between local variables, then the winner is more local.

Problem 92

Find the output of the following program?

```
#include <stdio.h>
#include <conio.h>
void main()
{
int k;
for (;scanf ("%d", &k); printf ("%d", k))
getch();
}
```

Output:

For loop would get executed infinite times.

Problem 93

Define scope of a variable? What are the different types of scopes that a variable can have?

Output:

Scope indicated the region over which the variable's declaration has an effect.

There are four kinds of scopes are – file, function, block and prototype.

Problem 94

Is the following statement a declaration or a definition?

```
extem int i;
```

Output:

```
Declaration
```

Problem 95

What are the differences between a declaration and a definition?

Output:

There are two differences between a declaration and a definition:

In the definition of a variable space is reserved for the variable and some initial value is given to it, whereas a declaration only identifiers the type of the variable for a function. Thus definition is the place where the variable is created or assigned storage, whereas declaration refers to places where the nature of the variable is stated but no storage is allocated.

Secondly, redefinition is an error, whereas, redeclaration is not an error.

Problem 96

Find the declarations and definitions from the following statements:

```
extem int i;
float k;
double add (double, double);
float divide (float j) {..}
```

Output:

```
extem int i;                              /*Declaration */
float k;                                  /*Definition*/
double add (double, double);              /*Declaration */
float divide (float j) {..}               /*Definition */
```

Problem 97

Check the errors from the following program?

```
#include <stdio.h>
#include <conio.h>
void main()
{
extem int i;
i = 200;
```

```
printf ("%d", sizeof (i));
getch();
}
```

Output:

```
Error, i undefined
```

NOTE: extern int i is a declaration and not a definition.

Problem 98

Given statement is true or false.

Statement: Global variable may have several declarations, but only one definition?

Output:

```
True
```

Problem 99

Given statement is true or false.

Statement: A function may have several declarations, but only one definition?

Output:

```
True
```

B. FILL IN THE BLANKS

1. C language was developed by ....
2. An identifier name in C starts with a ....
3. One of the most important attributes of an identifier is its ....
4. int var; is a .... statement.
5. .... is a data object locator.
6. C is a .... programming language.
7. C supports .... number of primitive data types.

8. A .... may precede a data type in a data type declaration.
9. A hexadecimal constant is preceded by ....
10. Null string is represented by ....
11. Variables are also known as .... in C.
12. Nested comments are .... in ANSI C.
13. Value of the constants does not .... during the execution of the program.
14. .... quantifier is used to create a constant within the main program.
15. Value of the .... varies during the execution of the program.
16. The first argument of printf function should always be a ....
17. Floating point literal constant by default is assumed to be of .... type.
18. C program is made up of ....
19. Every statement in C is terminated with a ....
20. The printf function prints the value according to the .... specified in the ....
21. The .... operator is used to tell amount of memory a datatype can use.
22. The code that establishes the original value for a variable is known as a ....
23. The .... function reads data from the keyboard.
24. One of the most common for new programmers is forgetting to use the .... operator for variables in a scanf statement.
25. The .... can be used to create a new type that can be used anywhere a type is permitted.
26. The enumerated type (enum) is derived from the .... type.
27. A .... is a construct that allows a portion of memory to be shared by different types of data.
28. A compiler splits a program into a number of ....

29. Assigning a value to a variable in a declaration, is known as .... The value used for the assignment, is known as ....
30. A variable declaration fixes .... and .... of the variables.
31. C99 introduced support for characters from ....

Answers

1. Dennis Ritchie	2. letter or an underscore
3. data type	4. definition
5. l-vlaue	6. structured
7. four	8. qualifier
9. Ox or ox	10. " "
11. storage element	12. not allowed
13. vary	14. const
15. variable	16. string
17. float	18. functions
19. semicolon	20. format specifiers, format string
21. sizeof	22. intializer
23. scanf	24. address
25. type definition	26. structured
27. Union	28. tokens
29. initialization, initializer	30. name, data type
31. unicode character set	

C. TRUE OR FALSE

State whether each of the following is true or false

1. C is a strongly types language.
2. Variables are created with a type definition (typedef).
3. Enumerated data type is not a derived type.
4. C is a case-sensitive language, which means that distinguishes

between uppercase characters and lowercase characters.

5. The purpose of a header file, such as stdio.h, is to store a program's source code.
6. The sizes of short integer and long integer data type would vary from one platform to another.
7. The sizes of short integer and long integer data type can be verified using the sizeof( ) operator.
8. A float is 4 bytes wide, whereas a double is 8 bytes wide.
9. Range of float is -1.7e-308 to +1.7e-308.
10. Rang of a double is -3.4e34 to +3.4e34.
11. An identifier name in C cannot start with a letter.
12. Any valid printable ASCII character can be used in an identifier.
13. All the variable names must be declared before they are used in a C program.
14. An integer value can be assigned to only one enumeration constant in an enumerated type.
15. Comments play an important role in a C program and are processed by the C compiler to produce an executable code.
16. The identifier $salesAmount is not valid.
17. One and only one function may be named main in the structure of a C program.
18. Keyword or a reserved word cannot be used as a valid identifier name.
19. A short integer is at least 2bytes wide and a long integer is at least 32 bits wide.
20. By default the data type of a constant without a decimal point is int, whereas the one with a decimal point is a double.
21. C is not an object oriented programming language.
22. C allows long float type.
23. The first character of an identifier may be an underscore.
24. A declaration without any variable name is also a valid declaration.

25. Blank space is a white space character.
26. A long double should be used if range of a double is not enough to accommodate a real number.
27. The modulus operator cannot be used with a long double.
28. A structure variable is used to declare a type containing multiple fields.
29. int a=20, b=30, c; is an example of a longhand declaration statement.
30. Float data type is used to store character data.
31. A type qualifier modifies the base type to yield a new type.
32. Constants have both l-value and r-value.
33. The value of a constant may be changed during a program's execution.
34. A character literal constant can have one or at most two characters enclosed within single quotes.
35. A char data type variable can store either an ASCII character or a Unicode character.
36. If scanf( ) is used to store a value in a char variable then along with the value a carriage return (\r) also gets stored in it.
37. Octal constant is preceded by the alphabet o or O.
38. The data type char is an integral data type.
39. The following manifest is a valid one.

```
#define PI 3.141592 A 15
```

40. The internal representation of a string constant includes NUL character at the end.
41. C99 supports Boolean data type.
42. The constant 542 is equal to the constant Ox243.
43. The constant 0412 is a valid constant.
44. The C standard function that receives data from the keyboard is printf.
45. The scanf function can be used to read more than one value at a

time.

46. The indirect selection operator is used with a pointer to access individual fields in a structure.
47. The structured programming concept known as coupling describes how data are passed to functions.
48. Structures are derived types based on the integer standard type.

Answers

1. True	2. False	3. False	4. True
5. False	6. True	7. True	8. True
9. False	10. False	11. True	12. False
13. True	14. True	15. False	16. True
17. True	18. True	19. True	20. True
21. True	22. False	23. True	24. True
25. True	26. True	27. True	28. True
29. False	30. False	31. False	32. False
33. False	34. True	35. True	36. False
37. False	38. True	39. False	40. True
41. True	42. False	43. False	44. False
45. False	46. True	47. False	48. True

D. OBJECTIVE TYPE QUESTIONS

1. Which of the following language is predecessor to C Programming Language?
   (a) A (b) B
   (c) BCPL (d) C++
2. C language has been developed by
   (a) Ken Thompson (b) Dennis Ritchie
   (c) Peter Norton (d) Martin Richards
3. C was developed in the year ....
   (a) 1976 (b) 1972

(c) 1980 (d) 1978

4. C is a .... language
   (a) high level (b) low level
   (c) middle level (d) machine level
5. C can be used on
   (a) Only MS-DOS operating system
   (b) Only Linux operating system
   (c) Only Windows operating system
   (d) All the above
6. C programs are converted into machine language with the help of
   (a) An Editor (b) A compiler
   (c) An operating system (d) All of the above
7. The real constant in C can be expressed in which of the following forms
   (a) Fractional form only (b) Exponential form only
   (c) ASCII form only (d) Both (a) and (b)
8. Who developed the C language?
   (a) Ken Thompson (b) Bjarne Stroutstrup
   (c) Dennis Ritchie (d) Kernighan
9. When was the C language developed?
   (a) 1970 (b) 1972
   (c) 1975 (d) 1976
10. Where was the C language developed?
   (a) Microsoft Corporation
   (b) Sun Microsystem
   (c) AT & T Bell Laboratory
   (d) CERN, European Particle Physics Laboratory
11. Who developed the language B?
   (a) Pascal (b) Bjarne Stroutstrup

(c) Kernighan (d) Ken Thompson

12. Who developed the language BCPL?
    (a) Martin Richard
    (b) Bjarne Stroutstrup
    (c) Kernighan
    (d) Ken Thompson
13. Which language was the predecessor of C?
    (a) A (b) BCPL
    (c) B (d) CPL
14. Which is not a character of C?
    (a) S (b) ^
    (c) ~ (d) |
15. An identifier cannot start with
    (a) _ (b) uppercase alphabet
    (c) lowercase alphabet (d) #
16. Which is not a keyword in C?
    (a) const (b) main
    (c) sizeof (d) void
17. Tell the primary data type in C.
    (a) double (b) union
    (c) function (d) array
18. Tell the secondary data type in C.
    (a) int (b) float
    (c) union (d) char
19. Which data type can either be used to represent a primary data type or secondary data type?
    (a) pointer (b) double
    (c) structure (d) union
20. The modifier that may precede float is
    (a) signed (b) unsigned

(c) long (d) none of the above

21. The modifier that may precede char is
    (a) signed (b) unsigned
    (c) options a and b (d) none of the above
22. The modifier that may precede double is
    (a) signed (b) unsigned
    (c) short (d) long
23. Printable characters always use
    (a) negative integers (b) positive integers
    (c) both a and b (d) –1
24. Integral data type includes
    (a) enum (b) int
    (c) char (d) all of the above
25. Which is not a valid integer constant?
    (a) 800000u (b) 587364 ul
    (c) 0Xajht (d) 0X685
26. Which is not a valid floating constant?
    (a) 6E-4f (b) 4E 11
    (c) 0.03e-5 (d) 1.23435F
27. Find the Octal constant
    (a) 457 (b) OX43
    (c) –0786 (d) 06.54
28. An octal constant is preceded by
    (a) X (b) OX
    (c) 0 (alphabet) (d) 0 (zero)
29. A hexadecimal constant is preceded by
    (a) OX (b) 0
    (c) hx (d) 0
30. A character variable can at a time store
    (a) 1 character (b) 8 characters

(c) 254 characters (d) None of the above

31. The statement char ch = 'Z' would store in ch
   (a) The character Z
   (b) ASCII value of Z
   (c) Z along with the single inverted commas
   (d) Both (a) and (b)

32. Which of the following is NOT a character constant
   (a) 'Thank You' (b) 'Enter values of P, N, R'
   (c) '23.56E-03' (d) All the above

33. The maximum value that an integer constant can have is
   (a) –32767 (b) 32767
   (c) 1.7014e+38 (d) –1.7014e+38

34. A C variable cannot start with
   (a) An alphabet
   (b) A number
   (c) A special symbol other than underscore
   (d) Both (b) & (c)

35. Which is not a character of C?
   (a) $ (b) ^
   (c) ~ (d) !

36. Which is not a keyword in C?
   (a) const (b) main
   (c) sizeof (d) void

37. Identify the scalar data type in C.
   (a) double (b) union
   (c) function (d) array

38. Identify the derived data type in C.
   (a) int (b) float

(c) union (d) char

39. Integral data type includes

(a) enum (b) int

(c) char (d) all the above

40. The qualifier that may proceed double is

(a) signed (b) unsigned

(c) short (d) long

41. A character constant is written within

(a) double quotes (b) single quotes

(c) options a and b (d) none of the above

42. String constants are represented within

(a) single quotes (b double quotes

(c) options a and b (d) * and *\

43. An integer constant in C must have:

(a) Atleast one digit (b) Atleast one decimal point

(c) A comma along with digits (d) Digits separated by commas

44. A character variable can never store more than

(a) 32 characters (b) 8 characters

(c) 254 characters (d) 1 character

45. Find the wrong statement.

(a) #define A 10 (b) int a, b;

(c) char ch; (d) #define A 5;

46. Which is an invalid variable name?

(a) sum (b) As

(c) net-salary (d) Sticks

47. Find the correct statement.

(a) The variable names VOLUME and volume are identical

(b) The variable names Sum and sum are identical

(c) Variables are not declared before use

(d) Variable names may be absent in a declaration

48. Find the invalid identifier.

(a) MUTE_S (b) SELL

(c) _DIVIDE (d) _24

49. Where does the execution of every C program starts?

(a) Every C program starts in the main ( ) function

(b) Every C program starts in the begin () function

(c) Every C program starts in the initialize ( ) function

(d) Every C program starts in the start ( ) function

50. Which of the following is TRUE about float?

1. A float occupies less memory than a double.
2. The range of real numbers that can be represented by a double is less than those represented by a float.

(a) only option 1 (b) only option 2

(c) both options 1 and 2 (d) Neither option 1 nor 2

51. What is the maximum value of a signed data type that is 8 bits in size?

(a) 2 to the power of 7

(b) 2 to the power of 8

(c) (2 to the power of 7) minus 1

(d) (2 to the power of 8) minus 1

52. What is the largest value an integer can hold in an ANSI C compiler?

(a) 65536 (b) 2147483647

(c) INT_MAX (d) 1 << INT_BITS

53. Which is not escape sequence character?

(a) '\t' (b) '\a'

(c) '\b' (d) '\d'

54. The escape sequence character '\x07' is equivalent to the character.

(a) '\a' (b) '\b'

(c) '\t' (d) '\r'

55. Which one is an invalid identifier?
    (a) stu-dent (b) stu_dent
    (c) stu3dent (d) student
56. In C a variable cannot contain
    (a) Blank spaces (b) Hyphen
    (c) Decimal point (d) All the above
57. Which of the following is FALSE in C?
    (a) Keywords can be used as variable names
    (b) Variable names can contain a digit
    (c) Variable names do not contain a blank space
    (d) Capital letters can be used in variable names
58. A declaration float a, b; occupies .... of memory
    (a) 1byte (b) 4bytes
    (c) 8bytes (d) 16 bytes
59. What will be the maximum size of a double variable?
    (a) 1byte (b) 4bytes
    (c) 8bytes (d) 16 bytes
60. What will be the maximum size of a float variable?
    (a) 1byte (b) 4bytes
    (c) 8bytes (d) 16 bytes
61. Find the most appropriate variable initialization?
    (a) # define A 10 (b) int x, y; y = 5
    (c) float y = 3.14; (d) char ch; ch = 'O';
62. Tokens are separated by using
    (a) : (b) .
    (c) ; (d) separator
63. An escape sequence commences with
    (a) \ (b) /

(c) ? (d) #

64. Find the wrong declaration.

(a) int n = {7}; (b) char ch = 'A' + 25, cd = 'Z';

(c) int x ; y; (d) int x = 10, y = x * 5, year;

65. Find the wrong statement.

(a) unsigned long int x, y; (b) long float f;

(c) long double d; (d) signed e;

66. Find the wrong sentence.

(a) # define is a preprocessor

(b) # define used for a constant value throughout the program

(c) # define statement terminated with semicolon

(d) # define improves the readability of the program

67. Which one is correct for variable declaration?

(a) Assignment of properties to a value

(b) Assignment of memory space to a variable

(c) Assignment of properties and memory space to a variable

(d) Assignment of properties and identification to a variable

68. Which one is correct for strings?

(a) Contiguous blocks of characters and a terminating NULL character

(b) Individual characters linked together to form a string

(c) Both options (a) and (b)

(d) None of the above

69. In addition to the length of the string, what must be considered while determining the minimum number of characters required to store a C string?

(a) An EOF at the end must be considered

(b) A '\0' at the end must be considered

(c) Apart from the string itself, there is nothing else to be considered when determining the length of the string

(d) A '\0n' at the end must be considered

70. Tell the white space character (s).

(a) blank (b) \f

(c) \r (d) all the above

71. Identify the invalid string constant.

(a) "4\t 12\t 14\t"

(b) "r = 40\x22\n"

(c) "\n C language"

(d) 'C is programming language'

72. If a constant is given a name if becomes

(a) a string constant (b) manifest

(c) const declaration (d) invalid

73. Symbolic constants are defined as

(a) # define S1 S2 (b) # define S1 S2;

(c) # define S1 = S2 (d) # define S1 = S2;

74. The symbol # in the # define statement must commence from

(a) Anywhere in a line (b) the first column of a line

(c) the first column of next line (d) the first line

75. What is an storage element in C?

(a) constant (b) variable

(c) identifier (d) keyword

76. Which one is C tokens?

(a) keywords (b) constants

(c) operators (d) all the above

77. Statement can be terminated by the use of

(a) : (b) blank

(c) ; (d) \n

78. A character constant is written within

(a) double quotes (b) single quotes

(c) options a and b (d) none of the above

79. String constants are represented within
    (a) single quotes (b) double quotes
    (c) options a and b (d) * and *\
80. Find the invalid string constant.
    (a) "X + Y" (b) """
    (c) " ' " (d) 'X'
81. Which is not a character constant?
    (a) '\40' (b) '\0412'
    (c) '\x12' (d) 'result'
82. Find the invalid constant.
    (a) " " (b) ' '
    (c) 'is' (d) '\b'
83. Find the escape sequences.
    (a) \0 (b) \n
    (c) \f (d) all the above
84. Which is not a white space character?
    (a) \f (b) \v
    (c) \0 (d) blank
85. Which statement is true in case of ANSI C?
    (a) Comments use /* and */
    (b) Nested comments are not allowed
    (c) Nested comments are allowed
    (d) Comments are not allowed within a string constant
86. Tell the correct statement(s) related to token.
    (a) Token is an individual entity of a program
    (b) Tokens are identified during the compilation
    (c) Compiler always constitutes the longest possible token
    (d) All the above
87. Find the number of tokens in the following:

```
if(a = 5)
```

(a) 4 (b) 5

(c) 6 (d) 7

88. Find the separator in C language.

(a) white space character (b) comment

(c) options a and b (d) semicolon

89. String constants should be enclosed between ....

(a) Single quotes (b) double quotes

(c) both a and b (d) none of these

90. Character constants should be enclosed between ....

(a) Single quotes (b) double quotes

(c) both a and b (d) none of these

91. Identify the escape sequence(s)

(a) \0 (b) \n

(c) \f (d) all the above

92. Which is not a white space character(s)

(a) \f (b) \v

(c) \0 (d) blank

93. What is an object in C?

(a) constant (b) variable

(c) identifier (d) keyword

94. Identify the C token(s)

(a) keywords (b) constants

(c) operators (d) all the above

95. Statement terminator is represented by

(a) : (b) blank

(c) ; (d) \n

96. C has position in the world of language

(a) high (b) middle

(c) low (d) All of above

97. Where was the C language developed?
    (a) Microsoft Corporation
    (b) Sun Microsystems
    (c) AT&T Bell Laboratory
    (d) CERN, European Particle Physics Laboratory

Answers

1. (b)	2. (b)	3. (b)	4. (c)	5. (d)
6. (b)	7. (d)	8. (c)	9. (b)	10. (c)
11. (d)	12. (a)	13. (c)	14. (a)	15. (d)
16. (b)	17. (a)	18. (c)	19. (a)	20. (d)
21. (c)	22. (d)	23. (b)	24. (d)	25. (c)
26. (b)	27. (c)	28. (d)	29. (a)	30. (a)
31. (d)	32. (d)	33. (b)	34. (d)	35. (a)
36. (b)	37. (a)	38. (c)	39. (d)	40. (d)
41. (d)	42. (b)	43. (a)	44. (d)	45. (d)
46. (c)	47. (d)	48. (a)	49. (a)	50. (a)
51. (c)	52. (c)	53. (d)	54. (a)	55. (a)
56. (d)	57. (a)	58. (c)	59. (c)	60. (b)
61. (c)	62. (d)	63. (a)	64. (c)	65. (b)
66. (c)	67. (d)	68. (c)	69. (b)	70. (d)
71. (d)	72. (b)	73. (a)	74. (a)	75. (b)
76. (d)	77. (c)	78. (b)	79. (b)	80. (d)
81. (d)	82. (c)	83. (d)	84. (c)	85. (d)
86. (d)	87. (c)	88. (c)	89. (b)	90. (a)
91. (d)	92. (d)	93. (b)	94. (d)	95. (c)
96. (b)	97. (c)			

CHAPTER

2

Operators and Expressions

A. CODE SNIPPETS

Problem 1

Find the output of the following program?

```
#include<stdio.h>
#include<conio.h>
void main( )
{
float f = 0.8;
int r;
r=f<0.8;
printf ("%d",r);
getch();
}
```

Output:

1

Problem 2

Find the output of the following program?

```
#include<stdio.h>
```

```
#include<conio.h>
void main( )
{
float f = 0.1;
int r;
r=f<0.1;
printf ("%d",r);
getch();
}
```

Output:

0

Problem 3

Find the output of the following program?

```
#include<stdio.h>
#include<conio.h>
void main( )
{
float f = 0.8;
int r;
r=f<0.8f;
printf ("%d",r);
getch();
}
```

Output:

0

Problem 4

Find the output of the following program?

```
#include<stdio.h>
#include<conio.h>
void main( )
{
int i = 0, j=0;
++i = = 0||++j = =11;
printf("%d%d",i,j);
getch();
}
```

Output:

11

Problem 5

Find the output of the following program?

```
#include<stdio.h>
#include<conio.h>
void main( )
{
int r =4+2%-8;
printf("%d",r);
getch();
}
```

Output:

6

Problem 6

Find the output of the following program?

```
#include<stdio.h>
#include<conio.h>
void main( )
```

```
{
int x =8;
x=!x>5;
printf("%d",x);
getch();
}
```

Output:

0

Problem 7

Find the output of the following program?

```
#include<stdio.h>
#include<conio.h>
void main( )
{
int i =10, j=50, k;
k=j=i*=2;
printf("%d%d%d",i,j,k);
getch();
}
```

Output:

20 20 20

Problem 8

Find the output of the following program?

```
#include<stdio.h>
#include<conio.h>
void main( )
{
printf("%x",-1<<4);
getch();
```

```
}
```

Output:

```
fff0
```

Problem 9

Find the output of the following program?

```
#include<stdio.h>
#include<conio.h>
void main( )
{
int i =-4;
printf("%d",i);
getch();
}
```

Output:

```
4
```

NOTE: minus operator is used twice.

Problem 10

Check the errors from the following program?

```
#include<stdio.h>
#include<conio.h>
void main( )
{
int c =-2;
printf("%d",c);
getch();
}
```

Output:

```
Compilation error
```

NOTE: L-value required. Decrement operator is used.

Problem 11

Find the output of the following program?

```
#include<stdio.h>
#include<conio.h>
void main( )
{
int i=7;
printf ("%d%d%d%d",i++,i–,++i,–i,i);
getch();
}
```

Output:

6 7 7 6 7

Problem 12

Find the output of the following program?

```
#include<stdio.h>
#include<conio.h>
void main( )
{
412;
printf ("%d",412);
getch();
}
```

Output:

412

Problem 13

Find the output of the following program?

```
#include <stdio.h>
#include <conio.h>
void main()
{
int i = 6, j, k;
j = –i;
k = i–;
printf ("%d %d %d", i, j, k);
getch();
}
```

Output:

```
4 5 5
```

Problem 14

Will the expression *p++ = c be disallowed by the compiler?

Output:

No. Because here even though the value of p is accessed twice it is used to modify two different objects p and *p.

Problem 15

Write one of the correct conditional statement used in C?

Output:

```
max = a > b ? a > c ? a : c : b > c ? b : c;
```

Problem 16

Find the output of the following program?

```
#include <stdio.h>
#include <conio.h>
void main()
{
```

```
int i = 15;
printf ("%d %d %d", i <= 15, i = 100, i >= 5);
getch();
}
```

Output:

```
1 100 0
```

Problem 17

Find the output of the following program?

```
#include <stdio.h>
#include <conio.h>
void main()
{
int k, i = 30;
k = (i > 5? (i <= 10 ? 100 : 200) : 500);
printf ("%d", k);
getch();
}
```

Output:

```
500
```

Problem 18

Find the output of the following program?

```
#include <stdio.h>
#include <conio.h>
void main()
{
int i = 100, j = 200, k;
k = (i = = 100 || j > 200);
printf ("k = %d", k);
```

```
getch();
}
```

Output:

```
k = 1
```

Problem 19

Find the output of the following program?

```
#include <stdio.h>
#include <conio.h>
void main()
{
int i = 7, j = 5, k;
k = i != 6 || j = = 6;
printf ("k = %d", k);
getch();
}
```

Output:

```
k = 1
```

Problem 20

Check the errors from the following program?

```
#include<stdio.h>
#include<conio.h>
void main( )
{
int i=10, j=11, k,l;
k=i+++j;
l=i+++++j;
printf("%d%d", l,k);
getch();
```

```
}
```

Output:

```
Error
```

NOTE: L- value required

Problem 21

Find the output of the following program?

```
#include<stdio.h>
#include<conio.h>
void main( )
{
int i=10, j=11, k, l;
k=i+++j;
l=i++ + ++j;
printf("%d%d",l,k);
getch();
}
```

Output:

```
23 21
```

Problem 22

Check the errors from the following program?

```
#include<stdio.h>
#include<conio.h>
void main( )
{
int i=10, j=11, k,l;
k=i+++j;
l=i++ +++j;
printf ("%d %d", x,y);
getch();
```

```
}
```

Output:

```
Error
```

NOTE: L- value required

Problem 23

Find the output of the following program?

```
#include<stdio.h>
#include<conio.h>
void main( )
{
int x=20, y=35;
x=y++ + x++;
printf ("%d%d", x,y);
getch();
}
```

Output:

```
57 94
```

Problem 24

Check the errors from the following program?

```
#include<stdio.h>
#include<conio.h>
void main( )
{
int i=100,j=20;
i++=j;
printf("%d%d", i,j);
```

```
getch();
}
```

Output:

```
Error
```

NOTE: L- value required

Problem 25

Find the output of the following program?

```
#include<stdio.h>
#include<conio.h>
void main( )
{
int a=10,b;
a>=5?b=100,b=200;
printf("%d",b);
getch();
}
```

Output:

```
100
```

Problem 26

Find the output of the following program?

```
#include<stdio.h>
#include<conio.h>
void main( )
{
int i=0,j=1,k=2,l;
l=i||j++&&k;
printf ("%d%d%d%d",i,j,k,l);
getch();
```

```
}
```

Output:

```
0 2 3 1
```

Problem 27

Find the output of the following program?

```
#include<stdio.h>
#include<conio.h>
void main( )
{
int i=0, j=1, k=2,l;
l=i&&j++&&++k;
printf("%d%d%d%d",i,j,k,l);
getch();
}
```

Output:

```
0 1 2 0
```

Problem 28

Find the output of the following program?

```
#include <stdio.h>
#include <conio.h>
void main()
{
int i = 2, j = -1, k = 0, p, q, r, s;
p = i || j || k
q = i || && j && k;
r = i || j && k;
```

```
s = i && j || k;
printf ("%d %d %d %d", p, q, r, s);
getch();
}
```

Output:

```
1 0 1 1
```

Problem 29

Find the output of the following program?

```
#include <stdio.h>
#include <conio.h>
void main()
{
float a = 2.7, b = 2.77;
if (a = b)
printf ("a and b are equal");
else
printf ("a and be are not equal");
getch();
}
```

Output:

```
a and b are equal
```

Problem 30

Find the correct order of evaluation for the following expression?

```
result = i + j * k / 3 % 2 - 1;
1. * / % - + =
2. = * / % + -
3. / * % - + =
```

```
4. * / % + - =
```

Output:

```
1
```

Problem 31

Find the output of the following program?

```
#include<stdio.h>
#include<conio.h>
void main( )
{
int a;
a=2*3+4%5-3/2+6;
printf ("%d",a);
getch();
}
```

Output:

```
15
```

Problem 32

Find the output of the following program?

```
#include<stdio.h>
#include<conio.h>
void main( )
{
printf ("%d %d %d %d", 6/5,-6/5,6/-5);
getch();
}
```

Output:

```
1 -1 -11
```

Problem 33

Find the output of the following program?

```
#include<stdio.h>
#include<conio.h>
void main( )
{
printf ("%d %d %d %d", 6%5,-6%5,6%5,-6%-5);
getch();
}
```

Output:

```
1 -11 -1
```

Problem 34

Find the output of the following program?

```
#include<stdio.h>
#include<conio.h>
void main( )
{
int a=12b;
printf ("%d %d",b.b=a);
getch();
}
```

Output:

```
12 12
```

Problem 35

Find the output of the following program?

```
#include<stdio.h>
#include<conio.h>
void main( )
{
int a=23,b=12,c=10,d;
```

```
d=c+2=b+1=a;
printf ("%d %d %d %d",a,b,c,d);
getch();
}
```

Output:

```
23 23 23 23
```

Problem 36

Check the errors from the following program?

```
#include<stdio.h>
#include<conio.h>
void main( )
{
int a=23, b=12, c=10, d;
d=c+2=b+1=a;
printf ("%d %d %d %d", a,b,c,d);
getch();
}
```

Output:

```
Error
```

NOTE: L- value required

Problem 37

Find the output of the following program?

```
#include<stdio.h>
#include<conio.h>
void main( )
{
```

```
int a=2, b=3,c=1,d;
d=a<b>c;
printf ("%d", d);
getch();
}
```

Output:

```
0
```

Problem 38

Find the output of the following program?

```
#include <stdio.h>
#include <conio.h>
void main()
{
int i = -4, j = 2, k = 0, result;
result = ++i && ++j || ++k;
printf ("\n%d %d %d %d", i, j, k, result);
getch();
}
```

Output:

```
-3 3 0 1
```

Problem 39

Find the output of the following program?

```
#include <stdio.h>
#include <conio.h>
void main()
{
int i = 3, j = 2, k = 0, result;
result = ++i || ++j && ++k;
```

```
printf ("\n%d %d %d %d", i, j, k, result);
getch();
}
```

Output:

```
-2 2 0 1
```

Problem 40

Find the output of the following program?

```
#include <stdio.h>
#include <conio.h>
void main()
{
int i = 3, j = 2, k = 0, result;
result = ++i && ++j && ++k;
printf ("\n%d %d %d %d", i, j, k, result);
getch();
}
```

Output:

```
-2 3 1 1
```

Problem 41

Find the output of the following program?

```
#include <stdio.h>
#include <conio.h>
void main()
{
int i = 2;
int j = i + (1, 2, 3, 4, 5);
printf ("%d", j);
getch();
```

```
}
```

Output:

```
7
```

Problem 42

Find the correct hierarchy of arithmetic operations in C?

```
1. / + * -
2. * / + -
3. + - / *
4. * - / +
```

Output:

```
2
```

Problem 43

Find the output of the following program?

```
#include<stdio.h>
#include<conio.h>
void main( )
{
int a=3,b=2,c=1,d;
d=a<b>c-1;
printf ("%d", d);
getch();
}
```

Output:

```
0
```

Problem 44

Check the errors from the following program?

```
#include<stdio.h>
```

```
#include<conio.h>
void main( )
{
int a=10, b=20, c=30;
c= =a=b;
printf ("%d %d %d", a,b,c);
getch();
}
```

Output:

Error

NOTE: L- value required

Problem 45

Find the output of the following program?

```
#include<stdio.h>
#include<conio.h>
void main( )
{
int a=10, b=20, c=30;
c=a= =b;
printf ("%d %d %d", a,b,c);
getch();
}
```

Output:

10 20 0

Problem 46

Find the output of the following program?

```
#include<stdio.h>
#include<conio.h>
void main( )
{
```

```
int a=10, b=20, c=30;
c= = a= =b;
printf ("%d %d %d", a,b,c);
getch();
}
```

Output:

10 20 30

Problem 47

Find the output of the following program?

```
#include<stdio.h>
#include<conio.h>
void main( )
{
int a=012, b=034;
int x=0x12, y=0x34;
int c,d,u,v;
c=a&b;
d=a|b;
u=x&y;
v=x|y;
printf ("%d %d %d %d", c,d,u,v);
getch();
}
```

Output:

8 30 16 54

Problem 48

Find the output of the following program?

```
#include<stdio.h>
```

```
#include<conio.h>
void main( )
{
int a=012, b=034;
int x=0x12, y=0x34;
int c,d,u,v;
c=a&&b;
d=a||b;
u=x&&y;
v=x||y;
printf ("%d %d %d %d", c,d,u,v);
getch();
}
```

Output:

1 1 1 1

Problem 49

Find the output of the following program?

```
#include<stdio.h>
#include<conio.h>
void main( )
{
int c=10, d, e;
d=!c;
e=~c;
printf ("%d%d", d,e);
getch();
}
```

Output:

0 -11

Problem 50

Find the output of the following program?

```
#include<stdio.h>
#include<conio.h>
void main( )
{
int c = -4, d=4;
printf ("%d%d%d%d", ~c, ~d, c^d, ~c^-d);
getch();
}
```

Output:

```
3 -5 -8 -8
```

Problem 51

Find the output of the following program?

```
#include<stdio.h>
#include<conio.h>
void main( )
{
int i=10;
printf("%d", i++*i++);
getch();
}
```

Output:

```
110
```

Problem 52

Check the errors from the following program?

```
#include<stdio.h>
#include<conio.h>
void main( )
```

```
{
int i=10;
j=++i++;
printf("%d%d", i,j);
getch();
}
```

Output:

```
Error
```

NOTE: L- value required

Problem 53

Find the output of the following program?

```
#include<stdio.h>
#include<conio.h>
void main( )
{
int i=0,j=1,k=2,l,
l=++i&&j++&&++k;
printf("%d%d%d%d", i,j,k,l);
getch();
}
```

Output:

```
1 2 3 1
```

Problem 54

Find the output of the following program?

```
#include<stdio.h>
#include<conio.h>
void main( )
{
int i=0, j=1, k=2, l;
```

```
l=++i||j++&&++k;
printf("%d%d%d%d", i,j,k,l);
getch();
}
```

Output:

```
1 1 2 1
```

Problem 55

Find the output of the following program?

```
#include<stdio.h>
#include<conio.h>
void main( )
{
int i=0, j=1, k=2, l;
l=++i&&j++||++k;
printf("%d%d%d%d", i,j,k,l);
getch();
}
```

Output:

```
1 2 2 1
```

Problem 56

Find the output of the following program?

```
#include<stdio.h>
#include<conio.h>
void main( )
{
int i=0, j=1, k=2, l;
l=++i&&j-||++k;
printf("%d%d%d%d", i,j,k,l);
```

```
getch();
}
```

Output:

1 0 3 1

Problem 57

Find the output of the following program?

```
#include<stdio.h>
#include<conio.h>
void main( )
{
int i=0, j=1, k=2, l;
l=++i&&j-||++k;
printf("%d%d%d%d", i,j,k,l);
getch();
}
```

Output:

1 0 2 1

Problem 58

Find the output of the following program?

```
#include<stdio.h>
#include<conio.h>
void main( )
{
int x=4;
printf("%d%d%d", x,x<<2,x>>2);
getch();
}
```

Output:

```
4 16 1
```

Problem 59

Find the output of the following program?

```
#include<stdio.h>
#include<conio.h>
void main( )
{
int n= 5,i=1;
printf ("%d", (n<<i&1<<15?1:0);
getch();
}
```

Output:

```
0
```

Problem 60

Find the output of the following program?

```
#include<stdio.h>
#include<conio.h>
void main( )
{
int n= 5,i=1;
printf ("%d", (n<<i&&1<<15?1:0);
getch();
}
```

Output:

```
1
```

Problem 61

Find the output of the following program?

```
#include<stdio.h>
#include<conio.h>
void main( )
{
int i=-12;
+i;
printf("%d%d",i,+i);
getch();
}
```

Output:

-12 -12

Problem 62

Find the output of the following program?

```
#include<stdio.h>
#include<conio.h>
void main( )
{
char ch;
ch=!4;
printf ("%d",ch);
getch();
}
```

Output:

0

Problem 63

Find the output of the following program?

```
#include<stdio.h>
#include<conio.h>
void main( )
```

```
{
int k=1;
printf("%d= =1 is ""%s",k,k= =1?"True": "False");
getch();
}
```

Output:

```
True
```

Problem 64

Check the errors from the following program?

```
#include<stdio.h>
#include<conio.h>
void main( )
{
const int x=5;
float y;
y=++x;
printf("%d%d",x,++y);
getch();
}
```

Output:

```
Error
```

NOTE: Cannnot modify a constant type

Problem 65

Find the output of the following program?

```
#include<stdio.h>
#include<conio.h>
void main( )
```

```
{
int x=8;
printf ("%d",x=++x= =9);
getch();
}
```

Output:

```
1
```

Problem 66

Find the output of the following program?

```
#include<stdio.h>
#include<conio.h>
void main( )
{
int x=5,y=10;
y=x&=y&&10;
printf ("%d%d",x,y);
getch();
}
```

Output:

```
1 1
```

Problem 67

Find the output of the following program?

```
#include<stdio.h>
#include<conio.h>
void main( )
{
```

```
float x,y;
x=7;y=10;
x* =y*=y+28.5;
printf("%f%f",x,y);
getch();
}
```

Output:

```
2695.0000000 385.000000
```

Problem 68

Find the output of the following program?

```
#include<stdio.h>
#include<conio.h>
void main( )
{
unsigned int i=0xfff;
~i;
printf ("%x",i);
getch();
}
```

Output:

```
ffff
```

Problem 69

Find the output of the following program?

```
#include<stdio.h>
#include<conio.h>
void main( )
{
unsigned char i=0x80;
```

```
printf("%d",i<<1);
getch();
}
```

Output:

256

Problem 70

Find the output of the following program?

```
#include<stdio.h>
#include<conio.h>
void main( )
{
unsigned int i = -1;
int j;
printf ("%u",i);
printf("%u",++i);
getch();
}
```

Output:

65535 0

Problem 71

Find the output of the following program?

```
#include<stdio.h>
#include<conio.h>
void main( )
{
float i=3.5;
int j,k,l,m;
j=(int)(i+0.5);
```

```
k=(int)i+0.5;
l=(int)((int)i+0.5);
m=(i+(int)0.5);
printf("%d%d%d%d",j,k,l,m);
getch();
}
```

Output:

```
4 3 3 3
```

Problem 72

Find the output of the following program?

```
#include<stdio.h>
#include<conio.h>
void main( )
{
int i=3.5,j,k,l,m;
j=(int)(i+0.5);
k=(int)i+0.5;
l=(int)((int)i+0.5);
m=(i+(int)0.5);
printf("%d%d%d%d",j,k,l,m);
getch();
}
```

Output:

```
3 3 3 3
```

Problem 73

Tell the order of evaluation of the Relational, Arithmetic, Logical and Assignment operators in C?

Output:

Arithmetic, Relational, Logical, Assignment

Problem 74

Which of the following are unary operators in C?

1. ==
2. sizeof
3. >
4. &&

Output:

2

Problem 75

Find the output of the following program?

```
#include <stdio.h>
#include <conio.h>
void main()
{
static int a[50];
int i = 0;
a[i] = i++;
printf ("\n%d %d %d", a[0], a[1], i);
getch();
}
```

Output:

0 0 1

Problem 76

Find the output of the following program?

```
#include <stdio.h>
#include <conio.h>
```

```
void main()
{
int i = 5;
i = i++;
printf ("%d", i);
getch();
}
```

Output:

6

Problem 77

Find the output of the following program?

```
#include <stdio.h>
#include <conio.h>
void main()
{
int i = 6;
printf ("\n%d %d", ++i, ++i);
getch();
}
```

Output:

Output may vary from compiler to compiler.

Problem 78

Are the following two statements same?

```
i <= 10 ? j = 20: k = 20;
(i <= 10) ? j : k = 20;
```

Output:

No

B. FILL IN THE BLANKS

1. An .... specifies an entity on which we can perform an operation.
2. An operator that has only one operand is known as ....
3. Assignment operator is .... associative.
4. The operands of a modulus operator must be of .... type.
5. An .... is a sequence of operands and operators that reduces to a single value.
6. The result of evaluation of a relational expression is a ....
7. In a compound expression, if operators of different precedence appear together, the operator of .... precedence operates first.
8. The order in which operators operate depends upon the .... and the .... of the operators.
9. If the operands of an operator are of different types, C automatically applies .... bring the operands to a common type.
10. The second operand of the operators % and / must be ....
11. The operator divide(/) can be applied to both .... and .... types.
12. The modulus operator can be applied only to .... types.
13. The bits shifted in from the left are the same as the bit value formerly occupying the leftmost bit position in .... shift.
14. The symbol .... is one's complement operator.
15. The symbol .... is logical AND operator and the symbol .... is bitwise AND operator.
16. i + + + + + j is evaluated as ....
17. Cast operator uses the format ....
18. The .... operator returns the number of bytes the variable occupies.

19. .... operator has least precedence.
20. An operator that can use two operands is known as ....
21. The relational operators are of two types: .... and .... operators.
22. The .... expression evaluates the operand on the right side of the operator and places its value in the variable on the left side of the operator.
23. .... is used to determine the order in which different operators in a complex expression are evaluated.
24. The result of bitwise and,ing of two bits is 1 if ....
25. The result of bitwise inclusive or'ing of two bits is 0 if ....
26. The result of bitwise exclusive or'ing of two bits is 1 if ....
27. To change every bit in a variable from a 1 to a 0 or from a 0 to a 1, we need to use the .... operator.
28. The bitwise................... operator is used to divide a data item by a power of 2.
29. The sizeof( ) is an ....
30. Assignment operators use the associativity of ....
31. The expression (float) (22/7) yields ....
32. The expression (double) (22/7) yields ....

Answers

1. operand
2. unary operator
3. right to left
4. integer
5. expression
6. Boolean value
7. higher
8. precedence, associativity
9. type casting
10. non-zero
11. integer, float
12. integral

13. arithmetic right
14. ~
15. && &
16. (i++) + (++j)
17. (datatype)variable
18. sizeof
19. Comma
20. binary operator
21. comparison, equality
22. assignment
23. precedence
24. both bits are 1s
25. both bits are 0s
26. bits are different
27. ~
28. <<
29. operator
30. right to left
31. 3.142857
32. 3.000000

C. TRUE OR FALSE

State whether each of the following is true or false

1. The expression +a is a unary expression.
2. A unary expression consists of only one operand with no operator.
3. The operators with the same precedence always have the same associativity.
4. The multiplication and division operators are left-to-right associative.
5. The sign of the result of evaluation of the modulus operator depends upon the sign of both the numerator as well as the denominator.
6. Two different operators would always have different Associativity.
7. In the expression x = y = 45 the order of assignment is NOT decided by Associativity of operators.
8. A constant or a variable alone may also be treated as an expression.
9. One's complement operator ~ is a binary operator.
10. Assignment operation is performed during execution of the program.
11. If both the operands of the operator/are integers, the result is a float value.

12. The sizeof() operator determines the memory space required by its operand.
13. A char data type always occupies one byte.
14. Side effect is an action that results from the evaluation of an expression.
15. An expression statement is terminated with a period.
16. The knowledge of precedence alone is sufficient to evaluate a compound expression.
17. Conditional operator is a binary operator.
18. The left operand in an assignment expression must be a single variable.
19. Given expression is valid ++(x+y).
20. Given expression is valid a&&= b.
21. Associativity of operator is either Left to Right or Right to Left.
22. Every operator has an Associativity.
23. Associativity has no role to play unless the precedence of operators is same.
24. Given expression (long double) (10 + 25) converts integer constant 35, to long double.
25. The expression ++5 ia valid.
26. Cast operator returns an rvalue.
27. The increment operator can only be applied to an operand that has a modification 1-value.
28. The expression ++a is equivalent to a+=1.
29. Some of the unary operators may precede or follow the operand.
30. The assignment statement i + j = k; is a valid statement.
31. The exponentiation operator in C is **.
32. The logical constant false is represented by zero and true by non-zero.
33. In C language, there is no operator available for logical eXclusive-OR(XOR) operation.
34. Qualified constant cannot be initialized with a value.

35. The expression !(x>=y) is equivalent to the expression x<y.
36. Associativity is used to determine which of several different expressions is evaluated first.

Answers

1. True	2. False	3. True	4. True
5. False	6. False	7. False	8. True
9. False	10. True	11. False	12. True
13. True	14. True	15. False	16. False
17. False	18. True	19. False	20. False
21. True	22. True	23. True	24. True
25. False	26. True	27. True	28. True
29. True	30. False	31. False	32. True
33. True	34. False	35. True	36. True

D. OBJECTIVE TYPE QUESTIONS

1. The bitwise AND is used for
   (a) masking (b) comparison
   (c) division (d) shifting bits
2. The bitwise OR is used to
   (a) set the desired bits to 1 (b) multiply numbers
   (c) divide numbers (d) set the desired bits to 0
3. The bitwise XOR is used to
   (a) complement the desired bits
   (b) multiply the numbers
   (c) divide the numbers
   (d) mask the bits
4. Logical right shift results in
   (a) maintaining the leftmost bit value
   (b) zero is shifted to the leftmost bit position

(c) one is shifted to the rightmost bit value
(d) zero is shifted to the rightmost position

5. Arithmetic right shift results in
   (a) zero is shifted to the leftmost bit position
   (b) one is shifted to the rightmost bit value
   (c) maintains the leftmost bit value
   (d) zero is shifted to the rightmost bit position
6. The result of the expression ~ ~ 7 is
   (a) 7 (b) 1
   (c) 0 (d) invalid expression
7. The operator that can be used for simple encryption is
   (a) ~ (b) &
   (c) ^ (d) all the above
8. Identify the invalid compound assignment.
   (a) += (b) ^=
   (c) <<= (d) ~=
9. Identify the valid compound assignment.
   (a) <<= (b) >>=
   (c) options a and b (d) >>>=
10. Identify the valid expression(s).
   (a) a = 0 (b) a = b = 0
   (c) a%= (x % 10) (d) all the above
11. What is the value of x after executing the following statement?

```
int x = 011 | 0x10;
```

   (a) 13 (b) 19
   (c) 25 (d) 27
12. What is the function of the modulus in most languages?
   (a) Sets a system environmental value to either base 10, base 8, or base 16

(b) Returns the first argument raised to the second argument power

(c) Prints out the actual code written to standard output rather than executing the code

(d) Rcturns the remainder after dividing one number by another

13. What is the value of x in the sample code below?

```
double x; x = (2 + 3) * 2 + 3;
```

(a) 10 (b) 13

(c) 25 (d) 28

14. What value will be stored in z if the following code is executed?

```
main( )
{
int x = 5, y = -10, z;
int a = 4, b = 2;
z = x+++++y * b / a;
}
```

(a) –2 (b) 0

(c) 1 (d) 2

15. Explicit type conversion is known as

(a) casting (b) coercion

(c) options a and b (d) upward type conversion

16. Which expression yields correct value for the expression 1/3?

(a) 1*/3 (b) (float) 1/3

(c) options a and b (d) float(1/3)

17. The associativity of ++ operator is

(a) right to left

(b) left to right

(c) a for arithmetic expression and b for pointer expression

(d) a for pointer expression and b for arithmetic expression

18. The associativity of assignment operators is

(a) right to left

(b) left to right
(c) a for arithmetic expression and b for pointer expression
(d) a for pointer expression and b for arithmetic expression

19. The associativity of comma operator is
(a) right to left
(b) left to right
(c) a for arithmetic expression and b for pointer expression
(d) a for pointer expression and b for arithmetic expression

20. The associative of ! operator is
(a) right to left
(b) left to right
(c) a for arithmetic expression and b for pointer expression
(d) a for pointer expression and b for arithmetic expression

21. The associativity of ~ operator is
(a) right to left
(b) left to right
(c) a for arithmetic expression and b for pointer expression
(d) a for pointer expression and b for arithmetic expression

22. The associativity of indirection operator is
(a) right to left
(b) left to right
(c) a for arithmetic expression and b for pointer expression
(d) a for pointer expression and b for arithmetic expression

23. The number of binary arithmetic operators in C is
(a) 5 (b) 4
(c) 6 (d) 7

24. The number of unary arithmetic operators in C is
(a) 1 (b) 4
(c) 3 (d) 2

25. If both the operands of the operator/are integers, the result is

(a) a float value (b) an integer value

(c) Options a or b (d) undefined

26. Which is not a valid expression?

(a) +0XAB5 (b) –0525

(c) 15– (d) +a

27. Identify the logical operator

(a) ! (b) ! =

(c) ~ (d) = =

28. Identify the relational operator

(a) && (b) >

(c) || (d) !

29. Which of the following statement is wrong?

(a) mes = 123.56 (b) con = 'T' * 'A'

(c) this = 'T' * 20 (d) 3 + a = b ;

30. Which of the following shows the correct hierarchy of arithmetic operators in C?

(a) **, * or /, + or - (b) **, *, /, +, -

(c) **, /, *, +, - (d) / or *, - or +

31. In b = 6.6 / a + 2 * n ; which operation will be performed first?

(a) 6.6 / a (b) a + 2

(c) 2 * n (d) Depends upon compiler

32. Which of the following is allowed in a C Arithmetic Instruction?

(a) [ ] (b) { }

(c) ( ) (d) None of the above

33. If a is an integer variable, a = 5 / 2; will return a value

(a) 2.5 (b) 3

(c) 2 (d) 0

34. The expression, a = 30 * 1000 + 2768; evaluates to

(a) 32768 (b) –32768

(c) 113040 (d) 0

35. The expression x = 4 + 2 % –8 evaluates to
    (a) –6 (b) 6
    (c) 4 (d) None of the above
36. The operator/when applied to floating values yields
    (a) remainder value
    (b) negative value of the remainder
    (c) quotient including fractional part
    (d) integer quotient value only
37. The operator % can be applied only to
    (a) float values (b) double values
    (c) options a and b (d) integer values
38. x % y is equal to
    (a) (x – (x/y)) (b) (x – (x/y) * y)
    (c) (y – (x/y)) (d) (y – (x/y) * y)
39. The operator can be applied to
    (a) integer values (b) float values
    (c) double values (d) all the above
40. The second operand of the operator % must always be
    (a) negative value (b) non-zero
    (c) zero (d) positive value
41. If both the operands of the operators / are integers, the result is
    (a) a float value (b) an integer value
    (c) option a or b (d) undefined
42. Integer division result in
    (a) rounding of the fractional part of the quotient
    (b) truncating the fractional part of the quotient
    (c) floating value
    (d) syntax error
43. Assume c1 and c2 as char variables. If c1 = 'A" c2 = '2'; what are the results of the statements putchar (c1 + 3) and putchar (c2 – 1)?

(a) D, 1 (b) C, 2
(c) d, 1 (d) C, 1

44. Which is not a valid expression?
(a) +0XAB5 (b) –0525
(c) 15– (d) +a

45. Which is not a valid expression?
(a) –p++ (b) ++p—
(c) ++6 (d) ++x++

46. Which is not a valid expression?
(a) ++(a + b) (b) y– –
(c) — x — (d) ++p + q

47. The equality operator is represented by
(a) := (b) .EQ.
(c) = (d) = =

48. Identify the logical operator
(a) ! (b) !=
(c) ~ (d) = =

49. Identify the relational operator
(a) && (b) >
(c) || (d) !

50. The number of binary bitwise operators in C is
(a) 3 (b) 4
(c) 5 (d) 6

51. The number of bitwise operator in C is
(a) 4 (b) 5
(c) 6 (d) 7

52. Identify the operator not used in C
(a) ~ (b) %
(c) ^ (d) * *

53. The operator % yields

(a) quotient value
(b) remainder value
(c) percentage value
(d) fractional part of the division

54. The operator % can be applied only to
(a) float values
(b) double values
(c) option a and b
(d) integral values

55. The second operand of the operator % must always be
(a) negative value
(b) non zero
(c) zero
(d) positive value

56. Tell the number of binary arithmetic operators in C is
(a) 5
(b) 4
(c) 6
(d) 7

57. Tell the number of unary arithmetic operators in C is
(a) 1
(b) 4
(c) 3
(d) 2

58. Identify the operator not used in C
(a) ~
(b) %
(c) ^
(d) **

59. The operator % yields
(a) Quotient value
(b) remainder value
(c) percentage value
(d) fractional part of the division

60. Which of the following expressions will correctly swap two integers without using a temporary variable?
(a) (x ^= y), (y ^= x)
(b) (x = y), (y = x)
(c) (x ^= y), (y ^= x), (x ^=y)
(d) x ^= (y ^= x)

61. What is the correct and full portable way to obtain the most significant byte of an unsigned integer x?
(a) x & 0xFF00

(b) x>>24

(c) x >> (CHAR – BIT * (sizeof(int) – 3))

(d) x >> (CHAR_BIT * (sizeof(int) -1))

62. What is the value of the following expression?

```
i = 1;
i << 1 % 2
```

(a) 2 (b) –2

(c) 1 (d) 0

63. What is the value of the following expression?

```
i = 1;
i = (i<<= 1 % 2)
```

(a) 2 (b) 1

(c) 0 (d) syntax error

64. For the following statements find the values generated for p and q?

```
int p = 0, q = 1;
p = q++;
p = q –;
p –q;
```

The value of p and q are

(a) 1, 1 (b) 0, 0

(c) 3, 2 (d) 1, 2

65. Which of the following is a better approach to do the operation i = i* 16;?

(a) multiply i by 16 and keep it (b) shift left by 4 bits

(c) add i 16 times (d) none of the above

66. Which of the following is an example of compounded assignment statement?

(a) a =5 (b) a+=5

(c) a=b=c (d) a=b

67. The operator && is an example for .... operator

(a) Assignment (b) Increment
(c) Logical (d) Rational

68. The operator & is used for
(a) Bitwise AND (b) Bitwise OR
(c) Logical AND (d) Logical OR

69. The operator/can be applied to
(a) integer values (b) float values
(c) double values (d) all of these

70. The equality operator is represented by
(a) := (b) EQ:
(c) = (d) = =

71. Operators have hierarchy. It is used to know which operator
(a) is most important (b) is used first
(c) is faster (d) operates on large numbers

72. The bitwise AND operator is used for
(a) Masking (b) Comparison
(c) Division (d) Shifting bits

73. The bitwise OR operator is used to
(a) set the desired bits to 1 (b) set the desired bits to 0
(c) divide numbers (d) multiply numbers

74. Which of the following operator has the highest precedence?
(a) * (b) ==
(c) => (d) ()

75. Which operator has the lowest priority?
(a) ++ (b) %
(c) + (d) ,

76. Which operator has the highest priority?
(a) ++ (b) %
(c) addition + (d) ||

77. The operator + in a+=4 means

(a) a = a + 4 (b) a + 4 = a
(c) a = 4 (d) a = 4 + 4

78. The number of bitwise operators in C is
(a) 4 (b) 5
(c) 6 (d) 7

79. The symbol of exclusive OR operator is
(a) ^ (b) ~
(c) & (d) |

80. The symbol of one's complement operator is
(a) & (b) ^
(c) ~ (d) |

81. The symbol of bitwise AND operator is
(a) << (b) &=
(c) && (d) &

82. The symbol of bitwise OR operator is
(a) | (b) ||
(c) != (d) >>

83. The symbol of left shift operator is
(a) < (b) <<
(c) <= (d) <<<

84. The symbol of right shift operator is
(a) >= (b) >>>
(c) >> (d) >

85. Identify the invalid compound statement
(a) += (b) ^=
(c) <<= (d) ~=

86. Which operator has the lowest priority?
(a) Assignment (b) Division
(c) Comma (d) Conditional operator

87. Which operator has the highest priority?

(a) ( ) (b) ->
(c) . (d) all the above

88. Of the following, which are logical operators?
(a) && (b) !
(c) || (d) options a , b and c

89. The symbol of exclusive OR operator is
(a) ^ (b) ~
(c) & (d) |

90. The symbol of one's complement operator is
(a) & (b) ^
(c) ~ (d) |

91. The symbol of bitwise AND operator is
(a) << (b) &=
(c) && (d) &

92. The symbol of bitwise OR operator is
(a) | (b) ||
(c) ! = (d) >>

93. The symbol of left shift operator is
(a) < (b) <<
(c) < = (d) <<<

94. The symbol of right shift operator is
(a) >= (b) >>>
(c) >> (d) >

95. The associativity of bitwise AND, OR, XOR is
(a) right to left
(b) left to right
(c) a for arithmetic expression and b for pointer expression
(d) a for pointer expression and b for arithmetic expression

96. The associativity of logical AND, OR is
    (a) right to left
    (b) left to right
    (c) a for arithmetic expression and b for pointer expression
    (d) a for pointer expression and b for arithmetic expression
97. Which operator has the lowest priority?
    (a) Assignment (b) Division
    (c) Comma (d) Conditional operator
98. Which operator has the highest priority?
    (a) ( ) (b) →
    (c) . (d) all the above
99. Which operator has the highest priority?
    (a) ++ (b) %
    (c) + (d) /
100. Which operator has the lowest priority?
    (a) & (b) +
    (c) <= (d) ||
101. Which is executed quickly?
    (a) p++ (b) ++p
    (c) options a and b (d) p + 1
102. p++ executes faster than p + 1 since
    (a) p uses registers
    (b) single machine instruction is required for p++
    (c) options a and b
    (d) none of the above
103. Of the following, which are logical operators?
    (a) && (b) !
    (c) || (d) options a, b, and c
104. In a C expression, how is a logical AND represented?

(a) ||
(b) .AND
(c) @@
(d) &&

105. Which of the following is ternary operator?
(a) ? :
(b) *
(c) sizeof
(d) ^

106. Which of the following is NOT a bitwise operator?
(a) &
(b) ^
(c) |
(d) ||

107. The type char operator is
(a) (type)
(b) cast( )
(c) //
(d) " "

108. Which of the following statements is/are TRUE?
1. A char data type variable always occupies one byte independent of the system architecture.
2. The sizeof operator is used to determine the amount of memory occupied by a variable.
(a) both 1 and 2
(b) 1 only
(c) 2 only
(d) neither 1 nor 2

109. What might be the minimum value for the data type int, for 32 bit compiler?
(a) 0
(b) –2,147,483,648
(c) –2,147,483,647
(d) –32768

110. If the value of a = 10 and b = –1, the value of x after executing the following expression is

```
x = (a! = 10) && (b = 1)
```

(a) 0
(b) 1
(c) –1
(d) none

111. What would be the output of the expression 11 ^ 5?
(a) 6
(b) 8
(c) 14
(d) 15

Answers

1. (a)	2. (a)	3. (a)	4. (b)	5. (c)
6. (a)	7. (d)	8. (d)	9. (c)	10. (d)
11. (c)	12. (d)	13. (b)	14. (c)	15. (c)
16. (c)	17. (a)	18. (a)	19. (b)	20. (a)
21. (a)	22. (a)	23. (a)	24. (b)	25. (b)
26. (c)	27. (a)	28. (b)	29. (d)	30. (d)
31. (c)	32. (c)	33. (c)	34. (b)	35. (b)
36. (c)	37. (d)	38. (b)	39. (d)	40. (b)
41. (b)	42. (b)	43. (a)	44. (c)	45. (c)
46. (a)	47. (d)	48. (a)	49. (b)	50. (c)
51. (c)	52. (d)	53. (b)	54. (d)	55. (d)
56. (a)	57. (b)	58. (d)	59. (b)	60. (c)
61. (d)	62. (a)	63. (a)	64. (a)	65. (b)
66. (b)	67. (c)	68. (a)	69. (d)	70. (d)
71. (b)	72. (c)	73. (d)	74. (d)	75. (d)
76. (a)	77. (a)	78. (c)	79. (a)	80. (c)
81. (d)	82. (a)	83. (b)	84. (c)	85. (d)
86. (c)	87. (a)	88. (d)	89. (a)	90. (c)
91. (d)	92. (a)	93. (b)	94. (c)	95. (b)
96. (b)	97. (c)	98. (d)	99. (a)	100. (d)
101. (c)	102. (b)	103. (d)	104. (d)	105. (a)
106. (d)	107. (a)	108. (a)	109. (b)	110. (a)
111. (c)				

CHAPTER 3

Console Input and Output

A. CODE SNIPPETS

Problem 1

Find the output of the following program?

```
#include<stdio.h>
#include <conio.h>
void main( )
{
int rn;
printf("%d", scanf("%d", &rn));
getch();
}
```

Output:

1

NOTE: value 12 is given to scanf.

Problem 2

Find the output of the following program?

```
#include<stdio.h>
#include <conio.h>
```

```
void main( )
{
int i = 12;
printf("%d", i);
getch();
}
```

Output:

```
12
```

Problem 3

Find the output of the following program?

```
#include<stdio.h>
#include <conio.h>
void main( )
{
float f = 5.13316;
printf("\n%6.1f", f);
printf("\n%6.3f", f);
printf("\n%5.4f", f);
printf("\n%2.2f", f);
printf("\n%0.0f", f);
getch();
}
```

Output:

```
5.2
5.133
5.1331
5.13
5
```

Problem 4

To print out i and j given below, write printf( ) statement?

```
float i = 3.14;
double j = 3.14;
```

Output:

```
printf("%f %lf", i, j);
```

Problem 5

Find the output of the following program?

```
#include<stdio.h>
#include <conio.h>
void main( )
{
int i = 4;
printf("%d = = 4" "%s", i, i = = 4? "TRUE": "FALSE");
getch();
}
```

Output:

```
4 = = 4 TRUE
```

Problem 6

To scan i and j given below, write scanf( ) statement?

```
float i;
double j;
```

Output:

```
scanf("%f %lf", &i, &j);
```

Problem 7

Find the output of the following program?

```
#include<stdio.h>
```

```
#include<conio.h>
void main( )
{
char ch ;
ch = getchar( ) ;
if ( islower ( ch ) )
putchar ( toupper ( ch ) ) ;
else
putchar ( tolower ( ch ) ) ;
getch();
}
```

Output:

```
i to I
s to S
```

Problem 8

Find the output of the following program?

```
#include<stdio.h>
#include<conio.h>
void main( )
{
int rn = 12;
float fees = 4.653;
char name[ ] = "Ikvinderpal Singh";
printf ( "\n%4d\t%3.3f\t%4s", rn, fees, name );
getch();
}
```

Output:

```
12 4.653 End of Life
```

Problem 9

Find the output of the following program?

```
#include<stdio.h>
#include<conio.h>
void main( )
{
printf ( "the data structures \b\b not \rthe relevant
   book \
for the postgraduate students." ) ;
getch();
}
```

Output:

```
the relevant book for the postgraduate students.
```

Problem 10

Check the errors from the following program?

```
#include<stdio.h>
#include <conio.h>
void main( )
{
char ch;
int i;
scanf("%c", &i);
scanf("%d", &ch);
printf("%c %d", ch, i);
getch();
}
```

Output:

```
Error
```

Problem 11

Find the output of the following program?

```
#include<stdio.h>
#include <conio.h>
void main( )
{
printf("%c", ~('E' * -1));
getch();
}
```

Output:

```
D
```

Problem 12

Find the output of the following program?

```
#include<stdio.h>
#include <conio.h>
void main( )
{
char *ptr;
ptr = "%d\n";
ptr++;
printf(ptr - 1, 15);
getch();
}
```

Output:

```
15
```

Problem 13

Find the output of the following program?

```
#include<stdio.h>
```

```
#include <conio.h>
void main( )
{
printf("\n%%%%");
getch();
}
```

Output:

%%

Problem 14

Find the output of the following program?

```
#include<stdio.h>
#include<conio.h>
char str[ ] = "Always speak the truth" ;

void main( )
{
int i = 0 ;
while ( str[i] != '\0' )
{
putch ( str[i] ) ;
i++;
}
getch();
}
```

Output:

Always speak the truth

Problem 15

Check the errors from the following program?

```
#include<stdio.h>
#include<conio.h>
void main( )
{
int i;
char str[ ] = "Ikvinder";
while ( str!= '\0' )
{
printf ( "%c", *str ) ;
str++ ;
}
getch();
}
```

Output:

```
Error.
```

NOTE: L-value required.

Problem 16

Find the output of the following program?

```
#include<stdio.h>
#include<conio.h>
void main( )
{
double d;
scanf ("%f", &d);
printf ("\nValue = %lf", d);
getch();
}
```

Output:

```
No error.
```

Problem 17

Find the output of the following program?

```
#include<stdio.h>
#include <conio.h>
void main( )
{
int i = 2;
printf("\ni=%*d", i, i);
getch();
}
```

Output:

```
i = 2
```

Problem 18

Can we specify variable field width in a scanf( ) format string?

Output:

No.

Problem 19

Check the errors from the following program?

```
#include<stdio.h>
#include<conio.h>
void main( )
{
int i;
scanf ("%d\n", &j);
printf ("\nValue = %d", i);
getch();
}
```

Output:

```
Error.
```

NOTE: undefined symbol j.

Problem 20

Check the errors from the following program?

```
#include<stdio.h>
#include<conio.h>
void main( )
{
char *str[5] ;
for ( i = 0 ; i < 5 ; i++ )
scanf ( "%s", str[i]);
getch();
}
```

Output:

```
Error.
```

NOTE: undefined symbol i.

Problem 21

Check the errors from the following program?

```
#include<stdio.h>
#include<conio.h>
void main( )
{
int d, m, y;
printf ( "\nEnter day, month and year\n" );
scanf ( "%d%*c%d%*c%d", &d, &m, &y );
printf ( "The date is: %d - %d - %d", d, m, y);
getch();
}
```

Output:

No error.

Problem 22

Check the errors from the following program?

```
#include<stdio.h>
#include<conio.h>
void main( )
{
char ch;
sprintf (ch,"%4d\t%2.3f\n%s", 1, 7.534, "Ikvinder pal
   singh");
printf ("\n%s", ch);
getch();
}
```

Output:

No error.

Problem 23

Check the errors from the following program?

```
#include<stdio.h>
#include<conio.h>
void main( )
{
char buffer[50];
int num = 47;
double d = 4.62312;
char name[20] = "Bajwa";
sprintf ( buffer, "%d %lf %s", num, d, name ) ;
printf ( "\n%s", buffer);
```

```
sscanf ( buffer, "%4d %2.2lf %s", &num, &d, name);
printf ( "\n%s", buffer);
printf ( "\n%d %lf %s", num, d, name);
getch();
}
```

Output:

```
No error.
```

B. FILL IN THE BLANKS

1. The .... function can be used to read a character from the standard input device.
2. The .... function can be used for writing characters one at a time to the output terminal.
3. The .... function is used to get a character from console but does not echo to the screen.
4. The character .... is used as suppression character in conversion specification.
5. The function putchar( ) uses ...., as its argument.
6. The statement .... reads the value of an int variable i.
7. Execution of scanf("%[^\n]",str); reads the input, to store in a char array str, until a .... is encountered.
8. Execution of printf("%d", 'A'); displays .... and printf("%c", 'A'); displays ....
9. Execution of printf("%-5d", 20); displays the output as ....
10. The .... function is used to get a character from console, and echoes to the screen.
11. The functions .... and .... are used to reading and writing strings.
12. Execution of printf("%+d", 5); displays the output as ....
13. Execution of printf("%4.3f", 3.1478); displays the output as ....

14. The library functions are made available to a program, by using ....

15. Conversion specification is represented by .... and a ....

Answers

1. getchar()	2. putchar()
3. getch()	4. *
5. ASCII value	6. scanf("%d", &i);
7. new line	8. 65 A
9. 20	10. getche()
11. gets(), puts()	12. +5
13. 3.148	14. # include facility
15. %, conversion character	

C. TRUE OR FALSE

State whether each of the following is true or false

1. There are two types of console I/O statements: formatted and unformatted.
2. The gets() function is used to read single character.
3. The getch() is used to display numeric values.
4. C doesn't have inherent I/O facilities.
5. The function scanf( ) returns the number of input data, that has been read successfully.
6. The function getchar( ) uses one parameter only.
7. The symbol % is printed using printf("\%"); in a program.
8. The conversion specification %f is equivalent to %F.
9. The conversion specification %h is used to read hexadecimal values.
10. The conversion specification %0 is used to print octal values.
11. Conversion specification starts with\.

12. Unlike the scanf function, the gets function reads the entire line of text until a new line character is encountered and does not stop upon encountering any other white-space character.
13. The printf function can print a string on the screen without using any format specifier.
14. If an error occurs, printf( ) returns a negative value.
15. The format specification %1c is used to print a character using printf( ).
16. The puts() function is to write string.
17. The getch() and getche() are the same.

Answers

1. True	2. False	3. False	4. True
5. True	6. False	7. False	8. False
9. False	10. False	11. False	12. True
13. False	14. True	15. False	16. True
17. False			

D. OBJECTIVE TYPE QUESTIONS

1. If an integer is to be entered through the keyboard, which function would you use?

   (a) scanf( )   (b) gets( )
   (c) getche( )   (d) getchar( )

2. If a character string is to be received through the keyboard which function would work faster?

   (a) scanf( )   (b) gets( )
   (c) getche( )   (d) getchar( )

3. The format string of a printf( ) function can contain:

   (a) Characters, format specifications and escape sequences
   (b) Character, integers and floats

(c) Strings, integers and escape sequences
(d) Inverted commas, percentage sign and backslash character

4. A field-width specifier in a printf( ) function:
   (a) Controls the margins of the program listing
   (b) Specifies the maximum value of a number
   (c) Controls the size of type used to print numbers
   (d) Specifies how many columns will be used to print the number
5. Header files in C contain
   (a) compiler commands
   (b) library functions
   (c) header information of C programs
   (d) operators for file
6. What format is used to print a character with the printf function?
   (a) %s (b) %c
   (c) %char (d) %1c
7. "The stock's value increased by 15%"
   (a) printf ("\"The stock\'s value increased by %d%%.\", 15)
   (b) printf ("\"The stock\'s value increased by %d%n\", 15)
   (c) printf ("\"The stock\'s value increased by %d%%.\n", 15)
   (d) printf ("\"The stock\'s value increased by %d%%.\"\n);
8. main( )

```
{
double x = ½ .0 - ½;
printf ("x=%.2f\n", x);
}
```

   What will be printed when the above code is executed?
   (a) x = 0.00 (b) x = 0.25
   (c) x = 0.50 (d) x = 1.00
9. main( )

```
{
```

```
int x = 5, y = 10;
double z;
z = (double) (x / y);
printf ("z = %.2f\n", z);
}
```

What will be printed when the above code is executed?

(a) z = 0.00 (b) z = 0.50
(c) z = 1.00 (d) 2.00

10. What will be printed when the following code is executed?

```
main( )
{
int i = 4, a = 6;
double z;
z = a /i;
printf ("z=%.2f\n", z);
}
```

(a) z = 0.00 (b) z = 1.00
(c) z = 1.50 (d) z = 2.00

11. main( )

```
{
int x = 3, y = 3, z = 3;
z - = x- - - - -y;
printf ("x = %d y = %d z = %d", x, y, z);
}
```

What will be the values of x, y and z?

(a) x = 2 y = 2 z = 2 (b) x = 1 y = 2 z = 2
(c) x = 2 x = 2 y = 0) (c) x = 2 y = 2 z = 1

12. main( )

```
{
int x, y, z;
```

```
printf ("%d\n", (z>= y>= x ? 10 : 20));
}
```

What might be the values of x, y and z, if 20 has to be printed?

(a) 0, 0, 0 (b) –1, –1, –2

(c) –1, 0, 1 (d) none

13. How the library functions are made available to a program?
    (a) by using # define statements
    (b) by linking loader to the program
    (c) by using # include statements
    (d) by using function declarations
14. The function putchar( ) uses
    (a) no argument
    (b) one argument that is the ASCII value of a character
    (c) two arguments; first one is ASCII value and the second one is number of characters
    (d) one argument that is a string
15. The function getchar( ) uses
    (a) no argument
    (b) one argument that is a character variable
    (c) one argument that is the ASCII value of a character
    (d) one argument that is the string
16. The function scanf( ) returns
    (a) the actual values read for each argument
    (b) the number of successfully read input values
    (c) no value (void)
    (d) ASCII values of the character read
17. The function printf( ) returns
    (a) the actual values displayed for each argument
    (b) no value(void)
    (c) the number of characters displayed
    (d) ASCII values of the character read

18. Identify the correct statement.
    (a) C library functions provide I/O facilities
    (b) C has inherent I/O facilities
    (c) C doesn't have inherent I/O facilities
    (d) options a and c
19. Header files in C contain
    (a) compiler commands
    (b) library functions
    (c) header information of C programs
    (d) operators for files
20. How are the library functions made available to a program?
    (a) by using # define statements
    (b) by linking loader to the program
    (c) by using # include statements
    (d) by using function declarations
21. Identify the character-oriented console I/O functions.
    (a) getchar( ) and putchar( ) (b) gets( ) and puts( )
    (c) scanf( ) and printf( ) (d) fgets( ) and fputs( )
22. Identify the formatted console I/O functions.
    (a) getchar( ) and putchar( ) (b) gets( ) and puts( )
    (c) scanf( ) and printf( ) (d) fgets( ) and fputs( )
23. What is the value returned by getchar( ) when an alphabet key is pressed?
    (a) the alphabet entered from the keyboard
    (b) one argument that is an ASCII value of a character
    (c) two arguments; first one is ASCII value and the second one is number of characters
    (d) one argument, that is a string
24. The function putchar( ) uses
    (a) no argument

(b) one argument that is an ASCII value of a character

(c) two arguments; first one is ASCII value and the second one is number of characters

(d) one argument, that is a string

25. The function getchar( ) uses

(a) no argument

(b) one argument that is a character variable

(c) one argument that is the ASCII value of a character

(d) one argument, that is a string

26. Identify the wrong statement.

(a) putchar(65) (b) putchar('x')

(c) putchar("x") (d) putchar('\n')

27. The function scanf( ) returns

(a) the actual values read for each argument

(b) the number of successfully read input values

(c) no value (void)

(d) ASCII values of the characters read

28. Conversion specification include

(a) \ and a conversion character

(b) / and a conversion character

(c) & and a conversion character

(d) % and a conversion character

29. Identify the correct statement given double x;

(a) scanf("%d", &x); (b) scanf("%f", x);

(c) scanf("%d", *x); (d) scanf("%f", &x);

30. Identify the wrong statements given, int x; float y; char z;

(a) scanf("%d, %f, %c", &x, &y, &z);

(b) scanf("%d, %f, %c", &x, &y, z);

(c) scanf("Rs. %d, %f, %c", &x, &y, &z);

(d) options a and c

31. What is the value returned by printf( ) function if an error occurs
   (a) Positive value (b) 0
   (c) Negative value (d) 1

32. What is the purpose of flag– in printf( ) function ?
   (a) Centered (b) right justified
   (c) Putting sign (d) left justified

33. What is the purpose of flag + in printf( ) function ?
   (a) left justified
   (b) + or – precedes the signed numbers
   (c) right justified
   (d) centered

34. What is the purpose of the flag # used in printf( ) function ?
   (a) left justified
   (b) right justified
   (c) 0 And 0x precedes non zero octal and hexa values respectively
   (d) Leading zeros appear

35. What is the purpose of the flag 0 used in printf( ) function ?
   (a) leading blanks are displayed
   (b) leading zeros are displayed
   (c) -- sign precedes
   (d) + or – sign precedes

36. What are the values of x, y and z, if 25 20 30 are given as inputs for scanf ("%d %* d %d", &x, &y, &z); ?
   (a) x = 25, y is not assigned, z = 30
   (b) x = 25, y = 20, z = 30
   (c) x = 25, y = 30, z is not assigned
   (d) x = 25, y is not assigned, z = 20

37. What are the values of a, b, c, given int a, c; float b; with inputs as 50, 3.52, 20 for the statement scanf("%d%*c% f%*c%d", &a, &b, &c); ?

(a) a = 50 b = , c = 3.52
(b) a = 50 b is not assigned, c = 3
(c) a = 50 b = 3.52 c = 20
(d) a = 50 b and c are not assigned

38. What are the values of p and q (integer variables) with inputs given as 50356 for the statement scanf("%2d %2d", &p, &q);?
(a) p = 50 q = 35
(b) p = 50q = 356
(c) p = 50 b = 3.52 c = 20
(d) a = 50 a and c are not assigned

39. What are the values of x and y (integer variables) with inputs given as 356 47 3 for the statement scanf("%2d %2d", &x, &y);?
(a) x = 356 y = 47 (b) x = 35 y = 6
(c) x = 35 y = 4 (d) x = 35 y = 47

40. char p, q; scanf("%c%1s", &p, &q);
What are the values assigned, if x and y are given as inputs?
(a) p = x and q = blank (b) p = x and q is not assigned
(c) p = x and q = y (d) p = x and q = x

41. Identify the correct statement(s) given the declaration char x, y;
(a) scanf ("%c%c", &x, &y);
(b) scanf ("%c%1s", &x, &y);
(c) scanf ("%* [ ] %c", &x, &y);
(d) all the above

42. What is the output of the statement

```
scanf ("%0%d %f%1s", &a, &b, &c, &d);
```

for the inputs 45 25 32 20 A given the declarations int a, b; float c; char d;?
(a) a = $(45)_8$ b is not assigned c = 25.32 d = A
(b) a = $(45)_8$ b = 25 c = 0.32 d = 2

(c) a = (45), b = 25   c = 20.0   d = A
(d) all the above

43. The statement printf("%*d %*.*f", a, b, c, d, e); is interpreted for a = 5, c = 10 and d = 5 as
(a) printf ("%5d %10.5%f ", b, e);
(b) printf ("%5d %5.5f ", b, e);
(c) printf ("%5d %10*f", c, e);
(d) printf ("%*d %10.5f ", a, e);

44. What is the value returned by printf( ) function, if an error occurs?
(a) Positive value
(b) 0
(c) Negative value
(d) 1

45. What is the purpose of the flag – in printf( ) function?
(a) Centered
(b) Right justified
(c) Putting sign
(d) Left justified

46. What is the purpose of the flag + used in printf( ) function?
(a) Left Justified
(b) + or – precedes the signed numbers
(c) Right justified
(d) Centered

47. What is the purpose of the flag # used in printf( ) function?
(a) Left Justified
(b) Right justified
(c) 0 and 0x precede non-zero octal and hexa values respectively
(d) Leading zeros appear

48. What is the purpose of the flag 0 used in the function printf( )?
(a) Leading blanks are displayed
(b) Leading zero appears
(c) – sign precedes
(d) + or – sign precedes

49. Which pair of functions below is used for single character I/O.
    (a) Getchar() and putchar()
    (b) Scanf() and printf()
    (c) Input() and output()
    (d) None of these
50. The printf() function retunes which value when an error occurs?
    (a) Positive value
    (b) Zero
    (c) Negative value
    (d) None of these
51. Identify the wrong statement
    (a) putchar(65)
    (b) putchar('x')
    (c) putchar("x")
    (d) putchar('\n')
52. Which of the following is character oriented console I/O function?
    (a) getchar() and putchar()
    (b) gets() and puts()
    (c) scanf() and printf()
    (d) fgets() and fputs()
53. The output of printf("%u", –1) is
    (a) –1
    (b) minimum int value
    (c) maximum int value
    (d) Error message
54. An Ampersand before the name of a variable denotes
    (a) Actual Value
    (b) Variable Name
    (c) Address
    (d) Data Type
55. To receive the string "We have got the guts, you get the glory!!" in an array char str[100] which of the following functions would you use?
    (a) scanf ("%s", str) ;
    (b) gets (str) ;
    (c) getche (str) ;
    (d) fgetchar (str) ;
56. Which function would you use if a single key were to be received through the keyboard?
    (a) scanf( )
    (b) gets( )
    (c) getche( )
    (d) getchar( )
57. The function printf( ) returns
    (a) the actual values displayed for each argument
    (b) no value (void)

(c) the number of characters displayed

(d) ASCII values of the characters read

58. # include <stdio.h>

```
main( )
{
int a = 0xff;
(a << 4 >> 12) ? printf ("Sandeep") :printf
("Ikvinder");
}
```

What will be the output of the program?

(a) Ikvinder (b) Sandeep

(c) Error: Incorrect assignment (d) None

59. int x = 0x1234, y = 0x5555;

```
printf ("0x%04.4x\n", x | y);
printf ("0x%04.4x\n", x | y);
printf ("0x%04.4x\n", x ^ y);
printf ("0x%04.4x\n", ~x);
```

What is output from the above sample code?

(a) The code will not compile.

(b) 0x5775
0x1014
0x4761
0xfffedcb

(c) 0x15f3
0x0492
0x1161
0xffffb2d

(d) 0x55d7
0x0450
0x5187
0xffffb2b

60. printf ("Daily Click!");

In the code segment above, the words Daily Click! will be printed to what output device?

(a) to an E-mail message

(b) to the console

(c) to the default printer

(d) to whenever standard output has been directed of

61. If x = 2, y = 6 and z = 6 then, what will be the output of

```
x = y = = z;
printf (%d", x);
```

(a) 0 (b) 1

(c) 2 (d) 6

62. int i = 20;

```
printf ("%x", i);
```

What is the output?

(a) x14 (b) 14

(c) 20 (d) none of the above

63. float x, y, z;

```
scanf ("%f %f", &x, &y); printf ("%.2f, %.2f", x,
y);
```

if input stream contains "4.2 3.2 3..." what will be the output?

(a) 4.20, 3.00 (b) 4.2, 2.3

(c) 4.20, 2.30 (d) 4.20 3.20

64. What will be the result of executing the following statement?

```
int i = 10;
printf ("%d %d %d", i, ++i, ++i);
```

(a) 10 11 12

(b) 10 11 11

(c) result is operating system dependent

(d) result is compiler dependent

65. What will be the result of the following program if the inputs are 2 3?

```
main( )
{
int a, b;
printf ("enter two numbers :");
scanf ("%d%d", a, b);
printf ("%d+%d=%d", a, b, a+b);
}
```

(a) 2 + 3 = 5

(b) syntax error

(c) will generate run time error /code dump

(d) a+b=5

66. main( )

```
{
int a=10, b=5, c=3, d=3;
if ((a<b)&&(c=d++)) printf ("%d %d %d %d", a, b, c,
d);
else printf ("%d %d %d %d", a, b, c, d);
}
```

(a) 10 5 3 4 (b) 10 5 4 4

(c) 10 5 3 3 (d) none of the above

67. What is he output of the following statement?

```
printf ("%u", -1);
```

(a) –1 (b) minimum int value

(c) maximum int value (d) error

68. Conversion specification includes

(a) \ and a conversion character

(b) / and a conversion character

(c) & and a conversion character

(d) % and a conversion character

69. Identify the correct statement given double x;

(a) scanf ("%d", &x);
(b) scanf ("%f", x);
(c) scanf ("%d", *x);
(d) scanf ("%lf", &x);

70. Identify the correct statement(s) given float y;

(a) scanf ("%e", &y)
(b) scanf ("%f",&y)
(c) scanf ("%g", &y);
(d) options a and c

71. For the given scanf( ) statement, what is the form of input expected?

```
scanf ("%d. %d. %d", &date, &month, &year);
```

(a) 22. 4. 1972
(b) 22 4 1972
(c) 22/ 4/ 1972
(d) options a and b

72. Identify the wrong statement given, int x; float y; char z;

(a) scanf(" %d, %f, %c", &x, &y, &z);
(b) scanf ("%d, %f, %c", &x, &y, &z);
(c) scanf ("Rs. %d, %f, %c", &x, &y, &z);
(d) options a and c

73. Find the output of the following code?

```
main( )
{
printf ("%c", 'A');
}
```

(a) 65
(b) a
(c) A
(d) Error

74. Find the output of the following code?

```
main( )
printf ("%d", 'A');
}
```

(a) 65 (b) a

(c) A (d) Error

75. Find the output of the following code?

```
main( )
{
char name [10];
strcpy (name, "Sameria");
printf ("%c%c%c", name [4], name [5], name [6]);
}
```

(a) eria (b) ia

(c) ria (d) meri

76. What is the purpose of the flag blank used in the function printf()?

(a) – precedes negative value and blank precedes positive value

(b) – precedes negative value and + precedes positive value

(c) – sign precedes negative value and nothing precedes positive value

(d) Blank precedes negative and positive numbers

77. What is the output of the following statement?

```
printf ("%u", -1);
```

(a) –1 (b) Minimum int value

(c) Maximum int value (d) Error

78. What is the output of the following code?

```
main( )
{
printf("%c", 'A');
}
```

(a) 65 (b) a

(c) A (d) Error

79. What is the output of the following code?

```
main( )
```

```
{
printf("%d", 'A');
}
```

(a) 65 (b) a

(c) A (d) Error

80. What format is used to print a character with a printf( ) function

(a) % s (b) % c

(c) % char (d) % lc

81. main( )

```
{
double  x = 1/2.0 -1/2 ;
printf( "x = %.2f \n", x);
}
```

What will be the printed output when the above code is executed?

(a) x = 0.00 (b) x = 0.25

(c) x = 1.00 (d) x = 1.25

82. If x = 2, y = 6, and z = 6 then, what will be the output of

```
X =y = z;
printf( "%d", x);
```

(a) 0 (b) 1

(c) 2 (d) 6

83. int i = 20;

```
printf ( " %x", i );
```

What will be the output?

(a) x14 (b) 14

(c) 20 (d) none of these

84. What will be printed when the following code is executed?

```
main( )
{
int i = 4, a = 6;
```

```
double z;
z = a/i;
printf("z= %.2f\n",z);
}
```

(a) z = 0.00 (b) z = 1.00
(c) z = 1.50 (d) z = 2.00

Answers

1. (a)	2. (b)	3. (a)	4. (d)	5. (b)
6. (b)	7. (a)	8. (c)	9. (a)	10. (b)
11. (a)	12. (d)	13. (c)	14. (a)	15. (b)
16. (a)	17. (c)	18. (d)	19. (b)	20. (c)
21. (a)	22. (c)	23. (b)	24. (b)	25. (a)
26. (c)	27. (b)	28. (b)	29. (c)	30. (d)
31. (b)	32. (d)	33. (b)	34. (c)	35. (b)
36. (a)	37. (c)	38. (a)	39. (b)	40. (c)
41. (d)	42. (d)	43. (a)	44. (c)	45. (d)
46. (b)	47. (c)	48. (b)	49. (a)	50. (b)
51. (c)	52. (a)	53. (c)	54. (c)	55. (b)
56. (d)	57. (c)	58. (a)	59. (b)	60. (b)
61. (b)	62. (b)	63. (d)	64. (d)	65. (c)
66. (c)	67. (c)	68. (d)	69. (d)	70. (d)
71. (a)	72. (b)	73. (c)	74. (a)	75. (c)
76. (a)	77. (c)	78. (c)	79. (a)	80. (b)
81. (c)	82. (b)	83. (b)	84. (b)	

CHAPTER

4

Control Flow Statements

A. CODE SNIPPETS

Problem 1

Find the output of the following program?

```
#include<stdio.h>
#include<conio.h>
void main( )
{
int i = 1;
float j = 1.0;
if ( i = = j )
printf ( "\ni and j are equal" );
else
printf ( "\ni and j are not equal" );
getch();
}
```

Output:

```
i and j are equal
```

Problem 2

Find the output of the following program?

```
#include<stdio.h>
#include<conio.h>
void main( )
{
int i = 5, j, k;
j = i = 12;
k = i < 12;
printf ( "\ni = %d \nj = %d \nk = %d", i, j, k );
getch();
}
```

Output:

```
i=12
j=12
k=0
```

Problem 3

Find the output of the following program?

```
#include<stdio.h>
#include<conio.h>
void main( )
{
int i = 3;
printf ( "\n%d %d %d", i= = 3, i = 5, i > 4 );
getch();
}
```

Output:

```
0 5 0
```

Problem 4

Find the output of the following program?

```
#include<stdio.h>
#include<conio.h>
void main( )
{
int i = 67;
char j = 'C';
if ( i = = j )
printf ( "Expert C Programming" );
else
printf( "Programming in C" );
getch();
}
```

Output:

```
Expert C Programming
```

Problem 5

Find the output of the following program?

```
#include<stdio.h>
#include<conio.h>
void main( )
{
int i = 25, j, k;
j = i = 10;
k = i < 10;
printf ( "\ni = %d \nj = %d \nk = %d", i, j, k );
getch();
}
```

Output:

```
i=10
j=10
k=1
```

Problem 6

Find the output of the following program?

```
#include<stdio.h>
#include<conio.h>
void main( )
{
int i = 1;
printf ( "\n%d %d %d", i != 1, i = 2, i < 3);
getch();
}
```

Output:

```
1 2 1
```

Problem 7

Check the errors from the following program?

```
#include<stdio.h>
#include<conio.h>
void main( )
{
float i = 1.5, j = 1.5;
if ( i = j )
printf ( "\ni and j are equal" );
getch();
}
```

Output:

```
No Error.
```

NOTE: The value 1.5 is assigned to i (i=j), then condition will be evaluated to true and printf() would get executed.

Problem 8

Check the errors from the following program?

```
#include<stdio.h>
#include<conio.h>
void main( )
{
int i = 34, j = 47;
if ( j >= i )
{
{
j = i;
i = j;
}
}
getch();
}
```

Output:

```
No Error.
```

NOTE: We can use any number of braces pairs{}.

Problem 9

Find the output of the following program?

```
#include<stdio.h>
#include<conio.h>
void main( )
```

```
{
int i = -1, j = 1, k ,p;
k = !i && j;
p = !i || j;
printf ( "%d %d", i, j );
getch();
}
```

Output:

```
-1 1
```

Problem 10

Find the output of the following program?

```
#include<stdio.h>
#include<conio.h>
void main( )
{
int i = 2, j;
j = !5 && i;
printf ( "\nj = %d", j ) ;
getch();
}
```

Output:

```
j=0
```

Problem 11

Check the errors from the following program?

```
#include<stdio.h>
#include<conio.h>
void main( )
{
```

```
int i = 4, j = 7;
if ( i = = 4 && j = = 7 )
printf ( "\nSatisfied at last" );
getch();
}
```

Output:

```
No error.
```

Problem 12

Check the errors from the following program?

```
#include<stdio.h>
#include<conio.h>
void main( )
{
int i,j ;
if ( i = = 1 & j = = 0 )
printf ( "\nWelcome" ) ;
getch();
}
```

Output:

```
Error.
```

NOTE: To concatenate two conditions we can use logical AND(&&) and not &.

Problem 13

Check the errors from the following program?

```
#include<stdio.h>
#include<conio.h>
void main( )
{
```

```
int i =1, j = 0;
if ( i = = 1 or j = = 0 )
printf ( "\nWelcome" ) ;
getch();
}
```

Output:

Error.

NOTE: Use logical OR(||) not or.

Problem 14

Check the errors from the following program?

```
#include<stdio.h>
#include<conio.h>
void main( )
{
int i = 12, j = 25;
if ( i = 1 ) && if ( j = 2 )
printf ( "\nProgramming" );
getch();
}
```

Output:

Error.

NOTE: The if statement is written like this way if (i==1 && j==2).

Problem 15

Check the errors from the following program?

```
#include<stdio.h>
#include<conio.h>
void main( )
{
```

```
int i = 5 , j = 35;
if ( i >= 3 and j <=40 )
printf ( "\n%d", i );
getch();
}
```

Output:

```
Error.
```

NOTE: Use logical AND(&&) not and.

Problem 16

Check the errors from the following program?

```
#include<stdio.h>
#include<conio.h>
void main( )
{
int i,j;
if ( i = = 1 & j = = 0 )
printf ( "\nProgramming secrets" );
getch();
}
```

Output:

```
Error.
```

NOTE: To concatenate two conditions we can use logical AND(&&) and not &.

Problem 17

Check the errors from the following program?

```
#include<stdio.h>
#include<conio.h>
void main( )
```

```
{
if ( 'A' < 'a' )
printf ( "\nASCII value of A is smaller than that of
   a" );
getch();
}
```

Output:

```
No Error.
```

NOTE: An ASCII value of A(65) is smaller than that of a(97).

Problem 18

Check the errors from the following program?

```
#include<stdio.h>
#include<conio.h>
void main( )
{
int i = 10;
if ( i >= 6 ) then
printf ( "\n%d", i );
getch();
}
```

Output:

```
Error.
```

NOTE: 'then' is not a keyword of C.

Problem 19

Check the errors from the following program?

```
#include<stdio.h>
#include<conio.h>
void main( )
```

```
{
int i = 10 ;
if i >= 2
printf ( "\n%d", i ) ;
getch();
}
```

Output:

```
Error.
```

NOTE: () missing in if statement.

Problem 20

Check the errors from the following program?

```
#include<stdio.h>
#include<conio.h>
void main( )
{
int i= 12, j = 15;
if ( x % 2 = y % 3 )
printf ( "\nExpert C Programming" ) ;
getch();
}
```

Output:

```
Error.
```

NOTE: For the purpose of comparison use = = operator not =.

Problem 21

Check the errors from the following program?

```
#include<stdio.h>
#include<conio.h>
void main( )
```

```
{
int i = 3, j = 4;
if ( i = = j )
printf( "i is equal to j" ) ;
elseif ( i > j )
printf( "i is greater than j" ) ;
elseif ( i < j )
printf( "i is less than j" ) ;
getch();
}
```

Output:

```
Error.
```

NOTE: elseif is not used like this way. Correction syntax is else if.

Problem 22

Check the errors from the following program?

```
#include<stdio.h>
#include<conio.h>
void main( )
{
int i, j;
scanf ( "%d %d",i, j );
if ( i > j );
printf ( "Expert C Programming" );
else
printf ( "Programming in C");
getch();
}
```

Output:

```
Error.
```

NOTE: Address operator (&) is not present in scanf().

Problem 23

Find the output of the following program?

```
#include<stdio.h>
#include<conio.h>
void main( )
{
int i = 4, j = 15;
if ( i = = 4 || j > 20 )
printf ( "\nExpert C Programming" );
else
printf ( "\nProgramming in C" );
getch();
}
```

Output:

```
Expert C Programming
```

Problem 24

Find the output of the following program?

```
#include<stdio.h>
#include<conio.h>
void main( )
{
int i = 7, j = 10;
if ( i = 5 && j > 5 )
printf ( "\nExpert C Programming" );
else
```

```
printf ( "\nProgramming in C" );
getch();
}
```

Output:

```
Expert C Programming
```

Problem 25

Find the output of the following program?

```
#include<stdio.h>
#include<conio.h>
void main( )
{
int i = 4, j = -1, k = 0, p, q, r, s ;
p = i || j || k;
q = i && j && k;
r = i || j && k;
s = i && j || k;
printf ( "\np = %d q = %d r = %d s = %d", p, q, r, s );
getch();
}
```

Output:

```
p= 1 q=0 r=1 s=1
```

Problem 26

Find the output of the following program?

```
#include<stdio.h>
#include<conio.h>
void main( )
{
int i = 4, j = -1, k = 0, p, q;
```

```
p = i + 5 && j + 1 || k + 2;
q = i + 5 || j + 1 && k + 2;
printf ( "\np = %d q = %d", p, q ) ;
getch();
}
```

Output:

```
p=1 q=1
```

Problem 27

Find the output of the following program?

```
#include<stdio.h>
#include<conio.h>
void main( )
{
int i = -5, j = 5;
if ( !i + !j * 1 )
printf ( "\nProgramming in C" );
else
printf ( "\nExpert C Programming" );
getch();
}
```

Output:

```
Expert C Programming
```

Problem 28

Find the output of the following program?

```
#include<stdio.h>
#include<conio.h>
void main( )
{
```

```
int i = 12;
if ( i > 20 && i < 25 )
printf ( " AND (&&) operator not working " );
else
printf ( "AND (&&) operator working" );
getch();
}
```

Output:

```
AND (&&) operator working
```

Problem 29

Find the output of the following program?

```
#include<stdio.h>
#include<conio.h>
void main( )
{
int i = 1, j = 7 ;
if ( i = = 2 && j > 1 )
printf ( " AND (&&) operator not working " );
else
printf ( "AND (&&) operator working" );
getch();
}
```

Output:

```
AND (&&) operator working
```

Problem 30

Find the output of the following program?

```
#include<stdio.h>
#include<conio.h>
```

```
void main( )
{
int i = -1, j = 1, k ,p;
k = i && j;
p = i || j;
printf ( "%d %d", i, j ) ;
getch();
}
```

Output:

```
-1 1
```

Problem 31

Find the output of the following program?

```
#include<stdio.h>
#include<conio.h>
void main( )
{
int i = 30, j, k;
if ( i >= 40 )
j = 30;
k = 20;
printf ( "\n%d %d", j, k );
getch();
}
```

Output:

j will contain some garbage value and k will be equal to 20

Problem 32

Find the output of the following program?

```
#include<stdio.h>
```

```
#include<conio.h>
void main( )
{
int i = 5, j, k;
if ( i >= 4 )
j = 3;
k = 2;
printf ( "\n%d \n%d", j, k );
getch();
}
```

Output:

3

2

Problem 33

Find the output of the following program?

```
#include<stdio.h>
#include<conio.h>
void main( )
{
int i = 10, j = 20;
if ( i = = j );
printf ( "\n%d \n%d", i, j );
getch();
}
```

Output:

10

20

Problem 34

Find the output of the following program?

```
#include<stdio.h>
#include<conio.h>
void main( )
{
int i = 3, j = 5;
if ( i == 3 )
printf ( "\n%d", i );
else;
printf ( "\n%d", j );
getch();
}
```

Output:

```
3
5
```

Problem 35

Find the output of the following program?

```
#include<stdio.h>
#include<conio.h>
void main( )
{
int i = 10, j = 20, k = 25;
if ( i > j && i > k )
printf( "i is big" );
else if ( j > i && j > k )
printf( "j is big" );
else if ( k > i && k > j )
```

```
printf( "k is big" );
getch();
}
```

Output:

```
k is big
```

Problem 36

Check the errors from the following program?

```
#include<stdio.h>
#include<conio.h>
void main( )
{
int i = 1;
if ( i = = 5 && i != 0 );
{
printf ( "\nWorking" );
printf( "\nWell" );
}
else
printf( "Not Working" );
getch();
}
```

Output:

```
Error.
```

NOTE: The if statement should not be terminated by a semicolon.

Problem 37

Check the errors from the following program?

```
#include<stdio.h>
#include<conio.h>
```

```
void main( )
{
int i = 10, j = 10;
if ( i && j - - 10)
printf ( "\nThat's like a good programmer" ) ;
getch();
}
```

Output:

No error.

Problem 38

Check the errors from the following program?

```
#include<stdio.h>
#include<conio.h>
void main( )
{
int i = -1, j, k;
j = ( k < 0 ? 0 : k * k);
printf ( "\n%d", j );
getch();
}
```

Output:

Error.

NOTE: k is not intialized.

Problem 39

Find the output of the following program?

```
#include<stdio.h>
#include<conio.h>
void main( )
```

```
{
int i, k = 12;
i = ( k > 3 ? ( k <= 10 ? 150 : 300 ) : 800);
printf ( "\n%d", k);
getch();
}
```

Output:

```
30
```

Problem 40

Find the output of the following program?

```
#include<stdio.h>
#include<conio.h>
void main( )
{
int x = 12, y = 24;
x = = 24 && y != 12 ? printf( "True" ) : printf(
   "False" ) ;
getch();
}
```

Output:

```
False
```

Problem 41

Find the output of the following program?

```
#include<stdio.h>
#include<conio.h>
void main( )
{
int i, j, k;
```

```
scanf ( "\n%d %d", &i, &j ) ;
if ( i > j )
k = i;
else
k = j;
getch();
}
```

Output:

```
#include<stdio.h>
#include<conio.h>
void main( )
{
int i, j, k;
scanf ( "\n%d %d", &i, &j);
( i > j ? (k = i) ; (k = j));
getch();
}
```

Problem 42

Find the output of the following program?

```
#include<stdio.h>
#include<conio.h>
void main( )
{
int code;
scanf ("%d", &code);
if (code > 1)
printf ("\nRed");
else
if (code < 1)
```

```
printf ("\nBlue");
else
printf ("\nOrange");
getch();
}
```

Output:

```
#include<stdio.h>
#include<conio.h>
void main( )
{
int code;
scanf ("%d", &code);
(code > 1 ? printf ("Red") : (code < 1 ? printf
   ("Blue") : printf ("Orange")));
getch();
}
```

Problem 43

Find the output of the following program?

```
#include<stdio.h>
#include<conio.h>
void main( )
{
float salary;
printf ("Enter the salary" );
scanf ( "%f", &salary );
if ( salary < 100000 && salary > 50000 )
printf ( "Programmer" );
else
if ( salary < 50000 && salary > 35000 )
```

```
printf ( "Lecturer" );
else
printf ( "Lab instructor" );
getch();
}
```

Output:

```
#include<stdio.h>
#include<conio.h>
void main( )
{
float salary;
printf ("Enter the salary");
scanf ( "%f", &salary);
( salary < 100000 && salary > 50000 ? printf (
   "Programmer" ) : ( salary < 50000 && salary > 35000
   ? printf ( "Lecturer" ) : printf ( "Lab instructor"
   )));
getch();
}
```

Problem 44

Find the output of the following program?

```
#include<stdio.h>
#include<conio.h>
void main( )
{
int i = 5;
( !i != 3 ? printf ( "\nExpert C Programming") :
   printf ( "\nProgramming in C") ) ;
getch();
```

```
}
```

Output:

```
Expert C Programming
```

Problem 45

Check the errors from the following program?

```
#include<stdio.h>
#include<conio.h>
void main( )
{
int i = 0, j = 1;
if ( i =v= 0 )
(j > 1 ? printf ( "\nExpert C Programming" ) ? printf
   ( "\nProgramming in C" ) );
else
printf ( "\nEND !!" ) ;
getch();
}
```

Output:

```
Error.
```

NOTE: missing (colon)

Problem 46

Check the errors from the following program?

```
#include<stdio.h>
#include<conio.h>
void main( )
{
int i = 65;
printf ( "\ni >= 65 ? %d: %c",i ) ;
```

```
getch();
}
```

Output:

No error.

Problem 47

Check the errors from the following program?

```
#include<stdio.h>
#include<conio.h>
void main( )
{
int i = 20, j ;
i >= 7 ? ( j = 12 ) : ( j = 17 ) ;
printf ( "\n%d %d", i, j ) ;
getch();
}
```

Output:

No error.

Problem 48

Check the errors from the following program?

```
#include<stdio.h>
#include<conio.h>
void main( )
{
int i = 1 , j = 2 ;
( i = = j ? printf( "%d",i) ) ;
getch();
}
```

Output:

```
Error.
```

NOTE: The ? operator must be followed with the : operator.

Problem 49

Check the errors from the following program?

```
#include<stdio.h>
#include<conio.h>
void main( )
{
int n = 9;
( n = = 9 ? printf( "Correct" ) ; : printf( "Incorrect"
   ) ;) ;
getch();
}
```

Output:

```
Error.
```

NOTE: Syntax of conditional statement is wrong.

Problem 50

Check the errors from the following program?

```
#include<stdio.h>
#include<conio.h>
void main( )
{
int i = 65, j;
j = ( i = = 65 : printf ( "\n i is equal to 65" ) :
   printf ( "\n i is not equal to 65" ) ) ;
printf( "%d", j );
getch();
}
```

Output:

```
Error.
```

NOTE: The ? operator is missing in conditional statement.

Problem 51

Find the output of the following program?

```
#include<stdio.h>
#include<conio.h>
void main( )
{
while ( ‘i’ < ‘j’ )
printf ( “\nWelcome” );
getch();
}
```

Output:

```
Indefinite loop
```

Problem 52

Find the output of the following program?

```
#include<stdio.h>
#include<conio.h>
void main( )
{
int i = 10;
while ( i = 20)
printf ( “\nYou Are Programmer! HAHA” );
getch();
}
```

Output:

```
Indefinite loop
```

Problem 53

Find the output of the following program?

```
#include<stdio.h>
#include<conio.h>
void main( )
{
int i ;
while ( i = 100 )
{
printf ( "\n%d", i );
i = i + 1;
}
getch();
}
```

Output:

100 will be print indefinitely

Problem 54

Find the output of the following program?

```
#include<stdio.h>
#include<conio.h>
void main( )
{
float i = 2.4;
while ( i = = 2.4)
{
printf ( "\n%f", i);
i = i - 0.2;
}
```

```
getch();
}
```

Output:

```
No output.
```

Problem 55

Find the output of the following program?

```
#include<stdio.h>
#include<conio.h>
void main( )
{
while ( '1' < '2' )
printf ( "\nWhile loop" ) ;
getch();
}
```

Output:

```
Indefinite loop
```

Problem 56

Find the output of the following program?

```
#include<stdio.h>
#include<conio.h>
void main( )
{
int i =4, j = 0, k;
while ( i >= 0 )
{
i–;
j++;
if(i = = j)
```

```
continue;
else
printf ( "\n%d %d", i, j) ;
}
getch();
}
```

Output:

```
3 1
1 3
0 4
-1 5
```

Problem 57

Find the output of the following program?

```
#include<stdio.h>
#include<conio.h>
void main( )
{
int i = 4, j = 0, k;
while ( i >= 0 )
{
if ( i == j )
break;
else
printf ( "\n%d %d", i, j ) ;
i–;
j++;
}
getch();
}
```

Output:

```
4 0
3 1
```

Problem 58

Find the output of the following program?

```
#include<stdio.h>
#include<conio.h>
void main( )
{
int i = 0 ;
for (; i ;)
printf ("\nThat's final");
getch();
}
```

Output:

```
No output
```

Problem 59

Find the output of the following program?

```
#include<stdio.h>
#include<conio.h>
void main( )
{
int i;
for ( i = 5; i <= 5; printf ("\n%d", i));
i++;
getch();
}
```

Output:

5 will be printed indefinite number of times.

Problem 60

Find the output of the following program?

```
#include<stdio.h>
#include<conio.h>
void main( )
{
int i = 1, j = 1;
for ( ; ; )
{
if ( i > 5 )
break;
else
j += i;
printf ( "\n%d", j ) ;
i += j;
}
getch();
}
```

Output:

2
5

Problem 61

Find the output of the following program?

```
#include<stdio.h>
#include<conio.h>
void main( )
{
int i ;
for ( i = 1 ; i <= 5 ; printf ( "\n%c", 65 ) ) ;
```

```
i++;
getch();
}
```

Output:

```
Indefinite loop
```

Problem 62

Find the output of the following program?

a. An expression contains relational operators, assignment operators, and arithmetic operators. In the absence of parentheses, they will be evaluated in which of the following order:

1. assignment, relational, arithmetic
2. arithmetic, relational, assignment
3. relational, arithmetic, assignment
4. assignment, arithmetic, relational

b. The **break** statement is used to exit from:

1. an **if** statement
2. a for loop
3. a program
4. the **main( )** function

c. A **do-while** loop is useful when we want that the statements within the loop must be executed:

1. Only once
2. At least once
3. More than once
4. None of the above

d. In what sequence the initialization, testing and execution of body is done in a do-while loop

1. Initialization, execution of body, testing
2. Execution of body, initialization, testing

3. Initialization, testing, execution of body
4. None of the above

Problem 63

Find the output of the following program?

```
#include<stdio.h>
#include<conio.h>
void main( )
{
char code = 3;
switch ( code )
{
case 1:
printf ( “\nBye” );
case 2:
printf ( “\nHi” );
default:
printf ( “\nHello”);
}
printf ( “\nI Love You” );
getch();
}
```

Output:

```
Hello
I Love You
```

Problem 64

Find the output of the following program?

```
#include<stdio.h>
#include<conio.h>
```

```
void main( )
{
int code = 4;
switch ( code )
{
case 'v':
printf ( "I am not programmer" ) ;
break;
case 4:
printf ( "Jagbir is a good programmer \n" ) ;
break;
case 12:
printf ( "I am not working \n" ) ;
break;
default:
printf ( "I am not intelligent \n" ) ;
}
getch();
}
```

Output:

```
Jagbir is a good programmer
```

Problem 65

Find the output of the following program?

```
#include<stdio.h>
#include<conio.h>
void main( )
{
int i=1, j ;
switch (  j= i + 2)
```

```
{
case 0 :
printf ( "\nYes") ;
case 1 :
printf ( "\nNo") ;
case 2 :
printf ( "\nThere") ;
default :
printf ( "\nGood Programmer!" ) ;
}
getch();
}
```

Output:

```
Good Programmer!
```

Problem 66

Find the output of the following program?

```
#include<stdio.h>
#include<conio.h>
void main( )
{
int i = 0;
switch (i)
{
case 0 :
printf ( "\nHello!" ) ;
case 1 :
printf ( "\nHow are you" ) ;
case 2 :
printf ( "\nAre you ok" ) ;
```

```
case 3 :
printf ( "\nYes" ) ;
}
getch();
}
```

Output:

```
Hello!
How are you
Are you ok
Yes
```

Problem 67

Find the output of the following program?

```
#include<stdio.h>
#include<conio.h>
void main( )
{
int i;
float j = 2.0 ;
switch ( i = j + 2 )
{
case 4:
printf ( "\nWelcome" ) ;
break ;
default :
printf ( "\nHello!" ) ;
}
getch();
}
```

Output:

```
Welcome
```

Problem 68

Find the output of the following program?

```
#include<stdio.h>
#include<conio.h>
void main( )
{
int ch = 'a' + 'b';
switch ( ch )
{
case 'a' :
case 'b' :
printf ( "\n Hello" );
case 'A' :
printf ( "\n How are you" );
case 'b' + 'a' :
printf ( "\nWelcome");
}
getch();
}
```

Output:

```
Welcome
```

Problem 69

Find the output of the following program?

```
#include<stdio.h>
#include<conio.h>
void main( )
{
int i = 3 ;
switch ( i - 4 )
```

```
{
case -1 :
printf ( "\nDo" ) ;
case 0 :
printf ( "\nDid" ) ;
case 1 : printf ( "\nDoes" ) ;
default :
printf ( "\nHaha" ) ;
}
getch();
}
```

Output:

```
Do
Did
Does
Haha
```

Problem 70

Check the errors from the following program?

```
#include<stdio.h>
#include<conio.h>
void main( )
{
int code = 1;
switch ( code ) ;
{
case 0 ;
printf ( "\nHello" ) ;
case 1 ;
printf ( "\nHi" ) ;
```

```
}
getch();
}
```

Output:

```
Error.
```

NOTE: Semi-colon after switch statement and after case 0 and case 1 is not permitted.

Problem 71

Check the errors from the following program?

```
#include<stdio.h>
#include<conio.h>
void main( )
{
int marks;
scanf ( "%d", &marks) ;
switch (marks)
{
case ( marks <= 20 ) :
printf ( "\nOoooooohhhh! fail!" ) ;
case ( marks > 20 && marks <= 30 ) :
printf ( "\nPoor performance!" ) ;
case ( marks > 30 && marks <= 40 ) :
printf ( "\nIts ok" ) ;
default :
printf ( "\nGood" ) ;
}
getch();
}
```

Output:

```
Error.
```

NOTE: Relational operators cannot be used in cases.

Problem 72

Check the errors from the following program?

```
#include<stdio.h>
#include<conio.h>
void main( )
{
float i = 1.5 ;
switch ( i )
{
case 0.0:
printf ( "\nExpert C Programming" ) ;
break ;
case 1.0 :
printf ( "\nProgramming in C" ) ;
break ;
case 1.5 :
printf ( "\nLet us C" ) ;
break ;
case 2.5 :
printf ( "\nObjective C" ) ;
}
getch();
}
```

Output:

```
Error.
```

NOTE: Floats cannot be used in cases.

Problem 73

Check the errors from the following program?

```
#include<stdio.h>
#include<conio.h>
void main( )
{
int i = 33, j = 34, k;
k = j - i;
switch (k)
{
case 1 || 2:
printf ("Expert C Programming");
break;
case a || b:
printf ("Solved Programming in C");
break;
}
getch();
}
```

Output:

```
Error.
```

NOTE: Logical operators cannot used in cases.

Problem 74

Find the output of the following program?

```
#include <stdio.h>
#include <conio.h>
void main()
{
```

```
int i = 4;
switch (i)
{
case 1:
printf ("\n How are you");
break;
case 2:
printf ("\n Hello");
break;
case 3:
printf ("\n Khalsa college");
default:
printf ("\n Amritsar to Delhi ");
}
getch();
}
```

Output:

```
Amritsar to Delhi
```

Problem 75

Find the output of the following program?

```
#include <stdio.h>
#include <conio.h>
void main()
{
int i = 4;
switch (i)
{
default:
printf ("\n Amritsar to Delhi ");
```

```
case 1:
printf ("\n How are you");
break;
case 2:
printf ("\n Hello");
break;
case 3:
printf ("\n Khalsa college");
}
getch();
}
```

Output:

```
Amritsar to Delhi
How are you
```

Problem 76

Find the output of the following program?

```
#include <stdio.h>
#include <conio.h>
void main()
{
int i = 1;
switch (i)
{
case 1:
printf ("\n How are you");
case 2:
printf ("\n Hello");
case 3:
printf ("\n Khalsa college");
```

```
default:
printf ("\n Amritsar to Delhi ");
}
getch();
}
```

Output:

```
How are you
Hello
Khalsa college
Amritsar to Delhi
```

Problem 77

Find the error, if any, in the for loop.

```
#include <stdio.h>
#include <conio.h>
void main()
{
int i = 1;
for (;;)
{
printf ("\n%d", i++);
if (i > 100)
break;
}
getch();
}
```

Output:

No error.

Problem 78

Find the error, if any, in the while loop.

```
#include <stdio.h>
#include <conio.h>
void main()
{
int i = 1;
while ( )
{
printf ("\n%d", i++);
if (i>100)
break;
}
getch();
}
```

Output:

Error

NOTE: In while statement, condition is must.

Problem 79

Find the error, if any, in the do-while loop.

```
#include <stdio.h>
#include <conio.h>
void main()
{
int i = 1;
do
{
printf ("\n%d", i++);
```

```
if (i>100)
break;
}while();
getch();
}
```

Output:

```
Error
```

NOTE: In while statement, condition is must.

Problem 80

Find the output of the following program?

```
#include <stdio.h>
#include <conio.h>
void main()
{
int i = 100, j = 200;
if (! (!i) && i)
printf ("i = %d", i);
else
printf ("j = %d", i);
getch();
}
```

Output:

```
i= 100
```

Problem 81

Find the error, if any, in the while loop.

```
#include <stdio.h>
#include <conio.h>
void main()
```

```
{
void show( );
int i = 1;
while (i <= 50)
{
printf ("%d", i);
if (i > 10)
goto here;
getch();
}
}
void show( )
{
here:
printf ("\n hello.");
}
```

Output:

```
Error.
```

NOTE: goto statement cannot perform a non-local jump.

Problem 82

Find the output of the following program?

```
#include <stdio.h>
#include <conio.h>
void main()
{
short int i = 0;
for (i <= 5 && i >= 1; ++i; i > 0)
printf ("%u\n", i);
```

```
getch();
}
```

Output:

```
1...65535
```

Problem 83

Find the output of the following program?

```
#include <stdio.h>
#include <conio.h>
void main()
{
int i = 1;
switch (i)
{
printf ("Hello");
case 1:
printf ("\nHi");
break;
case 2:
printf ("\nBye");
break;
}
   getch();
}
```

Output:

```
Hi
```

Problem 84

Find the output of the following program?

```
#include<stdio.h>
```

```
#include<conio.h>
void main()
{
int x=1;
while (x<=3)
{
printf("%d", x):
x=x+1;
}
printf("\nValue of x after loop is %d", x);
getch();
}
```

Output:

```
1 2 3
Value of of x after loop is 4
```

Problem 85

Find the output of the following program?

```
#include<stdio.h>
#include<conio.h>
void main()
{
int x=1;
while (x<=3);
{
printf("Value of x after loop is %d",x);
}
getch();
}
```

Output:

```
No output
```

NOTE: while statement is terminated by semicolon.

Problem 86

Find the output of the following program?

```
#include<stdio.h>
#include<conio.h>
void main( )
{
int x=1;
while (x<=3)
printf("%d", x);
printf("Value of x after loop is %d", x);
getch();
}
```

Output:

```
1111...... Infinite loop
```

Problem 87

Check the errors from the following program?

```
#include<stdio.h>
#include<conio.h>
void main()
{
int x=1;
for ( )
{
printf("%d",x);
if(x=3)
```

```
break;
}
getch();
}
```

Output:

```
Error
```

NOTE: Syntax of for statement is incorrect.

Problem 88

Find the output of the following program?

```
#include<stdio.h>
#include<conio.h>
void main( )
{
int x;
for (x=1; x<=32767;x++)
printf("%d", x);
getch();
}
```

Output:

```
1 2 3 ....... 32767 -32768 -32767.... 32767 -32768 -32767.......
```

NOTE: Infinite loop

Problem 89

Find the output of the following program?

```
#include<stdio.h>
#include<conio.h>
void main( )
{
```

```
int x=2;
for (;;)
{
printf("%d",x);
if (x= =3)
break;
}
getch();
}
```

Output:

```
2 2 2 2...... infinite loop
```

Problem 90

Find the output of the following program?

```
#include<stdio.h>
#include<conio.h>
void main( )
{
int x=2;
for (;;)
{
printf("%d", x);
if (x=3)
break;
}
getch();
}
```

Output:

```
2
```

Problem 91

Find the output of the following program?

```
#include<stdio.h>
#include<conio.h>
void main()
{
int x=1;
for (;x<=5; printf("%d", x++);
getch();
}
```

Output:

```
1 2 3 4 5
```

Problem 92

Find the output of the following program?

```
#include <stdio.h>
#include <conio.h>
void main()
{
unsigned int i = 65535;
while (i++ ! = 0)
printf ("%d", ++i);
}
```

Output:

```
Infinite loop
```

Problem 93

Find the output of the following program?

```
#include <stdio.h>
#include <conio.h>
```

```
void main()
{
char str[] = "Khalsa College Amritsar";
int a = 3;
printf (a > 5? "%50s": "%s:, str);
getch();
}
```

Output:

```
Khalsa College Amritsar
```

Problem 94

Find the output of the following program?

```
#include <stdio.h>
#include <conio.h>
void main()
{
int i = 15, j, k;
if (i >= 30)
j = 20;
k = 10;
printf ("\n%d %d", i, j, k);
getch();
}
```

Output:

```
15 Garbage 10
```

Problem 95

Check the errors from the following program?

```
#include <stdio.h>
#include <conio.h>
```

```
void main()
{
int i = 20, j = 35;
if(i = = j)
printf("i is equal to j");
elseif(i > j)
printf("i is greater than j");
elseif(i < j)
printf("i is less than j");
getch();
}
```

Output:

Error.

NOTE: Else Statement missing

Problem 96

Find the output of the following program?

```
#include <stdio.h>
#include <conio.h>
void main()
{
float i = 0.2;
if (0.2 > i)
printf ("Hi");
else
printf ("Hello");
getch();
}
```

Output:

Hi

Problem 97

Find the output of the following program?

```
#include <stdio.h>
#include <conio.h>
void main()
{
int i, j, k;
i = j = k = 1;
k = ++i || ++j && ++k;
printf("i = %d j = %d k = %d\n", i, j, k);
getch();
}
```

Output:

```
i = 2 j = 1 k = 1
```

Problem 98

Check the errors from the following program?

```
#include <stdio.h>
#include <conio.h>
void main()
{
int i = 3;
switch (i)
{
case 1:
printf ("Hello");
case 2:
printf ("Hi");
break;
```

```
case 3:
continue;
default:
printf ("Bye");
}
getch();
}
```

Output:

Error.

Problem 99

Check the errors from the following program?

```
#include <stdio.h>
#include <conio.h>
void main()
{
char ch;
while (ch = 0; ch <= 255; ch++)
printf ("Ascii value = %d Character = %c", ch, ch);
getch();
}
```

Output:

Error.

Problem 100

Find the output of the following program?

```
#include<stdio.h>
#include<conio.h>
void main()
{
```

```
int i=0;
for (;++i;)
printf("%d",i);
getch();
}
```

Output:

```
1 2 ...... 32767 -32768 -32767...-1
Infinite loop
```

Problem 101

Find the output of the following program?

```
#include<stdio.h>
#include<conio.h>
void main()
{
int i=3,j=3;
for (;i<6, j<4;i++,j++)
printf("%d%d\n", i, j);
getch();
}
```

Output:

```
3 3
```

Problem 102

Check the errors from the following program?

```
#include<stdio.h>
#include<conio.h>
void main( )
{
int i=1;
```

```
while (i<=3)
{
printf("%d", i);
if(i>2)
goto first;
i++;
}
getch();
}
fun( )
{
first:
printf("Call function");
}
```

Output:

Error

Problem 103

Find the output of the following program?

```
#include<stdio.h>
#include<conio.h>
void main()
{
int i=3;
goto label;
for (i=0;i<5;i++)
{
label:
printf("%d",i);
}
```

```
getch();
}
```

Output:

```
3 4
```

Problem 104

Find the output of the following program?

```
#include <stdio.h>
#include <conio.h>
void main()
{
int result, i = 30;
result = (i > 5? (i <= 10 ? 100 : 200) : 500);
printf ("%d", i);
getch();
}
```

Output:

```
30
```

Problem 105

Which of the following is not a logical operator?

```
1. &
2. &&
3. ||
4. !
```

Output:

```
1
```

Problem 106

Which of the datatype cannot be checked in a switch – case statement?

```
1. float
2. Integer
```

3. charater
4. enum

Output:

1

Problem 107

Find the incorrect statement about for loop?

1. for loop works faster than a while loop.
2. All things that can be done using a for loop can also be done using a while loop.
3. for (;;) implements an infinite loop.
4. for loop can be used if we want statements in a loop to get executed at least once.

Output:

1

Problem 108

Check the errors from the following program?

```
#include <stdio.h>
#include <conio.h>
void main()
{
int i = 5, j = 50;
if (i = 15) && if (j = 100)
printf ("Have a nice day");
getch();
}
```

Output:

Error:

NOTE: Syntax of if statcment is wrong.

Problem 109

Check the errors from the following program?

```
#include <stdio.h>
#include <conio.h>
void main()
{
int i = 0, j = 1;
j = = 1 ? i = 0: i = 1;
if (i)
printf ("true");
else
printf ("false");
getch();
}
```

Output:

```
Error.
```

NOTE: Lvalue required

Problem 110

Which of the following statements are correct about a switch statement in a C program?

A. switch is useful when we wish to check the value of a variable against a particular set of values.

B. switch is useful when we with to check whether a value falls in different ranges.

C. Compiler implements a jump table for cases used in a switch.

D. It is NOT necessary to use a break in every switch statement.

E. A common set of statements CANNOT be used for multiple cases in a switch.

Output:

A, C, D

Problem 111

Find the output of the following program?

```
#include <stdio.h>
#include <conio.h>
void main()
{
int i = 0;
i++;
if (i <= 5)
{
printf ("Welcome to Amritsar");
exit ( );
main ( );
}
getch();
}
```

Output:

Welcome to Amritsar

Problem 112

Find the output of the following program?

```
#include <stdio.h>
#include <conio.h>
void main()
{
```

```
int i = 6;
float j = 6.0;
if (i = = j)
{printf ("i and j are equal");}
else
{printf ("i and j are not equal");}
getch();
}
```

Output:

```
i and j are equal
```

Problem 113

Find the output of the following program?

```
#include <stdio.h>
#include <conio.h>
void main()
{
int i = 8, j = 9;
if (i % 2 = j % 3)
printf ("\nPowerful");
getch();
}
```

Output:

```
Lvalue required
```

Problem 114

Find the output of the following program?

```
#include <stdio.h>
#include <conio.h>
void main()
```

```
{
int i = 0, j = 1, k = 3;
*((i) ? &j: &i) = i ? j: k;
printf ("%d %d %d", i, j, k);
getch();
}
```

Output:

```
3 1 3
```

Problem 115

Find the output of the following program?

```
#include<stdio.h>
#include<conio.h>
void main( )
{
int i = 1;
while ( i <= 10)
{
printf ( "%d", i );
i = i + 1;
}
getch();
}
```

Output:

```
12345678910
```

Problem 116

Find the output of the following program?

```
#include<stdio.h>
#include<conio.h>
```

```
void main( )
{
int i = 1;
while ( i <= 10);
{
printf ( "\n%d", i);
i++;
}
getch();
}
```

Output:

No output indefinite while loop check semicolon';' at the end of while.

Problem 117

Find the output of the following program?

```
#include<stdio.h>
#include<conio.h>
void main( )
{
int i = 2;
while ( i = = 1 )
{
i = i - 1;
printf ( "\n%d", i);
i–;
}
getch();
}
```

Output:

No output.

Problem 118

Find the output of the following program?

```
#include<stdio.h>
#include<conio.h>
void main( )
{
int i = 1;
while ( i = = 1 )
i = i - 1;
printf ( "\n%d", i ) ;
getch();
}
```

Output:

0

Problem 119

Find the output of the following program?

```
#include<stdio.h>
#include<conio.h>
void main( )
{
char i;
while ( i = 0 ; i <= 255 ; i++ )
printf ( "\nAscii value %d Character %c", i, i ) ;
getch();
}
```

Output:

Do yourself

Problem 120

Find the output of the following program?

```
#include<stdio.h>
#include<conio.h>
void main( )
{
int i = 5, j, k;
j = –i;
k = i–;
printf ( “\n%d %d %d”, i, j, k);
getch();
}
```

Output:

```
3 4 4
```

Problem 121

Find the output of the following program?

```
#include<stdio.h>
#include<conio.h>
void main( )
{
int i = 5, j = 4, k;
k = i– -j;
printf ( “\n%d %d %d”, i, j, k);
getch();
}
```

Output:

```
4 4 1
```

Problem 122

Check the errors from the following program?

```
#include<stdio.h>
#include<conio.h>
int i = 5, j= 6, k;
k =i+j;
void main( )
{
printf("Value of k is %d",k);
getch();
}
```

Output:

```
Error
```

NOTE: Non- executable statements can be placed outside the body of a function.

Problem 123

Check the errors from the following program?

```
#include<stdio.h>
#include<conio.h>
void main( )
{
int i=5, j=6, k;
k = i+2*j;
printf("The value of k is %d",k);
getch();
}
```

Output:

```
Error.
```

NOTE: statement missing ; in function main.

Problem 124

Find the output of the following program?

```
#include<stdio.h>
#include<conio.h>
void main( )
{
int i=5, j=10;
if (i= =j)
printf ("i=5,j=10");
printf ("i and j are not equal");
getch();
}
```

Output:

```
i and j are not equal
```

Problem 125

Find the output of the following program?

```
#include<stdio.h>
#include<conio.h>
void main( )
{
int i=5, j=10;
if (i= =j)
{
printf ("i=5,j=10");
printf ("i and j are not equal");
}
getch();
}
```

Output:

```
No output
```

Problem 126

Find the output of the following program?

```
#include<stdio.h>
#include<conio.h>
void main( )
{
int i=5, j=10;
if (i= j)
printf (“i and j are  equal”);
else
printf (“i and j are not equal”);
getch();
}
```

Output:

```
i and j are equal
```

Problem 127

Check the errors from the following program?

```
#include<stdio.h>
#include<conio.h>
void main( )
{
int i=5, j=10;
if (i= =j);
printf (“i and j are  equal”);
else
printf (“i and j are not equal”);
getch();
}
```

Output:

Error

NOTE: Misplaced else in function main

Problem 128

Find the output of the following program?

```
#include<stdio.h>
#include<conio.h>
void main( )
{
int i=5, j=10;
if (i= =j)
printf ("i and j are  equal\n");
else
printf ("i and j are not equal\n");
getch();
}
```

Output:

```
i and j are  equal
i and j are not equal
```

Problem 129

Find the output of the following program?

```
#include<stdio.h>
#include<conio.h>
void main( )
{
if(1)
printf("Executed");
else
```

```
printf("Not Executed");
getch();
}
```

Output:

```
Executed
```

Problem 130

Find the output of the following program?

```
#include<stdio.h>
#include<conio.h>
void main( )
{
if (printf("khalsa"))
printf("college");
getch();
}
```

Output:

```
khalsacollege
```

Problem 131

Find the output of the following program?

```
#include<stdio.h>
#include<conio.h>
void main( )
{
int i=5, j=10;
if(i = = 5)
if(j = = 5)
printf("values are same");
else
```

```
printf("values are not same");
getch();
}
```

Output:

```
values are not same
```

Problem 132

Find the output of the following program?

```
#include<stdio.h>
#include<conio.h>
void main( )
{
int i=5, j=10;
if(i = = 5)
{
if(j = = 5)
printf("values are same");
}
else
printf("values are not same");
getch();
}
```

Output:

```
No output
```

Problem 133

Find the output of the following program?

```
#include<stdio.h>
#include<conio.h>
void main()
```

```
{
int code=1;
switch(code)
printf("Done");
getch();
}
```

Output:

No output

Problem 134

Find the output of the following program?

```
#include<stdio.h>
#include<conio.h>
void main()
{
int code=1;
switch(code);
printf("Done");
getch();
}
```

Output:

Done

Problem 135

Check the errors from the following program?

```
#include<stdio.h>
#include<conio.h>
void main( )
{
```

```
float code=1.0;
switch(code)
{
case 1: printf("One");
case 2: printf("Two");
default: printf("Default");
}
getch();
}
```

Output:

```
Error
```

NOTE: switch takes the expression of integer or character type not float type.

Problem 136

Check the errors from the following program?

```
#include<stdio.h>
#include<conio.h>
void main( )
{
int code=2,j=1;
switch(code)
{
case j:
printf("This is case 1");
case 2:
printf("This is case 2");
default;
printf("This is default case");
```

```
}
getch();
}
```

Output:

```
Error
```

NOTE: case j is not permitted.

Problem 137

Check the errors from the following program?

```
#include<stdio.h>
#include<conio.h>
void main( )
{
char ch= 'A';
switch(ch)
{
case 'A':
printf("Case lable is A");
case "B";
printf ("Case label is B");
}
getch();
}
```

Output:

```
Error
```

NOTE: case label must be of integer or character type. String is not used in cases.(case "B")

Problem 138

Find the output of the following program?

```
#include<stdio.h>
#include<conio.h>
void main( )
{
int code =1;
switch (code)
{
case 1: printf("One \n");
case 2: printf ("Two \n");
default: printf("Three \n");
}
getch();
}
```

Output:

```
One
Two
Three
```

Problem 139

Find the output of the following program?

```
#include<stdio.h>
#include<conio.h>
void main( )
{
switch (code)
{
case 1:
printf ("One \n");
break;
```

```
case 2:
printf("Two \n);
break;
default: printf ("Three \n);
}
getch();
}
```

Output:

One

Problem 140

Find the output of the following program?

```
#include<stdio.h>
#include<conio.h>
void main( )
{
int code=5;
switch(code)
{
default: printf ("Three \n);
case 1: printf("One \n);
case 2: printf("Two \n);
}
getch();
}
```

Output:

Three

One

Two

Problem 141

Check the errors from the following program?

```
#include<stdio.h>
#include<conio.h>
void main()
{
int code =2;
switch(code)
{
case 1:
printf("This is case 1");
case 2-1:
printf("This is case 2");
}
getch();
}
```

Output:

Error.

NOTE: Case labels should be unique.

Problem 142

Find the output of the following program?

```
#include<stdio.h>
#include<conio.h>
void main()
{
int i=1, j=3;
switch(i)
{
```

```
case 1:
printf("This is outer case 1\n");
switch(j)
{
case 3:
printf("This is inner case 1\n");
break;
default:
printf("This is inner default case");
}
case 2;
printf("This is outer case 2");
}
getch();
}
```

Output:

```
This is outer case 1
This is inner case 1
This is outer case 2
```

Problem 143

Check the errors from the following program?

```
#include<stdio.h>
#include<conio.h>
void main ()
{
itn code = 2;
switch(code)
{
```

```
case 1:
printf("This is case 1");
break;
case 2:
printf("this is case 2");
continue;
default:
printf ("default");
}
getch();
}
```

Output:

Error

NOTE: Misplaced continue in function main().

Problem 144

Check the errors from the following program?

```
#include<stdio.h>
#include<conio.h>
void main()
{
default:
printf("Default Statement"):
goto default;
getch();
}
```

Output:

Error

NOTE: Default used in switch statement only. Default is not used as goto statement label.

Problem 145

Find the output of the following program?

```
#include <stdio.h>
#include <conio.h>
void main()
{
int i = 0;
for (; i < 7; i++);
printf ("%d", i);
getch();
}
```

Output:

7

Problem 146

Find the output of the following program?

```
#include <stdio.h>
#include <conio.h>
void main()
{
int i = 50, j = 10, k;
if (!i > = 40)
j = 30;
k = 20;
printf ("j = %d k = %d, j, k);
getch();
}
```

Output:

j = 10 k = 20

Problem 147

Find the output of the following program?

```
#include <stdio.h>
#include <conio.h>
void main()
{
int i = 10, j = 60 % 50;
for (k = 1; k <= 10; k++);
if (i != j);
printf ("i = %d\n j = %d", i, j);
getch();
}
```

Output:

```
i = 10
j = 10
```

NOTE: semicolon terminated if statement.

Problem 148

Check the errors from the following program?

```
#include <stdio.h>
#include <conio.h>
void main()
{
int i = 3, j = 1;
switch (i)
{
case 1:
printf ("\n Welcome");
break;
```

```
case j:
printf ("\n Khalsa college");
break;
}
getch();
}
```

Output:

```
Error.
```

NOTE: Cannot use j in second case.

Problem 149

Check the errors from the following program?

```
#include <stdio.h>
#include <conio.h>
void main()
{
int i = 1;
switch (i)
{
case 1:
printf ("\n Welcome");
break;
case 1 * 4 + 2;
printf ("\n Amritsar");
break;
}
getch();
}
```

Output:

```
No error.
```

Problem 150

Check the errors from the following program?

```
#include <stdio.h>
#include <conio.h>
void main()
{
int a = 10;
switch (a)
{ }
printf ("\n Welcome");
getch();
}
```

Output:

No error.

NOTE: There can exist a switch, which has no cases.

Problem 151

Find the output of the following program?

```
#include <stdio.h>
#include <conio.h>
void main()
{
int i = 5;
while (i– >= 0) printf (%d", i);
i = 5;
printf ("\n");
while (i– >= 0) printf ("%i", i);
printf ("\n");
while (i– >= 0) printf ("&d", i);
```

```
getch();
}
```

Output:

```
4 3 2 1 0 -1
4 3 2 1 0 -1
```

Problem 152

Check the errors from the following program?

```
#include <stdio.h>
#include <conio.h>
void main()
{
int i = 1;
switch (i)
{
printf ("\n Hello");
case 1:
printf ("\n Welcome");
break;
case 2:
printf ("\n Bye");
break;
}
getch();
}
```

Output:

```
No error.
```

Problem 153

Find the output of the following program?

```
#include <stdio.h>
#include <conio.h>
void main()
{
int i = 10, j;
i > 5 ? j = 100: j = 200;
printf ("\n%d", j);
getch();
}
```

Output:

Lvalue required in function main(). The second assignment should be written in parentheses as follows:

```
i >= 5? j = 100: (j = 200);
```

Problem 154

Find the output of the following program?

```
#include <stdio.h>
#include <conio.h>
void main()
{
unsigned int i = 65536;
while (i++ != 0)
printf ("%d", ++i);
getch();
}
```

Output:

```
No output
```

Problem 155

Find the output of the following program?

```
#include <stdio.h>
#include <conio.h>
void main()
{
char i = 1;
while (i <= 255)
{
printf ("%d", i);
i = i + 1;
}
getch();
}
```

Output:

Infinite loop

Problem 156

Find the output of the following program?

```
#include <stdio.h>
#include <conio.h>
void main()
{
int i = 1, j = 1;
for(;i; printf ("%d %d\n", i, j))
j = i++ <=5;
getch();
}
```

Output:

```
2 1
3 1
4 1
```

```
5 1
6 1
7 0
```

Problem 157

Find the output of the following program?

```
#include <stdio.h>
#include <conio.h>
void main()
{
int i;
for (i =-1; i <= 10; i++)
{
if (i < 5)
continue;
else
break;
printf ("Hello");
}
getch();
}
```

Output:

```
No message print
```

Problem 158

Find the output of the following program?

```
#include <stdio.h>
#include <conio.h>
void main()
{
```

```
int i = 1;
while (i <= 255);
{
printf ("%c %d", i, i);
i++;
}
getch();
}
```

Output:

Infinite times

Problem 159

Find the output of the following program?

```
#include<stdio.h>
#include<conio.h>
void main()
{
int x=1;
for (;x<=20;x++)
{
if (x%2= =0)
continue;
printf("%d", x);
}
getch();
}
```

Output:

1 3 5 7 9 11 13 15 17 19

Problem 160

Check the errors from the following program?

```
#include<stdio.h>
#include<conio.h>
void main( )
{
int x=1;
first:
printf (“%d”, x++);
if(x= =5) break;
goto first;
getch();
}
```

Output:

```
Error
```

Problem 161

Find the output of the following program?

```
#include<stdio.h>
#include<conio.h>
void main()
{
int x=1;
first:
printf(“%d”, x++);
if (x= =5) goto second;
goto first;
second:
;
```

```
}
getch();
}
```

Output:

```
1 2 3 4
```

Problem 162

Find the output of the following program?

```
#include<stdio.h>
#include<conio.h>
void main()
{
int i,j;
for (i=1;i<5;i++)
for (j=1;j<6;j++)
{
if(j= =2) break;
printf("%d%d\n",i,j);
}
getch();
}
```

Output:

```
1 1
2 1
```

Problem 163

Find the output of the following program?

```
#include<stdio.h>
#include<conio.h>
void main()
```

```
{
int i,j;
for (i=1;i<3;i++)
for (j=1;j<4;j++)
{
if(j= =2) continue;
printf("%d%d\n",i,j);
}
getch();
}
```

Output:

```
1 1
1 3
2 1
2 3
```

Problem 164

Check the errors from the following program?

```
#include<stdio.h>
#include<conio.h>
void main()
{
int x=1;
for (;x++=0;)
printf("%d",x);
getch();
}
```

Output:

```
Error
```

Problem 165

Check the errors from the following program?

```
#include<stdio.h>
#include<conio.h>
void main()
{
int i = 2, j = 4;
char x = 1, y = 10;
if (y, x, j, i)
printf ("Welcome");
getch();
}
```

Output:

```
No error No output
```

Problem 166

Find the output of the following program?

```
#include<stdio.h>
#include<conio.h>
void main( )
{
int i=0;
for (;i++;)
printf("%d", i);
getch();
}
```

Output:

```
No output
```

Problem 167

Check the errors from the following program?

```
#include<stdio.h>
#include<conio.h>
void main()
{
int i=5;
do
{
printf("%d", i);
i++;
}while(i<10)
getch();
}
```

Output:

Error

NOTE: semicolon missing in do while statement.

Problem 168

Find the output of the following program?

```
#include<stdio.h>
#include<conio.h>
void main( )
{
int i=1;
do
{
printf("%d", i);
i++;
```

```
}while (i<0);
getch();
}
```

Output:

```
1
```

B. FILL IN THE BLANKS

1. The smallest logical entity that can independently exist in a C program is ....
2. Statements in C language are terminated with a ....
3. .... is an entry-controlled loop.
4. .... is called single line and fast executable statement.
5. A case label should be a compile time constant expression of .... type.
6. The form of looping in which the number of iterations to be performed is known in advance is called ....
7. The execution or term ation of a sentinel-controlled loop depends upon a special value known as ....
8. The .... logical operator is true only when both operands are true.
9. Two-way selection is implemented with the .... statement.
10. Sentinel-controlled loop is also known as ....
11. The statements which are start using double slash (//) symbol are called ....
12. To alter the default flow of control, ... statements are used.
13 .... statement is used to terminate the current iteration of the enclosing loop.
14. A null statement is represented by a ....
15. The minimum number of times a while loop is executed is ....

16. The expression 5<10?6>8?5:3:7 is reduced to .... after evaluating the first expression in it.
17. The do-while loop is also known as .... loop.
18. for (; ;) {...} forms an .... loop.
19. After evaluation of the expression x= (a= 10,3*a) the value of a is ....
20. The case label in a switch-case must be an ....
21. An expression terminated with a semicolon is known as .... statement.
22. .... is an exit-controlled loop.
23. The .... statement when executed in a switch statement causes immediate exit from it.
24. Careless use of looping statement may lead to ....
25. All programs can be written in terms of three types of control structures: ...., ... and ....
26. The .... branching statement is used to execute one action when a condition is true or a different action when that condition is false.
27. Repeating a set of instructions a specific number of times is called .... looping.
28. For statement is in the category of .... control structures.
29. Goto is of two types: .... and ....
30. The optional case of switch selection statement is ....
31. The label in a goto is an ....
32. Structured goto statements are .... and .... statements.
33. while(i=10) {...} results in an .... loop.
34. A group of declarations and statements surrounds by {and} form a ....
35. The .... statement in a switch case statement skips all the remaining statements and exits the switch block.

Answers

1. statement
2. semicolon
3. while
4. for statement
5. integer
6. definite looping statements
7. sentinel value
8. logical AND(&&)
9. if-else
10. indefinite loop statement
11. non-executable statements or comments
12. flow control
13. continue
14. semicolon
15. Zero
16. 5<10?3:7
17. post tested
18. infinite
19. 30
20. integral constant
21. expression
22. do-while
23. break
24. infinite iterations
25. Branching, looping, and jumping
26. if-else
27. definite
28. Looping
29. Forward, backward
30. default
31. identifier
32. break, continue
33. infinite
34. block
35. break

C. TRUE OR FALSE

State whether each of the following is true or false

1. Logical data are that can be interpreted as true or false.
2. The expression in a selection statement can have no side effects.
3. Only non-executable statements can appear outside the body of a function.
4. A null block contains {} only.
5. The minimum number of times a for loop is executed is zero.
6. The continue statement can be used both in selective and loop constructs.

7. Ternary expression is evaluated from right to left.
8. The do-while loop is terminated when its conditional expression returns true value.
9. Null statement performs no operation.
10. An empty compound statement is equivalent to a null statement.
11. Each labelled statement may identify one or more statements.
12. The character classification functions are found in the standard library (stdlib.h).
13. To ensure that a character is uppercase, the toupper conversion function is used.
14. Ternary expression is a selective control construct.
15. The conditional expression need not be written within the parenthesis in any control construct.
16. A semicolon must be placed after closing the conditional expression in a do-while construct.
17. An entry-controlled loop is executed at least once.
18. Identifier-labelled statement is a branching statement and alters the flow of control.
19. One type of loop can be nested in another type of loop.
20. A break statement can be used both in loop and selective control construct.
21. A continue statement can appear inside, or as a body of switch statement or a loop.
22. Case-labelled statements can appear only inside the body of switch statement.
23. A break statement is used to terminate the current iteration of the loop.
24. A switch selection expression can be of any type.
25. Compound statement in case label must be enclosed within braces.
26. In a switch-case statement, labels must be declared in ascending order.

27. In an entry-controlled loop, if the body of the loop is executed n times the expression in the condition section is evaluated n + 1 times.
28. In a pre-test loop, the limit test condition is tested first.
29. The action that causes the loop limit test to change from true to false is the loop update.
30. The value of a comma expression is the value of the first expression.

Answers

1. False	2. True	3. True	4. True
5. True	6. False	7. True	8. False
9. True	10. True	11. True	12. True
13. True	14. True	15. False	16. True
17. False	18. False	19. True	20. True
21. False	22. True	23. False	24. False
25. False	26. False	27. True	28. True
29. True	30. True		

D. OBJECTIVE TYPE QUESTIONS

1. Structural programming approach makes use of
   (a) modules (b) control structures
   (c) user defined data types (d) all the above
2. A statement is differentiated from an expression
   (a) by terminating it by a semicolon
   (b) by terminating it by a newline character
   (c) by terminating it by a NULL
   (d) by terminating it by a blank space
3. A null statement can be represented by a
   (a) newline (b) blank space
   (c) semicolon (d) colon

4. A block is enclosed within a pair of

   (a) {} (b) ( )

   (c) [ ] (d) <>

5. Identify the unconditional control structure.

   (a) do-while (b) switch-case

   (c) goto (d) if

6. Identify the wrong statement

   (a) if-else (b) switch-case

   (c) goto (d) while

7. What is the result of a multiple expression separated by commas?

   (a) result of the leftmost expression after evaluation

   (b) result of the rightmost expression after evaluating all other previous expressions

   (c) no value is returned

   (d) result of arithmetic operations, if any

8. Which is the correct statement?

   (a) while loop can be nested

   (b) for loop can be nested

   (c) options a and b

   (d) one type of a loop cannot be nested n another type of loop

9. The break statement is used to

   (a) continue the next iteration of a loop construct

   (b) exit the block where it exists and continues further sequentially

   (c) exit the outermost block even if it occurs inside the innermost block and continues further sequentially

   (d) terminate the program

10. The continue statement is used to

    (a) continue the next iteration of a loop construct

    (b) exit the block where it exists and continues further sequentially

(c) exit the outermost block even if it occurs inside the innermost

(d) continue the compilation even an error occurs in a program

11. The continue statement is used in

(a) selective control structures only

(b) loop control structures only

(c) options a and b

(d) goto control structure only

12. The break statement is used in

(a) selective control structures only

(b) loop control structures only

(c) options a and b

(d) switch-case control structures only

13. If break statement is omitted in each case statement

(a) The program executes the statements following the case statement where a match is found and exits the switch-case construct

(b) The program executes the statements following the case statement where a match is found and also all the subsequent case statements and default statement

(c) The program executed default statements only and continues with the remaining code

(d) Syntax error is produced

14. If default statement is omitted and there is no match with case labels

(a) No statement within switch-case will be executed

(b) Syntax error is produced

(c) Executes all the statements in the switch-case construct

(d) Executes the last case statement only

15. In what sequence the initialization, testing and execution of body is done in a do-while loop?

(a) Initialization, execution of body, testing

(b) Execution of body, initialization, testing
(c) Initialization, testing, execution of body
(d) None of the above

16. Which of the following statement is used to take the control to the beginning of the loop?
(a) exit (b) break
(c) continue (d) None of the above

17. The minimum number of times the while loop is executed is
(a) 0 (b) 1
(c) 2 (d) cannot be determined

18. The minimum number of times the for loop is executed is
(a) 0 (b) 1
(c) 2 (d) cannot be determined

19. The minimum number of times the do-while loop executed is
(a) 0 (b) 1
(c) 2 (d) cannot be determined

20. The do-while loop is terminated when the conditional expression returns
(a) zero (b) 1
(c) non-zero (d) –1

21. Which conditional expression always returns false value?
(a) if (a = = 0) (b) if (a = 0)
(c) if (a = 10) (d) if (10 = = a)

22. Which conditional expression always returns true value?
(a) if (a = 1) (b) if (a = = 1)
(c) if (a = 0) (d) if (1 = = a)

23. What is (are) the statement(s) which results in infinite loop?
(a) for (i = 0; ; i++); (b) for (i = 0; ;);
(c) for (; ;); (d) all the above

24. In the following loop construct, which one is executed only once always.

```
for (expr1; expr2; expr3) (...)
```

(a) exprl (b) expr3

(c) exprl and expr3 (d) exprl, expr2 and expr3

25. Identify the wrong construct.

(a) for (exprl; expr2;) (b) for (exprl; expr3)

(c) for (; expr;) (d) for(;; expr3)

26. main( )

```
{
int x, y, z, k; int ch;
x = y = z = k = 0;
while ((ch = getchar ()) !_ '\n')
{
switch (ch)
{
case '1': ++x;
case '2': ++y;
case '3': ++z;
break;
default: ++k;
break;
}
}
printf ("%d%d", x, k);
}
```

If the input is 'lalble" what is the output?

(a) 13 (b) 34

(c) 33 (d) 31

27. Result of the following program is

```
main ( )
{
int i=0;
for (i=0; i<20; i++)
{
switch (i)
{
case 0: i+=5;
case 1: i+=2;
case 5: i+=5;
default: i+=4;
break;
}
printf ("%d,", i);
}
}
```

(a) 0.5, 9, 13, 17 (b) 5, 9, 13, 17

(c) 12, 17, 22 (d) 16, 21

28. What is the output of the following code?

```
main ( )
{
int i = 0;
switch (i)
{
case 0 : i++;
case 1 : i+++2
case 2 : ++i;
}
```

```
printf ("%d", i++);
}
```

(a) 1 (b) 3

(c) 4 (d) 5

29. if (! 3.14) printf ("Welcome\n"); else printf ("Hello\n");

What might be the result?

(a) Float value can't be given in conditional part

(b) Hello

(c) Welcome

(d) None of the above

30. main( )

```
{
int i;
if (i > 4) printf ("Ikvinder");
else if (i > 10) printf ("Sukhwant");
else if (i > 21) printf ("Karan");
else printf ("Sandeep");
}
```

What will be the value of x so that "Sukhwant" will be printed?

(a) from 10 to 21 (b) from 11 to 21

(c) greater than 10 (d) none

31. main( )

```
{
i = 0; j = 0;
for (j = 1; j < 10; j++)
{i = i+1;}
{
```

In the code above, what will be the value of the variable i on completion?

(a) 1 (b) 3

(c) 9 (d) 10

32. main( )

```
{
int i = 0;
for (i=1; i<4; i++);
printf ("i=%d\n", i);
}
```

What will be printed when the above sample is executed?

(a) i = 0 (b) i = 1

(c) i =3 (d) i = 4

33. main( )

```
{
int i = 0;
for (; ;)
{
if (i++ = 4) break;
continue;
}
printf ("i=%d\n", i);
}
```

What will be printed when the above code is executed

(a) i = 0 (b) i = 1

(c) i =4 (d) i = 5

34. int i;

```
for (i = 0; i<3; i++);
printf("i=%d\n", i);
```

What will be printed when the sample code above is executed?

(a) i = 0

(b) i = 0

i = 1

i = 2

(c) i = 2

(d) i = 3

35. main( )

```
{
int i=0;
for (; ++i;)
printf ("%d", i);
}
```

How many times the for loop will be executed?

(a) 0

(b) infinite

(c) 32767

(d) The maximum integer value that can be represented in the machine.

36. main( )

```
{
unsigned int i = 10;
while (i->= 0);
}
```

How many times the loop will be executed?

(a) 10

(b) zero time

(c) one time

(d) none of these

37. int i = 10;

Which of the following is the finite loop?

(a) while (1)

{

if (! (i!= 10))

```
continue;
....
}
```

(b) while (! = 0)

```
{
if (i = = 10)
continue;
....
}
```

(c) do

```
{
....
}while (! ( i > 10));
```

(d) while (i > 10)

```
{...};
```

38. main( )

```
{
int code = 4;
switch (code)
{
default:
;
case 3:
code+=5;
if (code = = 8)
{
code++;
if (code = = 9) break;
code *= 2;
}
```

```
code - = 4;
break;
case 8:
code +=5;
break;
}
printf ("CODE = %d\n", code);
}
```

What will be the output of the above code?

(a) CODE = 5 (b) CODE = 4

(c) CODE = 9 (d) CODE = 10

39. switch (s)

```
{
case 1 : printf ("Ikvinder")
case 2 :
case 3 : printf ("Avtar")
case 4 : printf ("Lovedeep ")
default : printf ("Sukhwant")
}
```

To print only Sukhwant, what will be the value of s?

(a) 2

(b) 2 or 3 or 4

(c) any int value other than 1, 2, 3 and 4

(d) 4

40. main( )

```
{
int i=-4, r, num = 1;
r = i& -3;
r = (r ? 0 : num * num);
```

```
printf ("%d", r);
}
```

What will be the output of the program?

(a) 0

(b) 1

(c) –ve is not allowed in the mod operands

(d) none

41. What is the value of in variable result if i = 50, j = 75 and k = 100?
result = (i + 50 ? j >= 75 ? k > 100 ? 1 : 2 : 3 : 4);

(a) 1 (b) 2

(c) 3 (d) 4

42. Omitting the break statement from a particular case

(a) leads to a syntax error

(b) causes execution to terminate after that case

(c) causes execution to continue all subsequent cases

(d) causes execution to branch to the statement after the switch statement

43. The number of loop constructs in C is

(a) 2 (b) 3

(c) 4 (d) 5

44. Identify the wrong statement.

(a) if (a<b); (b) if a<b;

(c) if (a<b) {;} (d) options b and c

45. Which is syntactically correct?

(a) if (a := 10) {…} else if (a< 10) {…}

(b) if (a = = 10) {…} else if (a< 10) {…}

(c) if (a eq 10) {,..} else if (a< 10) {…}

(d) if (a .eq. 10) {…} else if (a< 10) {…}

46. Which is the correct statement?

(a) printf ("Maximum = % = % d\n", (x..y)?x:y);

(b) printf ("%s\n", (mark > = 60)? "FIRST CLASS" : "NOT FIRST CLASS");

(c) printf ("%s \n", "PASS");

(d) all the above

47. A statement differs from expression by terminating with a

(a) ; (b) :

(c) NULL (d) .

48. What should be the expression return value for a do-while to terminate

(a) 1 (b) 0

(c) –1 (d) NULL

49. Which among the following is a unconditional control structure

(a) do-while (b) if-else

(c) goto (d) for

50. Continue statement is used

(a) to go to the next iteration in a loop

(b) come out of a loop

(c) exit and return to the main function

(d) restarts iterations from beginning of loop

51. Structural programming approach makes use of

(a) modules (b) control structures

(c) user defined data types (d) all the above

52. A statement is differentiated from an expression

(a) by terminating it with a semicolon

(b) by terminating it with a newline character

(c) by terminating it by a null

(d) by terminating it by a blank space

53. A null statement can be represented by a

(a) newline (b) blank space

(c) semicolon (d) colon

54. A block is enclosed within a pair of

(a) { } (b) ( )

(c) [ ] (d) < >

55. Identify the unconditional control structure

(a) do-while (b) switch case

(c) goto (d) if

56. The break statement is used to exit from:

(a) an if statement (b) a for loop

(c) a program (d) the main( ) function

57. A do-while loop is useful when we want that the statements within the loop must be executed:

(a) Only once (b) At least once

(c) More than once (d) None of the above

58. What is the value of x in the expression x (a = 10, a*a)?

(a) invalid expression (b) 0

(c) 10 (d) 100

59. When is default statement executed in switch-case construct?

(a) Whenever there is exactly one match

(b) Whenever break statement is omitted in all case statements

(c) Whenever there is no match with case labels

(d) options b and c

60. Infinite loop is

(a) useful for time delay (b) useless

(c) used to terminate execution (d) not possible

61. C is an example of

(a) object oriented language

(b) structured programming language

(c) object based language

(d) component based language

62. The syntax of if statement is
    (a) if expression then program statement
    (b) if (expression) program statement
    (c) if(expression) then program statement
    (d) if expression { program statement}
63. Identify the wrong statement where .... represents C code.
    (a) label: {......} ......goto label;
    (b) goto end; ......
        end: {......}
    (c) goto 50; ......
        50: {......}
    (d) begin: {......}
        if (a < 10) goto begin;
64. The syntax of if statement is
    (a) if expression then program-statement
    (b) if (expression) program-statement
    (c) if (expression) then program-statement
    (d) if expression {program-statement}
65. main( )

```
{
int i = 2, j = 4, k = 8, x = 4;
if (x = = i) x = i; else x = j;
if (x ! = j) k =k + j; else k = k + i;
printf ("k = %d\n", k);
}
```

What will be printed when the above code is executed?

(a) k = 4 (b) k = 8
(c) k = 10 (d) k = 12

66. main( )

```
{
unsigned int i = -10; int j = 10;
if (j <= i) printf ("Welcome\n");
if (j = = (i = -10)) printf ("Hello\n");
if ((int) i = = j) printf ("Hi\n");
}
```

What will be the output of above sample code?

(a) Hello (b) Welcome Hi

(c) Hi (d) Welcome

67. int i;

```
i=2;
i++;
if (i=4)
{
printf ("i=4");
}
else
{
printf ("i=3");
}
```

What is the output of the program?

(a) i = 4 (b) i = 3

(c) unpredictable (d) none

68. int i = 0, j = 2;

```
if (i = 0) j = 0;
else j *= 10;
```

What is the value of j?

(a) 0 (b) 20

(c) 2 (d) none

69. int i = 2, j = 2, k = 1;

What is the value of x after the following statements?

```
if (i = j%2) k +=10;
else k +=20;
```

(a) 0 (b) 2

(c) 1 (d) none

70. What is the result?

```
main( )
{
char ch = -64; int i = -32;
unsigned int u =-16;
if (ch>i)
{
printf ("pass1");
if (ch<u) printf ("pass2");
else printf ("Fail2");}
else printf ("Fail1");
if (i<u) printf ("pass2");
else printf ("Fail2");
}
```

(a) pass1pass2 (b) pass1Fail2

(c) Fail1pass2 (d) Fail1Fail2

71. How many x are printed?

```
for (i = 0, j = 10, i < j; i++, j-)
printf ("i");
```

(a) 10 (b) 5

(c) 4 (d) none

72. What is the output of the following program?

```
main ( )
{
```

```
unsigned int i;
for (i = 10; i >= 0; i–)
print ("%d", i);
}
```

(a) prints numbers 10 to 0 (b) prints numbers 10 to 1

(c) prints numbers 10 to –1 (d) goes into infinite loop

73. unsigned char ch;

```
for (ch=0; ch!=256; ch+2)
printf("%d", ch);
```

How many times the loop is executed?

(a) 127 (b) 128

(c) 256 (d) Infinitely

74. For the following code how many times the printf( ) function is executed?

```
int i, j;
for (i=0; i<=10; i++);
for (j=0; j<=10; j++);
printf ("i=%d, j=%d\n", i, j);
```

(a) 121 (b) 11

(c) 10 (d) none of the above

75. What output of the following code?

```
main ( )
{
int i=3;
while (i–)
{
int i=100;
i–;
printf ("%d..", i);
}
```

```
}
```

(a) Infinite loop (b) Error
(c) 99..99..99.. (d) 3..2..1..

76. What will be the output of the following code?

```
{
ch = 'A';
while (ch<='F')
{
switch (ch)
{
case 'A': case 'B' :case 'C' : case 'D' : ch++;
continue;
case 'E' :case 'F' : ch++;
}
putchar (ch);
}
}
```

(a) ABCDEF (b) EFG
(c) FG (d) Error

77. Comma is used as
(a) a separator in C (b) an operator in C
(c) a delimiter in C (d) terminator in C

Answers

1. (d)	2. (a)	3. (c)	4. (a)	5. (c)
6. (d)	7. (b)	8. (c)	9. (b)	10. (a)
11. (b)	12. (c)	13. (b)	14. (a)	15. (a)
16. (d)	17. (a)	18. (a)	19. (b)	20. (a)
21. (b)	22. (a)	23. (d)	24. (a)	25. (b)

26. (a)	27. (d)	28. (b)	29. (b)	30. (d)
31. (c)	32. (d)	33. (d)	34. (d)	35. (d)
36. (d)	37. (d)	38. (a)	39. (c)	40. (a)
41. (b)	42. (c)	43. (b)	44. (b)	45. (b)
46. (d)	47. (a)	48. (b)	49. (c)	50. (a)
51. (d)	52. (a)	53. (c)	54. (a)	55. (c)
56. (d)	57. (b)	58. (d)	59. (d)	60. (a)
61. (b)	62. (b)	63. (c)	64. (b)	65. (d)
66. (d)	67. (a)	68. (b)	69. (a)	70. (c)
71. (b)	72. (a)	73. (d)	74. (a)	75. (c)
76. (c)	77. (b)			

CHAPTER

5

Arrays

A. CODE SNIPPETS

Problem 1

Check the errors from the following program?

```
#include<stdio.h>
#include<conio.h>
void main( )
{
int a[];
a[0]=a[1]=a[2]=2;
printf(%d%d%d",a[0],a[1],a[2]);
getch();
}
```

Output:

Error

NOTE: size of arr is unknown

Problem 2

Check the errors from the following program?

```
#include<stdio.h>
#include<conio.h>
```

```
void main( )
{
int size=3;
int a[size];
a[0]=a[1],a[2]=5;
printf("%d%d%d",a[0],a[1],a[2]);
getch();
}
```

Output:

Error

NOTE: Constant expression required

Problem 3

Find the output of the following program?

```
#include<stdio.h>
#include<conio.h>
void main( )
{
int a[]={1, 2,3};
printf("%d%d%d",a[0],a[1],a[2]);
getch();
}
```

Output:

1 2 3

Problem 4

Check the errors from the following program?

```
#include<stdio.h>
#include<conio.h>
```

```
void main( )
{
int a[2]={1,2,3};
printf("%d%d%d",a[0],a[1],a[2]);
getch();
}
```

Output:

```
Error
```

NOTE: Too many intializers

Problem 5

Find the output of the following program?

```
#include<stdio.h>
#include<conio.h>
void main( )
{
int a[6]={1,2,3,4};
int i;
for (i=0;i<6;i++)
printf("%d",a[i]);
getch();
}
```

Output:

```
1 2 3 4 0 0
```

Problem 6

Find the output of the following program?

```
#include<stdio.h>
#include<conio.h>
```

```
void main( )
{
int a[3]={1,2,3};
printf("%d%d%d",arr[1],arr[2],arr[3]);
getch();
}
```

Output:

```
2 3 garbage value
```

Problem 7

Find the output of the following program?

```
#include<stdio.h>
#include<conio.h>
void main( )
{
int a[]={1,2,3};
a[0,1,2]=10;
printf("%d%d%d",a[0],a[1],a[2]);
getch();
}
```

Output:

```
1 2 10
```

Problem 8

Find the output of the following program?

```
#include<stdio.h>
#include<conio.h>
void main( )
{
int a[]={1,2,3,4,5},i;
```

```
a[1+2]=10;
for(i=0;i<5;i++)
printf("%d",a[i]);
getch();
}
```

Output:

```
1 2 3 10 5
```

Problem 9

Find the output of the following program?

```
#include<stdio.h>
#include<conio.h>
void main( )
{
int a[]={1,2,3,4,5},i;
a[2.5+1.5]=10;
for(i=0;i<5;i++)
printf("%d",a[i]);
getch();
}
```

Output:

```
Error
```

NOTE: Illegal use of float type

Problem 10

Find the output of the following program?

```
#include<stdio.h>
#include<conio.h>
void main( )
{
```

```
int a[]={1,2,3,4};
printf("Number of elements in array are %d", sizeof(a)/
    sizeof(a[0]));
getch();
}
```

Output:

```
Number of elements in array are 4
```

Problem 11

Find the output of the following program?

```
#include<stdio.h>
#include<conio.h>
void main( )
{
int a=4,b;
int a[]={1,2,3}, a1[3];
b=a;
a1=a;
printf("Array elements are %d%d%d",a1[0], a1[1], a1[2]);
getch();
}
```

Output:

```
Error
```

NOTE: L-value required

Problem 12

Find the output of the following program?

```
#include<stdio.h>
#include<conio.h>
void main( )
```

```
{
int a[]={1,2,3},a1[]={1,2,3};
if(a= =a1)
printf("Both arrays are same\n");
else
printf("Both arrays are different");
getch();
}
```

Output:

```
Both arrays are different
```

Problem 13

Check the errors from the following program?

```
#include<stdio.h>
#include<conio.h>
void main( )
{
int i, a = 4, b = 6;
int a[ 4 + 6 ] ;
for ( i = 0 ; i < a+b ; i++ )
{
scanf ("%d", &a[i]);
printf ("\n%d", a[i]);
}
getch();
}
```

Output:

```
No error.
```

Problem 14

Find the output of the following program?

```
#include<stdio.h>
#include<conio.h>
void main( )
{
int a[ ] = { 10, 20, 30, 40, 50 };
int i;
for ( i = 0 ; i <= 4 ; i++ )
printf ( "\n%d" *( a + i ) ) ;
getch();
}
```

Output:

```
10
20
30
40
50
```

Problem 15

Find the output of the following program?

```
#include<stdio.h>
#include<conio.h>
void main( )
{
int a[ ] = { 10, 20, 30, 40, 50 };
int i, *p ;
p = a;
for ( i = 0 ; i <= 4 ; i++ )
```

```
{
printf ( "\n%d", *p ) ;
p++;
}
getch();
}
```

Output:

```
0
20
0
40
5
```

Problem 16

Find the output of the following program?

```
#include<stdio.h>
#include<conio.h>
void display(int*,int);
void main( )
{
int a[ ] = { 2, 4, 6, 8, 10 };
int i;
display( a, 5);
for ( i = 0 ; i <= 4 ; i++ )
printf( "\n%d", a[i] );
getch();
}
void display( int *p, int n )
{
```

```
int i ;
for ( i = 0 ; i < n ; i++ )
*(p + i) = *(p + i) + 5;
}
```

Output:

```
7
9
11
13
15
```

Problem 17

Find the output of the following program?

```
#include<stdio.h>
#include<conio.h>
void main( )
{
static int a[5];
int i;
for ( i = 0 ; i <= 4 ; i++)
printf ( "\n%d", a[i] );
getch();
}
```

Output:

```
0
0
0
0
0
```

Problem 18

Check the errors from the following program?

```
#include<stdio.h>
#include<conio.h>
void main( )
{
int a[5] = { 1, 2, 3, 4, 5};
int i;
for (i = 0; i <= 25; i++)
printf ("\n%d", a[i]);
getch();
}
```

Output:

No error.

Problem 19

Check the errors from the following program?

```
#include<stdio.h>
#include<conio.h>
void main( )
{
int a[100], i;
for ( i = 1; i <= 100; i++ )
{
a[i] = i;
printf ( "\n%d" , a[i] ) ;
}
getch();
}
```

Output:

No error.

Problem 20

Check the errors from the following program?

```
#include<stdio.h>
#include<conio.h>
void main( )
{
int a[ ] = { 10, 20, 30, 40, 50 };
int j;
j = a;
j = j + 3;
printf ( "\n%d" *j );
getch();
}
```

Output:

```
Error.
```

NOTE: Declare the j as pointer variable int *j.

Problem 21

Find the output of the following program?

```
#include<stdio.h>
#include<conio.h>
void main( )
{
float a[ ] = { 1.6, 17.5, 21.5, 35.2, 23.8 };
float *j;
j = a;
j = j + 4;
printf ( "\n%d %f %f", j, *j, a[4] );
```

```
getch();
}
```

Output:

No error.

Problem 22

Check the errors from the following program?

```
#include<stdio.h>
#include<conio.h>
void main( )
{
float a[ ] = { 1.8, 21.6, 11.4, 15.2, 17.3 };
float *j, *k;
j = a;
k = a + 2;
j = j * 4;
k = k / 4;
printf ( "\n%d %d", *j, *k );
getch();
}
```

Output:

Error.

NOTE: multiplty (*) and divison (/) operators are not used with pointers.

Problem 23

Check the errors from the following program?

```
#include<stdio.h>
#include<conio.h>
void main( )
```

```
{
int size = 10;
float a[size];
for ( i = 0 ; i < size ; i++ )
scanf ( "%f", &a[i] );
getch();
}
```

Output:

```
Error.
```

NOTE: Array dimension cannot use variables.

Problem 24

Find the output of the following program?

```
#include<stdio.h>
#include<conio.h>
void main( )
{
int a[3][3] = { 1, 2, 3, 4, 5, 6, 7, 8,9 };
printf ( "\n%d %d %d", *a, a[3][3], a[2][2] );
getch();
}
```

Output:

```
<base address> <garbage value> 1
```

Problem 25

Find the output of the following program?

```
#include<stdio.h>
#include<conio.h>
void main( )
{
```

```
int a[3][3] = { 1, 2, 3, 4, 5, 6, 7, 8,9 };
int i, *ptr ;
ptr = a;
for ( i = 0 ; i <= 8 ; i++ )
printf ( "%d", *( ptr + i ) ) ;
getch();
}
```

Output:

```
1 2 3 4 5 6 7 8 9
```

Problem 26

Find the output of the following program?

```
#include<stdio.h>
#include<conio.h>
void main( )
{
int a[3][3] = { 1, 2, 3, 4, 5, 6, 7, 8,9 };
int i, j;
for ( i = 0 ; i <= 2 ; i++ )
for ( j = 0 ; j <= 2 ; j++ )
printf ( "\n%d %d", n[i][j], *( *( n + i ) + j ) );
getch();
}
```

Output:

```
1 1
2 2
3 3
4 4
5 5
–
–
9 9
```

Problem 27

Check the errors from the following program?

```
#include<stdio.h>
#include<conio.h>
void main( )
{
int twoD[ ][ ] = { 2, 4, 6, 8 };
printf ( "\n%d", twoD );
getch();
}
```

Output:

```
Error.
```

NOTE: Column dimension is necessary when we declaring two dimensional array.

Problem 28

Check the errors from the following program?

```
#include<stdio.h>
#include<conio.h>
void main( )
{
int a[3][ ] = { 2, 4, 3, 7, 4, 9, 2, 6, 4};
printf ( "\n%d", three[2][3] );
getch();
}
```

Output:

```
Error.
```

NOTE: Column dimension is necessary when we declaring two dimensional array.

Problem 29

Find the output of the following program?

```
#include<stdio.h>
#include<conio.h>
void main( )
{
int num[10], temp;
num[0] = 10;
num[9] = 20;
temp = num[9];
num[9] = num[0];
num[0] = temp;
printf ("\n%d %d", num[0], num[9]);
getch();
}
```

Output:

```
20 10
```

Problem 30

Find the output of the following program?

```
#include<stdio.h>
#include<conio.h>
void main( )
{
int array[100], i;
for ( i = 0 ; i <= 25 ; i++ )
{
array[i] = 'A' + i;
printf ("\n%d %c", array[i], array[i]);
```

```
}
getch();
}
```

Output:

```
65 A
66 B
.....
.....
90 Z
```

Problem 31

Find the output of the following program?

```
#include<stdio.h>
#include<conio.h>
void main( )
{
int a[50], i;
for ( i = 0 ; i <= 48 ; i++ );
{
a[i] = i;
printf ("\n%d", a[i]);
}
getch();
}
```

Output:

```
49. Variable i takes a value 49 when it reaches the
   statement a[i] = i;
```

Problem 32

Check the errors from the following program?

```
#include<stdio.h>
#include<conio.h>
int char mixed[100];
void main( )
{
int a[10], i;
for(i = 1; i <= 10; i++)
{
scanf("%d", a[i]);
printf("%d", a[i]);
}
getch();
}
```

Output:

```
Error.
```

NOTE: Logical error occur int char mixed[100]. Array bounds are exceeded.

Problem 33

Check the errors from the following program?

```
#include<stdio.h>
#include<conio.h>
void main( )
{
int size;
scanf("%d", &size);
int a[size];
for( i = 1; i <= size; i++)
{
scanf ("%d", a[i]);
```

```
printf ("%d", a[i]);
}
getch();
}
```

Output:

```
Error.
```

NOTE: Array dimensions should be constant and all declarations should be at the beginning.

Problem 34

Find the output of the following program?

```
// array starting address is 1000
#include<stdio.h>
#include <conio.h>
void main( )
{
int a[]= {1, 2, 3, 4, 5};
printf("%u %u %u", a, &a, &a[0]);
getch();
}
```

Output:

```
1000 1000 1000
```

Problem 35

Difference between **a** and **&a.**

Output:

In above problem these two gives the same addresses. But a given the address of the first int, whereas &a gives the address of array of integers. Suppose the expression a+1 will give the address of the next integer, whereas &a+1 will give the address of next array of integers.

Problem 36

Check the errors from the following program?

```
#include<stdio.h>
#include <conio.h>
void main( )
{
int size, a[size];
scanf("%d", &size);
for(i=1; i<=size; i++)
{
printf("%d", a[i]);
}
getch();
}
```

Output:

Error

NOTE: The statement declaring array is invalid.

Problem 37

Find the output of the following program?

```
// array starting address is 1000: each integer take
   2 bytes
#include<stdio.h>
#include <conio.h>
void main( )
{
int a[]= {1, 2, 3, 4, 5};
printf("%u %u", a+1, &a+1);
getch();
}
```

Output:

1000 1008

Problem 38

Find the output of the following program?

```
#include<stdio.h>
#include <conio.h>
void main( )
{
float a[]= {1.1, 1.2, 1.3, 1.4, 1.5};
printf("\n%d", sizeof (a) / sizeof (a[0]));
getch();
}
```

Output:

4

Problem 39

Find the output of the following program?

```
#include<stdio.h>
#include<conio.h>
void main( )
{
int a[2][3]={1,2,3,4};
printf("%d%d%d%d%d%d",a[0][0],a[0][1],a[0][2],a[1][0],
   a[1][1],a[1][2]);
getch();
}
```

Output:

1 2 3 4 0 0

Problem 40

Find the output of the following program?

```
#include<stdio.h>
#include<conio.h>
```

```
void main( )
{
int a[2][3]={{1,2},{3,4}};
printf("%d%d%d%d%d%d",a[0][0],a[0][1],a[0][2],
   a[1][0],a[1][1],a[1][2]);
getch();
}
```

Output:

```
1 2 0 3 4 0
```

Problem 41

Check the errors from the following program?

```
#include<stdio.h>
#include<conio.h>
void main( )
{
int a[][]={1,2,3,4};
printf("%d%d%d%d%d%d",a[0][0],a[0][1],a[0][2],a[1][0],a[1][1],
   a[1][2]);
getch();
}
```

Output:

```
Error
```

NOTE: size of type is unknown or zero

Problem 42

Check the errors from the following program?

```
#include<stdio.h>
#include<conio.h>
void main( )
```

```
{
int a[2][][]={1,2,3,4,5,6,7,8};
int i,j,k;
for (i=0;i<2;i++)
for(j=0;j<2;j++)
for(k=0;k<2;k++)
printf("%d",a[i][j][k]);
getch();
}
```

Output:

```
Error
```

NOTE: size of type is unknown or zero

Problem 43

Find the output of the following program?

```
#include<stdio.h>
#include<conio.h>
void main( )
{
int a[][3]={1,2,3,4};
printf("%d%d%d%d%d%d",a[0][0],a[0][1],a[0][2],a[1][0],
    a[1][1],a[1][2]);
getch();
}
```

Output:

```
1 2 3 4 0 0
```

Problem 44

Find the output of the following program?

```
#include<stdio.h>
#include <conio.h>
```

```
void main( )
{
int a[5], i=0;
while (i < 5)
a[i] = ++i;
for (i=0; i<5;i++)
printf("%d", a[i]);
getch();
}
```

Output:

```
Garbage value 1 2 3 4
```

Problem 45

Write the function fun1( ) in the program given below?

```
#include<stdio.h>
#include <conio.h>
void main( )
{
int a[2][6];
fun (a);
getch();
}
```

Output:

```
fun (int a1[][6])
{ }
```

Problem 46

Find the output of the following program?

```
#include<stdio.h>
#include <conio.h>
void main( )
```

```
{
int a[5], i=-1;
while (i<5)
a[i]=++i;
for (i=0; i<5; i++)
printf("%d", a[i]);
getch();
}
```

Output:

```
0 1 2 3 4
```

Problem 47

Explain the following statement:

```
int a[2];
a[2]=10;
```

Output:

The first statement tells the array size, whereas second statement specifies a particular element of the array.

Problem 48

Find the output of the following program?

```
#include<stdio.h>
#include <conio.h>
void main( )
{
int a[1]= {10};
printf("%d", 0[a]);
getch();
}
```

Output:

```
10
```

Problem 49

Find the output of the following program?

```
// array starting address is 1000
#include<stdio.h>
#include <conio.h>
void main( )
{
int a[] = {1, 2, 3, 4, 5};
printf("%u", a);
printf("%u", &a[0]);
printf("%u", &a);
getch();
}
```

Output:

1000 1000 1000

Problem 50

Is there any difference in the following declarations?

```
int f(int a[]);
int f(int a[10]);
```

Output:

No

Problem 51

Explain the following statements:

```
int a[10];
a[10]=1;
```

Output:

The first statement 10 tells the array size, whereas in the second statement specifies a particular element of the array.

B. FILL IN THE BLANKS

1. An array is a collection of .... data items.
2. Lists and tables of values can be stored in ....
3. Array is the collection of .... data elements.
4. The elements of an array are related by the fact that they have the same .... and ....
5. The array index in C language starts with ....
6. The elements of an array are always stored in .... memory locations.
7. The size specifier in an array declaration must be a compile time expression of .... type.
8. The elements of an array can be accessed by using .... operator.
9. A vector is a .... array.
10. Array name represents the .... of the starting element.
11. .... storage representation is used in a matrix.
12. Number of elements in a two-dimensional array having 5 rows and 3 columns is ....
13. ANSI C compiler supports at least .... dimensions of array.
14. Missing elements of partially initialized arrays are set to ....
15. The array subscript must always start at ....
16. In an array declaration, the value enclosed in [] specifies the .... of the array.
17. The .... of an array are stored in the consecutive memory locations.
18. The initializer char s[]= {'a', 'e', 'i', 'o', 'u'}; is different from char s[]= "aeiou"; since the first assignment does not include .... character.
19. The arrays are of two types: .... and ....

20. The number like a[3] used to refer to a particular element of an array is called its ....
21. The process of placing the elements of an array in order is called .... the array.
22. The process of finding an array element from an array is called .... the array.
23. An array that uses two subscripts is referred to as a .... array.
24. An .... is an integral value used to access an element in an array.
25. The .... search locates the target item by starting at the beginning and moving toward the end of the list.
26. The process through which data are arranged according to their values is known as ....
27. Whenever an error occurs or end of file reaches the function gets( ) returns ....
28. Whenever an error occurs the function puts( ) returns ....
29. The function scanf( ) is used to read a string by using a conversion specification ....
30. The function printf( ) is used to display a string by using a conversion specification ....
31. In a one-dimensional array declaration, the value within .... mentions the size of the array and in other places it represents the subscript value.

Answers

1. homogenous
2. arrays
3. homogeneous
4. name, type.
5. zero
6. contiguous
7. integral
8. Subscript
9. One-dimensional array
10. address
11. row major order
12. 15

13. 6
14. zero
15. zero
16. size
17. elements
18. NULL
19. Linear, Non-linear
20. subscript (or index)
21. sorting
22. searching
23. two-dimensional
24. index
25. linear or sequential
26. Sorting
27. NULL
28. EOF
29. %s
30. %s
31. [ ]

C. TRUE OR FALSE

State whether each of the following is true or false

1. The efficiency of the sequential search is O(n).
2. In an array declaration, the number of initializes in the initialization list should be less than or at most equal to the value of size specifier.
3. The type of all elements in an array must be the same.
4. The array int a[20]; can store twenty elements.
5. The expression a[1] is the starting index in the array.
6. It is necessary to initialize the array at the time of declaration.
7. When an array is passed to a function, C passes the value for each element.
8. A single array can be used to represent both integer and real numbers.
9. The values of an array b can be assigned to another array a by the statement a = b;
10. A list of strings can be stored in within a two dimensional array.
11. In a two-dimensional array a, the individual elements a[i][j] and a[i j] are the same.
12. The index of an array must be a positive integer greater than zero.
13. A pointer variable can be initialized with a constant value zero.

14. Any array can be searched using the sequential search.
15. A pointer to any type of object can be assigned to a pointer of type void* without explicit type casting.
16. Any expression that evaluates to an integral value may be used as an index.
17. The expression a[19] designates the twenty element in the array.
18. The declaration a[SIZE] is allowed is SIZE is a macro.
19. A pointer to a block of memory is effectively same as an array.
20. A void pointer can be assigned to a pointer variable without explicit type casting.
21. The name of the array refers to the base address of the complete array.
22. Only the size of the second dimension needs to be declared when the array is used as a parameter.
23. Array is an ordered sequence of finite data items of different data types.
24. Matrix is an array of one-dimensional array.
25. Array must be declared before use.
26. If the size of an array is less than the number of initializers, the size grows dynamically.
27. C has no checks on array bounds.
28. The size of an array cannot be changed at the run time.
29. If the size specifier is not mentioned in an array declaration, the size of the array is automatically initialized to a single element.
30. Multi-dimensional arrays in C are stored in the memory using column major order of storage.
31. Because of its efficiency, the binary search is the best search for any array, regardless of its size and order.
32. The size of an array which is initialized with a string constant is equal to the number of characters in the string.
33. Numeric array elements can be read as a single entity.

34. One-dimensional character array can be read as a single entity.
35. Array name and subscripted variables are different.
36. The expressions a[5] and 5[a] are identical.
37. The first dimension is known as the column dimension.
38. The selection, insertion and bubble sort are all $O(n^2)$ sorts.
39. The declaration statement int* a[10]; declares a as a pointer to an integer array of 10 elements.
40. When an array is defined, C automatically sets the value of its elements to zero.

Answers

1. True	2. True	3. True	4. True
5. False	6. False	7. True	8. False
9. False	10. True	11. False	12. False
13. True	14. True	15. True	16. True
17. True	18. True	19. True	20. False
21. False	22. True	23. False	24. False
25. True	26. False	27. True	28. True
29. False	30. False	31. True	32. False
33. False	34. True	35. True	36. True
37. False	38. True	39. False	40. True

D. OBJECTIVE TYPE QUESTIONS

1. An array of n elements will be declared in C as:
   (a) array[n] (b) array[n–1]
   (c) array[n+1] (d) array
2. The first element of a 0 based array can be accessed by:
   (a) array (b) array[0]
   (c) array[n–1] (d) array[n]

3. What will the piece of code reveal...

```
int a[] = {1,2,3,4,5,6,7,8,9,0};
printf("%d",a[2]);
printf("%d",2[a]);
```

** Regarding the fact that there are no syntax errors..

(a) a. 3 8 (b) Logical error
(c) 3 3 (d) 3

4. Memory is allocated in an array in:
   (a) Non Continues Way
   (b) Continues fashion
   (c) It may be any way, does not matter
   (d) Random but in some logical manner according to some algorithm.

5. A 'n' sized 1 based array indexed from:

(a) [1] – [n] (b) [0] – [n]
(c) [1] – [n-1] (d) [0] – [n-1]

6. In an Array the range specifies...
   (a) Scope of the Array
   (b) Nos. of Elements in the Array
   (c) The Group of the Array
   (d) Size – 1 of the Array

7. If Array's upper bound is specified by 'U' and lower bound is specified by 'L' then the range of the array will be

(a) U – L +1 (b) L + U – 1
(c) U – L – 1 (d) L – U + 1

8. If Upper bound is represented by 99 and lower bound by 0 in a o based array, then the range of the array is..

(a) 0 (b) 99
(c) 100 (d) 101

9. A string is ended by…
   (a) The Last Character
   (b) The Null Character
   (c) The Dot Character
   (d) The First Character
10. Suppose that you want to declare an array of characters to hold a C++ string with exactly 9 letters. Which declaration is best?
    (a) char s[8];
    (b) char s[9];
    (c) char s[10];
    (d) char s[11];
11. Which of the following can be used to describe arrays as well as hard disks?
    (a) static
    (b) dynamic
    (c) direct access
    (d) linked access
12. Of the following, which would access an element of an array of records?
    (a) Data[i]
    (b) Data(i)
    (c) Data(i,j)
    (d) Data.i
13. Arrays are also called as
    1. Dense lists; 2. Predefined variables; 3. Static data structures
    (a) 1 and 2
    (b) 2 and 3
    (c) 1 and 3
    (d) All
14. Array is used represent
    (a) a list of data items of integer data type
    (b) a list of data items of real data type
    (c) a list of data items of different data type
    (d) a list of data items of same data type
15. Array name is
    (a) an array variable
    (b) a keyword
    (c) a common name shared by all elements
    (d) not used in a program

16. One-dimensional array is known as
    (a) vector (b) table
    (c) matrix (d) an array of arrays
17. The array elements are represented by
    (a) index values (b) subscripted variables
    (c) array name (d) size of an array
18. Array elements occupy
    (a) subsequent memory locations
    (b) random location for each element
    (c) varying length of memory locations for each element
    (d) no space in memory
19. The address of the starting element of an array is
    (a) represented by subscripted variable of the starting element
    (b) cannot be specified
    (c) represented by the array name
    (d) no used by the compiler
20. Identify the wrong statement.
    (a) Subscripts are also known as indices
    (b) Array variables and subscripted variables are same
    (c) Array name and subscripted variables are different
    (d) Array name and subscripted variables are same.
21. Array subscripts in C always start at
    (a) –1 (b) 0
    (c) 1 (d) any value
22. Identify the correct declaration.
    (a) int a[10] [10]; (b) int a[10, 10];
    (c) int a(10) (10); (d) int a (10, 10);
23. Maximum number of elements in the array declaration int x[10];
    (a) 9 (b) 10
    (c) 11 (d) undefined

24. Identify the correct declaration

    (a) int a[10][10]; (b) int a[10,10];
    (c) int a (10) (10); (d) int a (10,10);

25. Maximum number of elements in the array declaration int x[10]; is

    (a) 9 (b) 10
    (c) 11 (d) undefined

26. Maximum number of elements in the array declaration int y[5][8]; is

    (a) 28 (b) 32
    (c) 35 (d) 40

27. Two-dimensional array elements are sorted in

    (a) column major order (b) row major order
    (c) both options a and b (d) random order

28. Two-dimensional array elements are sorted

    (a) row by row in the subsequent memory locations
    (b) column by column in the subsequent memory location
    (c) row by row in scattered memory locations
    (d) column by column scattered memory locations

29. ANSI C recommends a compiler to support at least dimensions of an array

    (a) 4 (b) 5
    (c) 6 (d) 7

30. Array declaration

    (a) requires the number of elements to be specified
    (b) does not require the number of elements to be specified
    (c) assumes default size as 0
    (d) is not necessary

31. Identify the wrong expression given int a[10];

    (a) a[–1] (b) a[10]
    (c) a[0] (d) + + a

32. What is the value of a[0][2] in int a[3][4] = { {1,2}, {4,8,15} }?
    (a) 4
    (b) 2
    (c) 0
    (d) not defined
33. Identify the correct statement
    (a) float array can be read as a whole
    (b) integer array can be read as a whole
    (c) character array can be read as a whole
    (d) double array can be read as a whole
34. Identify the correct statement
    (a) float array can be displayed by using single printf( ) without using a loop.
    (b) Integer array can be displayed by using single printf( ) without using a loop
    (c) Char array can be displayed by using single printf( ) without using a loop
    (d) Double array can be displayed by using single printf( ) without using a loop
35. Missing elements of partly initialized arrays, are
    (a) set to zero
    (b) set to one
    (c) not defined
    (d) invalid
36. main( )

```
{
char s[ ] = "Focal Point";
printf ("%d\n", ????);
}
```

Which of the following could replace the ???? in the code above to print the index of the first occurrence of the letter letter o in s (in this case the value would be 1)?

(a) strchr(s, 'o') – s
(b) strchr (s, "o")
(c) stchr(s, 'o')
(d) stchr(s, "o") – s

37. main( )

```
{
char s[6] = "Hello";
printf ("%s", s [5]);
}
```

What is the output of the above program?

(a) 0 (b) 48

(c) nothing (d) unpredictable

38. What is the result of the following declaration?

```
int A[ ] = {1, 2, 3, 4, 5};
&A[5] - &A[1];
```

(a) 8 (b) –4

(c) 4 (d) –8

39. char name [ ] = {'n', 'a', 'm', 'e'};

```
printf ("name = %s\n", name);
```

What will be the output?

(a) name = name

(b) name = name followed by junk characters

(c) name = \name

(d) options a or b

40. What would be the result of the following program?

```
main( )
{
char p[ ] = "string";
char t;
int i, j;
for (i=0; j=strlen (p); i<j;i++)
{
t=p[i];
```

```
p[i]= p[j - i];
p [j- i] = t;
}
printf("%s", p);
}
```

(a) will print:string

(b) will not print anything since p will be pointing to a null string

(c) will print:gnirts

(d) will result in a complication error

41. What is the output of the program?

```
main( )
{ int rows = 3, columns = 4;
int a[rows] [columns] = {1, 2, 3, 4, 5, 6, 7, 8, 9,
10, 11, 12};
i = j = k = 99;
for (i=0; i<rows; i++)
for (j = 0; j<columns; j++)
if (a[i] [j] < k) k=a [i] [j];
printf ("%d\n", k);}
```

(a) syntax error (b) routine error

(c) 1 (d) none of the above

42. What is the value of i in the following code?

```
main( )
{
int i=strlen ("BLUE") + strlen ("purple") /strlen
("red") - strlen ("green");
printf ("&d", i);
}
```

(a) –2 (b) 1

(c) –1.666667 (d) –1

43. What is the output of the following code?

```
int cap (int);
main( )
{
int n; n=cap (6);
printf ("%d", n);
}
int cap (int n)
{
if (n<=1) return 1;
else return (cap (n-3) + cap (n-1));
}
```

(a) 7 (b) 8

(c) 9 (d) 10

44. The elements of the following array x are

```
float x[5];
```

(a) x[0], x[1], x[3], x[4] (b) x[1], x[2], x[3], x[4], x[5]

(c) x(0), x(1), x(2), (3), x(4) (d) x(1), x(2), x(3), x(4), x(5)

45. Maximum number of elements in the declaration int y[5][8]; is

(a) 28 (b) 32

(c) 35 (d) 40

46. Two-dimensional array element are stored in

(a) column major order (b) row major order

(c) both options a and b (d) random order

47. Two-dimensional array elements are stored

(a) row by row in the subsequent memory locations

(b) column by column in the subsequent memory locations

(c) row by row in scattered memory locations

(d) column by column scattered memory locations

48. Arrays that do not have their dimension explicitly specified called
    (a) unsized array (b) one-dimensional arrays
    (c) initialized array (d) no size array
49. In C any arithmetic expression is equivalent to:
    (a) l-value (b) r-value
    (c) integer value (d) constant
50. Which conversion character display the address of variable:
    (a) u (b) d
    (c) x (d) i
51. The declarations float f[] [3] = {{1.0}, {2.0}, {3.0}}; represents
    (a) a one-by-three array (b) a three-by-one array
    (c) a three-by-three array (d) a one-by-one-array
52. A char array with the string value "aeiou" can be initialized as
    (a) char s[ ] = {'a, 'e', 'i', 'o', 'u'};
    (b) char s[ ] = "aeiou";
    (c) char s[ ] {'a, 'e', 'i', 'o', 'u' '\0'};
    (d) options b and c
53. If the size of an array is less than the number of initializers.
    (a) the extra values are neglected
    (b) it is an error
    (c) the size is automatically increased
    (d) the size is neglected
54. Identify the correct statement.
    (a) Float array can be read as a whole
    (b) Integer array can be read as a whole
    (c) Char array can be read as a whole
    (d) Double array can be read as a whole
55. Identify the correct statement
    (a) Float array can be displayed by using single printf( ) without using a loop

(b) Integer array can be displayed by using single printf( ) without using a loop

(c) Char array can be displayed by using single printf( ) without using a loop

(d) Double array can be displayed by using single printf( ) without using a loop

56. Missing elements of partly initialized arrays, are

(a) set to zero (b) set to one

(c) not defined (d) invalid

57. The declaration of array main( ) {int a[10]; —}

(a) reserves the space required for 11 elements

(b) reserves space for 9 elements

(c) does not initialize any element

(d) initializes the values of all elements to 0

58. The value within the [ ] in an array declaration specifies

(a) subscript value (b) index value

(c) size of an array (d) value of the array element

59. The value within the [ ] in an array variable specifies

(a) subscript value (b) size of the array

(c) value of the array element (d) array bound

60. In a multi-dimensional array with initialization

(a) The rightmost dimension may be omitted

(b) The leftmost dimension may be omitted

(c) Nothing must be omitted

(d) All may be omitted

61. When should an array be used?

(a) When we need to hold variable constants

(b) When we need to hold data of the same type

(c) When we need to obtain automatic memory cleanup functionality

(d) When we need to hold data of different types

62. x [2] = 5;

    2 [x] = 5;

    Are x[2] and 2[x] identical in the sample code above? Why or why not?

    (a) Not. Both variable assignments have invalid syntax
    (b) No. x[2] is correct, but 2[x] is correct, but 2[x] is invalid syntax
    (c) Yes. Both are identical because they are resolved to pointer references
    (d) No. 2[x] is correct, but x[2] is invalid syntax

63. main ( )

```
{
int a[100], i;
for (i = 1; i <= 100; ++i){… ;}
}
```

    (a) The above loop statement is incorrect since the last valid subscript of a is 99
    (b) The above loop statement is incorrect since i is not initialized to 0
    (c) The above loop statement is correct
    (d) The above loop statement is incorrect since i is pre-incremented

64. char sub [10] = ????;

    Which of the following statements cannot be used to replace the ???? in the above syntax to initialize sub with the string "Maths"?

    (a) }"Maths"}
    (b) {'M, 'a', 't', 'h', 's', '\0'}
    (c) {'M' "aths"}
    (d) {"Mat" "hs"}

65. main( )

```
{
const int size = 5;
int i, n, line [size];
for (i = 0; i< n; i++)
```

```
{
line [i]= i;
}
}
```

What will happen when the sample code fragment above is executed?

(a) The array will be initialized with the numbers 0 through 39

(b) The code will not compile

(c) The code will compile with warnings

(d) The code will compile, but not link.

66. Which of the following macros would properly return the number of elements in an array (not a pointer, an actual array)?

(a) #define NUM_ELEM(x) (sizeof(x)/sizeof(x[0]))

(b) #define NUM ELEM(x) (sizeof(x))

(c) #define NUM ELEM(x) (sizeof(x[0])/sizeof(x))

(d) #define NUM ELEM(x) (sizeof(x)/sizeof(x[O])) (e) #include <stdio.h>

67. main ( )

```
{
char s1[100]; char s2[100];
gets (s1);
fgets (s2, sizeof (s2), stdin);
printf ("%d\n", strlen (s1) - strlen (s2));
}
```

What will be printed when the above code is executed and the string "abcd" is entered twice on stdin?

(a) –1 (b) 0

(c) 1 (d) 4

68. int booklet [3] [2] [2] = {1, 2, 3, 4, 5, 6, 7, 8, 9, 10, 11, 12};

What value does booklet[2] [1] [0] in the sample code above contain?

(a) 5 (b) 7
(c) 9 (d) 11

69. int matrix [10] [4];
 (a) memset (matrix, –1, sizeof (matrix));
 (b) memset (matrix, 0, sizeof (matrix));
 (c) memset (matrix, 1, sizeof (matrix));
 Given the above choices, which one will fill the matrix with an integer value?
 (a) only A (b) only B
 (c) A and B (d) A, B and C
70. ANSI C recommends a compiler to support at least .... dimensions of an array.
 (a) 4 (b) 5
 (c) 6 (d) 7
71. Array declaration
 (a) requires the number of elements to be specified
 (b) does not require the number of elements to be specified
 (c) assumes default size as 0
 (d) is not necessary
72. Identify the wrong expression given int a[5];
 (a) a[–1] (b) a[10]
 (c) a[0] (d) ++a
73. What is the value of a[0][2] in int a[3][4] = {{1, 2}, {4, 8, 15}}?
 (a) 4 (b) 2
 (c) 0 (d) not defined
74. To initialize a 5 element array all having value 0 is given by
 (a) int num[5] = {0}; (b) int num[5] = {1, 1, 1, 1, 1};
 (c) int num [5] = {1, 1, 1, 1, 1};(d) int num [ ] = {1};
75. To initialize a 5 element array all having value 0 is given by
 (a) int num [5] = {0}; (b) int num[5] = {0, 0, 0, 0, 0};
 (c) options a and b (d) int num[5] = (1);

76. Which array has the high speed of execution?
    (a) Single dimensional
    (b) Double Dimensional
    (c) All
    (d) None of the above
77. Which array has the reliability and efficiency in working?
    (a) Single dimensional
    (b) Double Dimensional
    (c) All
    (d) None of the above
78. An array is a collection of
    (a) different data types scattered throughout memory
    (b) the same data type scattered throughout memory
    (c) the same data type placed next to each other in memory
    (d) different data types placed next to each other in memory
79. What is the difference between the 5's in these two expressions? (Select the correct answer)

```
int num[5];
num[5] = 11;
```

    (a) first is particular element, second is type
    (b) first is array size, second is particular element
    (c) first is particular element, second is array size
    (d) both specify array size

Answers

1. (a)	2. (b)	3. (c)	4. (b)	5. (a)
6. (b)	7. (a)	8. (c)	9. (b)	10. (c)
11. (d)	12. (a)	13. (d)	14. (d)	15. (c)
16. (a)	17. (b)	18. (a)	19. (c)	20. (d)
21. (b)	22. (a)	23. (b)	24. (a)	25. (b)
26. (d)	27. (b)	28. (a)	29. (c)	30. (a)
31. (d)	32. (c)	33. (c)	34. (c)	35. (a)
36. (a)	37. (c)	38. (c)	39. (d)	40. (b)
41. (a)	42. (b)	43. (c)	44. (d)	45. (d)

46. (b)	47. (a)	48. (d)	49. (b)	50. (a)
51. (c)	52. (d)	53. (b)	54. (c)	55. (c)
56. (a)	57. (c)	58. (c)	59. (a)	60. (b)
61. (b)	62. (c)	63. (c)	64. (c)	65. (b)
66. (d)	67. (a)	68. (d)	69. (c)	70. (c)
71. (a)	72. (d)	73. (c)	74. (c)	75. (c)
76. (a)	77. (c)	78. (c)	79. (b)	

CHAPTER

6

Strings

A. CODE SNIPPETS

Problem 1

Find the output of the following program?

```
#include<stdio.h>
#include<conio.h>
void main( )
{
printf("%d %d" sizeof('I'), sizeof("I"));
getch();
}
```

Output:

```
1 2
```

Problem 2

Find the output of the following program?

```
#include<stdio.h>
#include<conio.h>
void main( )
{
```

```
char str[]= "Welcome";
printf("%d %d", strlen(str), sizeof(str));
getch();
}
```

Output:

```
7 8
```

Problem 3

Find the output of the following program?

```
#include<stdio.h>
#include<conio.h>
void main( )
{
char str1[]= "Khalsa";
char  str2[]= "College";
printf("Khalsa" "College""\n");
puts("Khalsa" "College");
printf("%s %s", str1, str2);
getch();
}
```

Output:

```
Khalsa College
Khalsa College
Khalsa College
Khalsa College
```

Problem 4

Check the errors from the following program?

```
#include<stdio.h>
#include<conio.h>
```

```
void main( )
{
char str1[]= "Khalsa";
char str2[]= "College";
puts(str1, str2);
getch();
}
```

Output:

```
Error
```

NOTE: Extra parameter in call to puts

Problem 5

Find the output of the following program?

```
#include<stdio.h>
#include<conio.h>
void main( )
{
char str1[]= "Khalsa";
char str2[]= "College";
puts(str1, str2));
getch();
}
```

Output:

```
College
```

Problem 6

Find the output of the following program?

```
#include<stdio.h>
#include<conio.h>
```

```
void main( )
{
char str1[]= "Amritsar";
char str2[]= "Delhi"
printf(str1, str2);
getch();
}
```

Output:

```
Amritsar
```

Problem 7

Find the output of the following program?

```
#include<stdio.h>
#include<conio.h>
void main( )
{
printf("Hello Dear"+6);
getch();
}
```

Output:

```
Dear
```

Problem 8

Find the output of the following program?

```
#include<stdio.h>
#include<conio.h>
void main( )
{
putchar ("Hello Dear"[6]);
putchar(6["Hello Dear"]);
```

```
getch();
}
```

Output:

```
DD
```

Problem 9

Find the output of the following program?

```
#include<stdio.h>
#include<conio.h>
void main( )
{
char str1[] = “Strings!”;
char str2[]= “Strings!”;
if(str1= = str2)
printf(“Strings are same”);
else
printf(“Strings are different”);
getch();
}
```

Output:

```
Strings are different
```

Problem 10

Find the output of the following program?

```
#include<stdio.h>
#include<conio.h>
void main( )
{
printf ( “\n%d%d”, sizeof ( ‘4’ ), sizeof ( “5” ),
   sizeof ( 6 ) );
```

```
getch();
}
```

Output:

```
2 2 2
```

Problem 11

Find the output of the following program?

```
#include<stdio.h>
#include<conio.h>
void main( )
{
int a[ ] = { 'M', 'N', 'O', 'P' };
int i;
for ( i = 0 ; i <= 3 ; i++ )
printf ("\n%d", a[i]);
getch();
}
```

Output:

```
No error.
```

Problem 12

Find the output of the following program?

```
#include<stdio.h>
#include <conio.h>
void main( )
{
int i;
char a[] = "\0";
if(printf ("%s", a))
printf("String is not empty");
```

```
else
printf("String is empty");
getch();
}
```

Output:

```
String is not empty.
```

Problem 13

Find the output of the following program?

```
#include<stdio.h>
#include <conio.h>
void main( )
{
int i;
char str[]= "\0";
if printf("%s\n", str))
printf("String is empty");
else
printf("String is not empty");
getch();
}
```

Output:

```
String is empty.
```

Problem 14

Find the output of the following program?

```
#include<stdio.h>
#include <conio.h>
void main( )
{
```

```
char ptr[]= "%d\n";
ptr[1] = 'c';
printf(ptr, 67);
getch();
}
```

Output:

C

Problem 15

Find the output of the following program?

```
#include<stdio.h>
#include <conio.h>
void main( )
{
printf(4 + "Lovedeep");
getch();
}
```

Output:

deep

Problem 16

Find the output of the following program?

```
#include<stdio.h>
#include <conio.h>
#include<string.h>
void main( )
{
char ch1[5], ch2[5];
int i;
gets (ch1);
```

```
gets (ch2);
i = strcmp(ch1, ch2);
printf("%d", i);
getch();
}
```

Output:

```
Gives any integer value
```

Problem 17

Find the output of the following program?

```
#include<stdio.h>
#include <conio.h>
void main( )
{
char ch1[] = "Ikvinder";
char ch2[] = "Ikvinder";
if (ch1 = = ch2)
printf("\nEqual");
else
printf("\nNot Equal");
getch();
}
```

Output:

```
Not Equal
```

Problem 18

Find the output of the following program?

```
#include<stdio.h>
#include <conio.h>
void main( )
```

```
{
char str[7] = "Welcome";
printf("%s", str);
getch();
}
```

Output:

```
Unknown result
```

Problem 19

Write statement to print output \n on the screen?

Output:

```
printf ("\\n");
```

Problem 20

Find the output of the following program?

```
#include<stdio.h>
#include <conio.h
void main( )
{
char ch = 'S';
printf("%d %d", sizeof (ch), sizeof (sizeof ('S'))
   sizeof(3.14));
getch();
}
```

Output:

```
1 4 8
```

NOTE: Sizes of a char = 1 bytes, an int=4 bytes and a float = 4 bytes.

Problem 21

Find the output of the following program?

```
#include<stdio.h>
#include <conio.h>
void main( )
{
printf("\n%d %d %d", sizeof(6.0f), sizeof ("6"),
   sizeof(6.0));
getch();
}
```

Output:

```
4 2 8
```

Problem 22

Find the output of the following program?

```
#include<stdio.h>
#include<conio.h>
void main( )
{
char a[2] = "A";
printf ( "\n%c", a[0] );
printf ( "\n%s",a);
getch();
}
```

Output:

```
A
A
```

Problem 23

Find the output of the following program?

```
#include<stdio.h>
#include<conio.h>
```

```
void main( )
{
char str[ ] = "All is Well!!" ;
printf ( "\n%s", &str[2] ) ;
printf ( "\n%s", str ) ;
printf ( "\n%s", &str ) ;
printf ( "\n%c", str[2] ) ;
getch();
}
```

Output:

```
l is Well
All is Well
All is Well
l
```

Problem 24

Find the output of the following program?

```
#include<stdio.h>
#include<conio.h>
void main( )
{
char str1[ ] = {'H', 'e', 'l', 'l', 'o'};
char str2[ ] = "Hello";
printf ("\n%s", str1);
printf ("\n%s", str2);
getch();
}
```

Output:

```
Hello
Hello
```

Problem 25

Find the output of the following program?

```
#include<stdio.h>
#include<conio.h>
void main( )
{
printf (5 + “Good Morning”);
getch();
}
```

Output:

```
Morning
```

Problem 26

Find the output of the following program?

```
#include<stdio.h>
#include<conio.h>
void main( )
{
printf ( “%c”, “abcdefgh”[6] ) ;
getch();
}
```

Output:

```
g
```

Problem 27

Tell the function used to find the first occurrence of a given string in another string?

Output:

```
strstr( )
```

Problem 28

Tell the function used to concatenate strings?

Output:

```
strcat( )
```

Problem 29

Find the output of the following program?

```
#include<stdio.h>
#include<conio.h>
void main( )
{
char city[][20]={"Amritsar", "Jalandhar",
   "Rajpura","Chandigarh"};
int i;
for (i=0;i<3;i++)
puts (city[i]);
getch();
}
```

Output:

```
Amritsar
Jalandhar
Rajpura
Chandigarh
```

Problem 30

Check the errors from the following program?

```
#include<stdio.h>
#include<conio.h>
str(char[][]);
void main( )
```

```
{
char a[][10]={"Khalsa", "College");
str(a);
printf("%s %s", a[0], a[1]);
getch();
}
str(char a[][])
{
strcpy(a[1], "Amritsar");
}
```

Output:

Error

Problem 31

Find the output of the following program?

```
#include<stdio.h>
#include<conio.h>
str(char[][10]);
void main( )
{
char a[][10]={"Khalsa", "College");
str(a);
printf("%s %s", a[0], a[1]);
getch();
}
str(char a[][10])
{
strcpy(a[1], "Amritsar");
}
```

Output:

Khalsa Amritsar

Problem 32

Check the errors from the following program?

```
#include<stdio.h>
#include<conio.h>
char[20] display()
{
char str[20]= "Strings";
return str;
}
   void main( )
{
puts(display());
getch();
}
```

Output:

Error

Problem 33

Find the output of the following program?

```
#include<stdio.h>
#include<conio.h>
void main( )
{
char str1[]="Strings";
char str2[]={'S', 't', 'r', 'i', 'n', 'g', 's');
puts (str1);
puts (str2);
getch();
}
```

Output:

```
Strings
Strings! Some special characters
```

Problem 34

Find the output of the following program?

```
#include<stdio.h>
#include<conio.h>
void main( )
{
char str[]="Strings";
int i;
for (i=0;str[i];i++)
printf("%c",str[i]);
getch();
}
```

Output:

```
Strings
```

Problem 35

Find the output of the following program?

```
#include<stdio.h>
#include <conio.h>
void main( )
{
char a[20] = "Welcome";
a[8] = 'F';
printf("%s", a);
```

```
getch();
}
```

Output:

```
Welcome
```

Problem 36

Check the errors from the following program?

```
#include<stdio.h>
#include <conio.h>
#define ch ch[]
void main( )
{
char ch = "Khalsa college";
printf("%s", ch);
getch();
}
```

Output:

```
Error
```

Problem 37

Find the output of the following program?

```
#include<stdio.h>
#include <conio.h>
void main( )
{
printf("Khalsa College" "Amritsar");
getch();
}
```

Output:

```
Khalsa College Amritsar
```

Problem 38

Find the output of the following program?

```
#include<stdio.h>
#include <conio.h>
void main( )
{
char ch[50] = "Welcome to Khalsa College, Amritsar!";
printf("%s", &ch + 2);
getch();
}
```

Output:

Garbage value

Problem 39

Find the output of the following program?

```
#include<stdio.h>
#include <conio.h>
void main( )
{
void f();
f();
getch();
}
void f()
{
char ch;
if ((ch = getchar() ) != "\n')
f();
printf("%c", ch);
```

```
}
Input:
xyz
```

Output:

```
zyx
```

Problem 40

Find the output of the following program?

```
#include<stdio.h>
#include <conio.h>
#include<string.h>
void main( )
{
char str1[20] = "Khalsa", str2[20] = "College";
printf("%s", strcpy(str2, strcat (str1, str2)));
getch();
}
```

Output:

```
Khalsa College
```

Problem 41

Find the output of the following program?

```
#include<stdio.h>
#include <conio.h>
#include<string.h>
void main( )
{
char str[] = "Khalsa\0\College\0";
printf("%s", str);
```

```
getch();
}
```

Output:

```
Khalsa
```

Problem 42

Find the output of the following program?

```
#include<stdio.h>
#include <conio.h>
void main( )
{
char str[]= "Khalsa\0College\0";
printf("%d", sizeof (str));
getch();
}
```

Output:

```
16
```

Problem 43

Find the output of the following program?

```
#include<stdio.h>
#include <conio.h>
#include<string.h>
void main( )
{
char str[] = "Khalsa\0\College\0";
printf("%d", strlen(str));
getch();
}
```

Output:

```
6
```

Problem 44

Find the output of the following program?

```
#include<stdio.h>
#include <conio.h>
void main( )
{
printf("%d", strlen ("12345"));
getch();
}
```

Output:

5

NOTE: Size of an integer is 4 bytes.

Problem 45

Find the output of the following program?

```
#include<stdio.h>
#include <conio.h>
void main( )
{
printf("%c", "abcde"[2]);
getch();
}
```

Output:

c

Problem 46

Find the output of the following program?

```
#include<stdio.h>
#include<conio.h>
```

```
void main( )
{
char str1[] = “Strings!”;
char str2[]= “Strings!”;
if(strcmp(str1,str2)= =0)
printf(“Strings are same”);
else
printf(“Strings are different”);
getch();
}
```

Output:

```
Strings are same
```

Problem 47

Find the output of the following program?

```
#include<stdio.h>
#include<conio.h>
void main( )
{
char str1[] = “strings!”;
char str2[]= “STRINGS!”;
if(strcmp(str1,str2)= =0)
printf(“Strings are same”);
else
printf(“Strings are different”);
getch();
}
```

Output:

```
Strings are different
```

Problem 48

Find the output of the following program?

```
#include<stdio.h>
#include<conio.h>
void main( )
{
char str1[] = "strings!";
char str2[]= "STRINGS!";
if(strcmp(str1,str2)= =0)
printf("Strings are same");
else
printf("Strings are different");
getch();
}
```

Output:

```
Strings are same
```

Problem 49

Find the output of the following program?

```
#include<stdio.h>
#include<conio.h>
void main( )
{
if(strcmp("Strings", "Strings\0"))
printf("Strings are different");
else
printf("Strings are same");
getch();
}
```

Output:

```
Strings are same
```

Problem 50

Find the output of the following program?

```
#include<stdio.h>
#include<conio.h>
void main( )
{
char str1[]=[]={'S', 't', 'r', 'i', 'n', 'g', 's');
char str2[] = "Strings";
if(strcmp(str1, str2))
printf("Strings are different");
else
printf("Strings are same");
getch();
}
```

Output:

```
Strings are different
```

Problem 51

Find the output of the following program?

```
#include<stdio.h>
#include<conio.h>
void main( )
{
char str[]= "%d\n";
str[1]= 'd';
printf(str 67);
getch();
}
```

Output:

```
C
```

Problem 52

Check the errors from the following program?

```
#include<stdio.h>
#include<conio.h>
void main( )
{
char str1[]= "Strings";
char str2[10];
str2 = str1;
puts (str1);
puts (str2);
getch();
}
```

Output:

Error

NOTE: L-value requ ed

Problem 53

Find the output of the following program?

```
#include<stdio.h>
#include<conio.h>
void main( )
{
char str[]= "Strings";
char str1[10];
strcpy(str1, str);
puts(str);
puts(str1);
getch();
}
```

Output:

```
Strings
Strings
```

Problem 54

Find the output of the following program?

```
#include<stdio.h>
#include<conio.h>
void main( )
{
char dest[]="Visual Basic";
char src[]= "C++";
puts(strcpy(&dest[7], src));
getch();
}
```

Output:

```
C++
```

Problem 55

Find the output of the following program?

```
#include<stdio.h>
#include<conio.h>
void main( )
{
char str[]="Visual Basic";
char str1[]= "C++";
strcpy(&str[7], str1);
puts (str);
getch();
}
```

Output:

```
Visual C++
```

Problem 56

Find the output of the following program?

```
#include<stdio.h>
#include<conio.h>
void main( )
{
char str[]="Visual Basic";
char str1[]= "Visual C++";
strcpy(&str[7], &str1[7]);
puts (str);
getch();
}
```

Output:

```
Visual C++
```

Problem 57

Find the output of the following program?

```
#include<stdio.h>
#include<conio.h>
void main( )
{
if (printf("\0"))
printf("group of characters");
else
printf("Strings");
getch();
}
```

Output:

```
Strings
```

Problem 58

Find the output of the following program?

```
#include<stdio.h>
#include <conio.h>
#include<string.h>
void main( )
{
char str[100];
int i;
printf("Enter a String:");
gets (str);
for (i=strlen (str) -1; i>=0; i–)
putchar (str[i]);
getch();
}
```

Input:

Enter a String: come

Output:

eomc

Problem 59

The library function used to reverse a string is

1. strstr( )
2. strrev( )
3. revstr( )
4. None of the above

Output:

2

Problem 60

Find the output of the following program?

```
#include<stdio.h>
#include <conio.h>
#include<string.h>
void main( )
{
static char str1[] = "come";
static char str2[20];
static char str3[20]= "Wel";
int i;
i = strcmp (strcat(str3, strcpy (str3, str1)),
   "Welcome");
printf("%d", i);
getch();
}
```

Output:

0

Problem 61

Tell the function which is more appropriate for reading in a multi-word string?

Output:

gets( )

Problem 62

Find the output of the following program?

```
#include<stdio.h>
#include <conio.h>
void main( )
{
```

```
char str[]= "Khalsa";
str[0]= 'K''
printf("%s", str);
str= "College";
printf("%s", str + 1);
getch();
}
```

Output:

```
Error
```

Problem 63

The library function used to find the last occurrence of a character in a string is:

Output:

```
strchr( )
```

Problem 64

Find the output of the following program?

```
#include<stdio.h>
#include <conio.h>
void main( )
{
printf (5+ "Good Morning");
}
```

Output:

```
Morning
```

Problem 65

Given two strings are identical, then strcmp( ) function returns:

Output:

```
0
```

Problem 66

Which one is correct for string comparison?

1. `strcmp (str1, str2) returns a number less then 0 if str1>str2`
2. `strcmp (str1, str2) returns a number greater then 0 if str1 < str2`
3. `strcmp (str1, str2) returns 0 if str1 = = str2`

Output:

```
3
```

B. FILL IN THE BLANKS

1. Combination of characters (group of character) is called ....
2. String is terminated by a special character which is called as .... terminator
3. A string literal constant of zero length is called ....
4. Every string literal in C is terminated by ....
5. The amount of memory taken by an empty string literal is ....
6. Group of characters is called ....
7. A string literal constant is always enclosed within ....
8. .... string library function is used to concatenate two strings.
9. A string is an array of ....
10. The number of locations needed to store a string is .... more than the string's length.
11. A pair of double quotes with nothing between them is called ....
12. A string literal is enclosed within ....
13. The length of a null string is ....
14. The scanf function uses .... format specification to read to string from the user.

15. .... string library function is used to compare two strings.
16. .... string library function is used to find the length of the string.
17. .... function is used to read a character from the keyboard.
18. We can read the string by using the .... function.
19. String handling function strcat ( ) is to .... two different strings together.
20. Inputs to function main are given by making use of special arguments known as ....
21. The delimiter in a C string is ....
22. The .... string manipulation function returns the number of characters in the string excluding the null character.

Answers

1. string	2. null
3. empty string	4. a null character
5. 1 byte	6. string
7. double quotes	8. strcat()
9. characters	10. one
11. null string	12. double quotes
13. zero	14. %s
15. strcmp();	16. strlen()
17. getch	18. command line arguments
19. scanf	20. combine
21. null character	22. strlen()

C. TRUE OR FALSE

State whether each of the following is true or false

1. The length of a string literal constant is equal to the number of characters present in it.
2. The length of an empty string literal constant is one.

3. The amount of the memory space required for storing a string literal constant is not fixed and depends upon the number of characters present in the string literal.
4. There is no string data type in C.
5. The number of locations needed to store a string is the length of the string.
6. The length of a string can be obtained using strlen().
7. The strcat() function is used to compare strings.
8. The strcpy() function is used to copy string.
9. The number of bytes required to store a string literal is equal to the number of characters present in it.
10. The pointers CANNOT work on string.
11. Null string points to same byte filled with 0 bits.
12. The functions gets( ), puts( ) are string functions to read and write.
13. String parsing is an application of string.
14. The quotes are part of the literals in case of string constants.
15. A double quote included in the string literal as \" is recognized as part of the literal.
16. The length of null string is one.
17. It is not mandatory to use ampersand (i.e., address-of operator) with string variable names while reading string using the scanf function.
18. If the character array to be printed does not have a terminating null character, the output would be the content of the character array followed by some garbage character.
19. It is not mandatory to have the first argument of the printf function to be const char* type.
20. A string is a collection of characters terminated by '\0'.
21. The format specifier %s is used to print a string.
22. Pointer to char and character array are one and the same as far as memory allocation is concerned.

23. The string library function strrev() reverses all the characters of a string including the null character.
24. It is not possible to initialize a character array with string literal constant.
25. A list of strings can be stored by using a two-dimensional character array.

Answers

1. True	2. False	3. True	4. True
5. False	6. True	7. False	8. True
9. False	10. False	11. True	12. True
13. True	14. False	15. True	16. False
17. True	18. True	19. False	20. True
21. True	22. False	23. False	24. False
25. True			

D. OBJECTIVE TYPE QUESTIONS

1. Which of the following is the correct output for the program given?

```
char str[7] = "strings"; printf("%s", str);
```

(a) error (b) strings
(c) cannot predict (d) none of the above

2. If sizes of a char, an int, a float and a double are 1,4, 4 and 8 bytes respectively, which of the following is the correct output for the program given below?

```
{
char ch = 'A';
printf ("%d %d %d", sizeof (ch), sizeof
(sizeof('A')), sizeof (3.14));
}
```

(a) 1 4 2 (b) 1 4 8
(c) 2 2 4 (d) 2 4 8

3. What is the value of str3 and str1?

```
void main( )
{
char str1 [100] = "Khalsa";
char *str2= "College";
char *str3;
str3=strcat (str1, str2)
printf ("\n%s", str3);
}
```

(a) compilation error because strcat does not return a value

(b) Khalsa College

(c) segmentation fault because str3 might be pointing to a garbage value

(d) united

4. Which one is the string handling function

(a) strcat() (b) strupr()

(c) strlen() (d) all of these

5. Find the output for the program given?

```
main( )
{
char str[ ] = "Sales\0man\0";
printf ("%d %s %d \n", sizeof (str), strlen (str));
}
```

(a) 5 Sales 5 (b) 11 Sales 9

(c) 11 Sales man 9 (d) 11 Sales 5

6. The function strcpy(s1, s2) in string.h

(a) copies s1 to s2 (b) copies s2 to s1

(c) appends s1 to end of s2 (d) appends s2 to end of s1

7. The function strcat(s1, s2) returns zero

(a) copies s1 to s2 (b) copies s2 to s1

(c) appends s1 to end of s2 (d) appends s2 to end of s1

8. The function strcmp (s1, s2) returns zero
   (a) if s1 is lexicographically less than s2
   (b) if s1 is lexicographically greater than s2
   (c) if both s1 and s2 are equal
   (d) if s1 is empty string
9. The function toupper(ch) in ctype.h
   (a) returns the upper case alphabed of ch
   (b) returns the lowercase alphabet of ch
   (c) returns upper case if ch is lower case, and lower case if ch is upper case
   (d) is a user-defined function
10. The function tolower(ch) in ctype.h
   (a) returns the upper case alphabed of ch
   (b) returns the lowercase alphabet of ch
   (c) returns uppercase if ch is lowercase, and lower case if ch is upper case
   (d) is a user-defined function
11. Consider the following declarations:
```
char *a;
char a[5];
```
   Which of the following statements is/are true?
   1. both are of pointer type.
   2. memory allocation is different in both the cases
   3. the value of a in declaration char a[5] can be changed later.

   (a) 2 only (b) 1 only
   (c) 1 and 2 (d) 2 and 3
12. What will be the output?
```
char str[ ] = "India";
cahr *p;
```

```
strcpy (p, st);
printf ("%s and %s are same", st, p);
```

(a) India and India are same
(b) India and <some Garbage value> are same
(c) compilation error
(d) runtime segmentation fault

13. The function used to combine strings
(a) strcat() (b) strcpy()
(c) strlen() (d) strrev()

14. What will strcmp return, if both the strings are equal?
(a) Boolean TRUE (b) 0
(c) 2 (d) 1

15. Which of the following function is used to check the presence of a substring?
(a) strstr() (b) substr( )
(c) check strint( ) (d) none of the above

16. Given a declaration and initialization statement as shown below,

```
char a a[200] = {'0'};
```

What is the output of the following printf statement?

```
printf ("%d %c %c %d", a[0], a[0], a[3], a[3]);
```

(a) 48 0 0 (b) 44 0 0
(c) 46 0 (d) 49 0 49 0

17. Given a declaration and initialization as shown below,

```
char a[6] = {'1', '2', '3'};
```

What is the output of the following printf statement?

```
printf ("%c %c %c %c %c %c", a[0], a[3], a[4],
a[2], a[4], a[1]);
```

(a) 1 2 3 4 5 6 (b) 1 2 3 4 5
(c) 1 3 2 (d) 1 2 3 0 0 0

18. The function used to reverse a string
    (a) strcat() (b) strcpy()
    (c) strlen() (d) strrev()
19. Given an integer 'a' and a float 'b', write a statement that copies the integer and float data into a character array?
    (a) strcat (str, a); strcat (str, b); (b) sprintf(str, "%d %f', a, b);
    (c) sscanf(str, "&d &f', a, b); (d) none of the above
20. What does strlen( ) return for the following character array?
    (a) 5 (b) 6
    (c) 3 (d) 7
21. char *a= "23422";

```
printf ("%d%d", sizeof(a), strlen(a));
```

    From the above, what is the output of the printf function?
    (a) 4 4 (b) 5 5
    (c) 5 4 (d) 4 5
22. The function used to find length of a string
    (a) strcat() (b) strcpy()
    (c) strlen() (d) strrev()
23. char name[ ] = "BIT"

```
printf ("%s is department %s %d of %s/n", &name[1],
"no", ('A' 'a') /", name);
```

    From the above, what is the output of the printf statement?
    (a) IT is department no 1 of BIT
    (b) L value required RUNTIME ERROR
    (c) IT is department no -1 of BIT
    (d) compilation error
24. char *p;
    char name [25] = "MIT-IT";
    strcpy (p, name);
    printf ("%s", p);

What will be the output?

(a) segmentation fault because pointer p is only declared but no memory allocated

(b) compilation error

(c) MIT-IT

(d) none of the above

25. The function used to copy one string to another string

(a) strcat() (b) strcpy()

(c) strlen() (d) strrev()

26. char name [10];

```
scanf ("%s", name);
if (strcmp (name, "Chennai") = =0
{
char a[10] = "760008";
printf ("Danju has the pin code: %s\n", a);
}
```

What will be the amount of memory allocated in the following cases'?

case 1 input is not chennai,

case 2 input is chennai

(a) in both cases, the total amount of memory allocated will be the same

(b) the total amount of memory allocated differs based on the input

(c) based on the compiler options

(d) both a and c

27. The function used to result in uppercase string

(a) strcat() (b) strupr()

(c) strlen() (d) strrev()

28. char *name = ‘Delhi”;

```
printf (“%d %d”, sizeof (name), sizeof ((*name));
```

(a) 4 1 (b) 4 4

(c) 5 1 (d) 5 4

29. What does strcat append to the target string after the specified number of

Characters have been copied?

(a) nothing (b) null

(c) \0 (d) –0

30. What does atoi( ) function do?

(a) convert a string into an integer

(b) convert string into a float

(c) convert integer to string

(d) convert float to string

31. The number of bits used in extended ASCII is

(a) 7 (b) 8

(c) 16 (d) 32

Answers

1. (c)	2. (b)	3. (b)	4. (d)	5. (d)
6. (b)	7. (d)	8. (c)	9. (a)	10. (b)
11. (a)	12. (d)	13. (a)	14. (b)	15. (a)
16. (a)	17. (c)	18. (d)	19. (b)	20. (c)
21. (d)	22. (c)	23. (c)	24. (a)	25. (b)
26. (a)	27. (b)	28. (a)	29. (c)	30. (a)
31. (b)				

CHAPTER

7

Functions

A. CODE SNIPPETS

Problem 1

Find the output of the following program?

```
#include<stdio.h>
#include<conio.h>
int swap (int i, int j)
{
i^=j^=i^=j;
printf("Value of i and j in swap are %d %d\n", i, j);
}
void main( )
{
int i=10, j=20;
printf("Values of i and j before swap are %d %d\n", i,
j);
swap (i, j);
printf("Values of i and j after swap are %d %d\n", i,
j);
getch();
}
```

Output:

```
Values of i and j before swap are  10 20
Values of i and j in swap are 20 10
Values of i and j after swap are 10 20
```

Problem 2

Find the output of the following program?

```
#include<stdio.h>
#include<conio.h>
int swap (int i, int j)
{
*i^=*j^=*i^=*j;
printf("Values of i and j in swap are %d %d\n", *i,
*j);
}
void main( )
{
int i=10, j=20;
printf("Values of i and j before swap are %d %d\n", i,
j);
swap (&i, &j);
printf("The values of a and b after swap are %d %d\n",
i, j);
getch();
}
```

Output:

```
Values of i and j before swap are  10 20
Values of i and j in swap are 20 10
Values of i and j after swap are 20 10
```

Problem 3

Find the output of the following program?

```
#include<stdio.h>
#include<conio.h>
int add_sub(int i, int j)
{
int add=i+j;
int sub=i-j;
return add, sub;
}
void main()
{
int i=20, j=10;
printf("Addition is %d and Subtraction is %d\n",
   add_sub(i, j), add_sub(i, j));
getch();
}
```

Output:

```
Addition is 10 and Subtraction is 10
```

Problem 4

Check the errors from the following program?

```
#include<stdio.h>
#include<conio.h>
int add_sub(int i, int j)
{
int add=i+j;
int sub=i-j;
return add, return sub;
}
```

```
void main()
{
int i=20, j=10;
printf("Addition is %d and Subtraction is %d\n",
   add_sub(i, j), add_sub(i, j));
getch();
}
```

Output:

```
Error
```

NOTE: Expression syntax

Problem 5

Find the output of the following program?

```
#include<stdio.h>
#include<conio.h>
int add_sub(int i, int j)
{
int add=i+j;
int sub=i-j;
return add, return sub;
}
void main()
{
int i=20, j=10;
printf("Addition is %d and Subtraction is %d\n",
   add_sub(i, j), add_sub(i, j));
getch();
}
```

Output:

```
Addition is 30 and Subtraction is 30
```

Problem 6

Find the output of the following program?

```
#include<stdio.h>
#include<conio.h>
add_sub(int i, int j, int *add, int *sub)
{
*add=a+b;
*sub=a-b;
}
void main()
{
int i=20, j=10, add, sub;
add_sub(i, j, &add, &sub);
printf("Addition is %d and Subtraction is %d\n", add,
   sub);
getch();
}
```

Output:

```
Addition is 30 and Subtraction is 10
```

Problem 7

Find the output of the following program?

```
#include<stdio.h>
#include<conio.h>
fun1( )
{
return printf("Function1\n");
}
fun2( )
{
```

```
return printf("Function2\n");
}
void main( )
{
printf(%d %d", fun1( ), fun2( ));
getch();
}
```

Output:

```
Function2
Function1
10 10
```

Problem 8

Find the output of the following program?

```
#include<stdio.h>
#include<conio.h>
fun1( )
{
return printf("Function1\n");
}
fun2( )
{
return printf("Function2\n");
}
void main( )
{
printf("%d", fun1()+fun2());
getch();
}
```

Output:

```
Function1
Function2
20
```

Problem 9

Find the output of the following program?

```
#include<stdio.h>
#include<conio.h>
int fact(int num)
{
if(num = =1)
return 1;
else
return num *fact(num-1);
}
void main( )
{
int temp;
temp=fact(4);
printf("Value of factorial of 4 is %d", temp);
getch();
}
```

Output:

```
Value of factorial of 4 is 24
```

Problem 10

Find the output of the following program?

```
#include<stdio.h>
#include<conio.h>
```

```
void main( )
{
printf("Infinite recursion\n");
main( );
getch();
}
```

Output:

```
Infinite recursion (infinite loop)
```

Problem 11

Find the output of the following program?

```
#include<stdio.h>
#include<conio.h>
display (int[2][3]);
void main( )
{
int a[2][3]={1,2,3,4,5,6};
printf("Size of a in function main is %d", sizeof(a));
getch();
}
display(int a[2][3])
{
printf(" Size of a in function display is %d",
   sizeof(a));
}
```

Output:

```
Size of a in function main is 4
```

Problem 12

Find the output of the following program?

```
#include<stdio.h>
#include<conio.h>
```

```
int add(int i, int j)
{
return i+j;
}
void main( )
{
int (*ptr) (int, int);
ptr=add;
printf("Addition is %d\n", ptr(3, 3));
printf("Addition is %d", (*ptr)(3,3));
getch();
}
```

Output:

```
Addition is 9
Addition is 9
```

Problem 13

Check the errors from the following program?

```
#include<stdio.h>
#include<conio.h>
void main( )
{
int i = 5, j = 4, k, p;
k = mul( i, j );
p = mul( i, j );
printf ( "\n%d %d", k, p);
getch();
}
mul( int x, int y)
```

```
{
int z, w;
z = x + y;
w = x * y;
return ( z, w);
}
```

Output:

```
Error.
```

NOTE: A function cannot return two values at a time without the help of pointers.

Problem 14

Find the output of the following program?

```
#include<stdio.h>
#include<conio.h>
int message( );
void main( )
{
int i;
i = message( ) ;
getch();
}
int message( )
{
printf ( "\nC is a programming language");
return;
}
```

Output:

```
No error.
```

Problem 15

Check the errors from the following program?

```
#include<stdio.h>
#include<conio.h>
void print ( i, c )
void main( )
{
float i = 1.5;
char c = ‘C’ ;
print ( i, c ) ;
getch();
}
void print ( i, c )
{
printf ( “\n%f %c”, i, c);
}
```

Output:

```
Error.
```

NOTE: i and c should be declared as float and char respectively in the function print().

Problem 16

Find the output of the following program?

```
#include<stdio.h>
#include<conio.h>
void message( );
void main( )
{
message( );
```

```
message( );
getch();
}
void message( );
{
printf ( "\nExpert C Programming");
}
```

Output:

```
Error.
```

Note: Semicolon after message() in the function definition.

Problem 17

Check the errors from the following program?

```
#include<stdio.h>
#include<conio.h>
void display( );
void main( )
{
void display( )
{
printf ( "\nExpert C programming");
printf ( "\nSolved Programming in C");
}
getch();
}
```

Output:

```
Error.
```

NOTE: The display() function cannot be defined within another main() function.

Problem 18

Check the errors from the following program?

```
#include<stdio.h>
#include<conio.h>
void message( );
void main( )
{
message( message ( ));
getch();
}
void message( )
{
printf ("\nIs it possible");
}
```

Output:

Error.

NOTE: void cannot be passed as parameter.

Problem 19

Find the output of the following program?

```
#include<stdio.h>
#include<conio.h>
void circle(int);
void main( )
{
float area;
int rad = 2;
area = circle (rad);
printf ("\n%f", area);
```

```
getch();
}
void circle (int r)
{
float result;
a = 3.14 * r * r;
return(result);
}
```

Output:

```
12.56000
```

Problem 20

Check the errors from the following program?

```
#include<stdio.h>
#include<conio.h>
void display();
void main( )
{
void display( );
int i = 1;
i = display( );
printf ("\n%d", i);
getch();
}
void display( )
{
printf ("\nExpert C Programming");
}
```

Output:

```
Error message by compiler.
```

Problem 21

Find the output of the following program?

```
#include<stdio.h>
#include<conio.h>
void mul(int,int);
void main( )
{
int i = 2, j = 1;
mul( i, j );
printf ( "\n%d %d", i, j );
getch();
}
void mul( int i, int j )
{
i = i * i;
j = j * j;
}
```

Output:

```
2 1
```

Problem 22

Find the output of the following program?

```
#include<stdio.h>
#include<conio.h>
void mul(int*,int*);
void main( )
{
int i = 4, j = 3;
mul( &i, &j );
```

```
printf ( "\n%d %d", i, j );
getch();
}
void mul ( int *i, int *j )
{
*i = *i * *i;
*j = *j * *j;
}
```

Output:

```
16 9
```

Problem 23

Find the output of the following program?

```
#include<stdio.h>
#include<conio.h>
void mul(int*,int);
void main( )
{
int i = 4, j = 3;
mul( &i, j);
printf ( "\n%d %d", i, j);
getch();
}
void mul( int *i, int j )
{
*i = *i * *i;
j = j * j;
}
```

Output:

```
16 3
```

Problem 24

Find the output of the following program?

```
#include<stdio.h>
#include<conio.h>
void main( )
{
float i = 1.5;
float *j, *k;
j = &i;    /* suppose address of i is 1004 */
k = j;
printf ( "\n%u %u %u", &i, j, k);
printf ( "\n%f %f %f %f %f", i, *(&i), *&i, *j, *k);
getch();
}
```

Output:

```
1004 1004 1004
1.500000 1.500000 1.500000 1.500000 1.500000
```

NOTE: instead of 1004 you may get some other number

Problem 25

Check the errors from the following program?

```
#include<stdio.h>
#include<conio.h>
void pass ( int , int );
void main( )
{
int i = 5, j = 15, k ;
k = pass ( i, j ) ;
printf ( "\n%d", k ) ;
```

```
getch();
}
void pass ( int n, int j )
int m;
{
m = n + j;
return ( m ) ;
}
```

Output:

```
Error.
```

NOTE: int m can be declared inside the brace.

Problem 26

Check the errors from the following program?

```
#include<stdio.h>
#include<conio.h>
void display( int *, int *);
void main( )
{
int i = 2, j = 4;
display( &i, &j );
printf ( "\n%d %d", i, j );
getch();
}
void display( int m, int n )
{
m = m + m;
n = n + n;
}
```

Output:

```
Error.
```

NOTE: variables m and n should be declared as integer pointers.

Problem 27

Check the errors from the following program?

```
#include<stdio.h>
#include<conio.h>
int compare( int )
void main( )
{
int i = 5, k ;
k = compare ( i ) ;
printf ( "\n%d", k ) ;
getch();
}
int compare (m)
{
int m ;
if ( m > 40 )
return ( 1 ) ;
else
return ( 0 ) ;
}
```

Output:

```
Error.
```

NOTE: The declaration int m should be before opening brace.

Problem 28

Find the output of the following program?

```
#include<stdio.h>
#include<conio.h>
```

```
int * function (int*);
void main( )
{
int i = 3, *k;
k = function ( &i );
printf ( “\n%d”, k);
getch();
}
int *function ( int *m )
{
return ( m + 2 );
}
```

Output:

```
No error.
```

Problem 29

Find the output of the following program?

```
#include<stdio.h>
#include<conio.h>
void main( )
{
int i = 0;
i++;
if (i <= 2)
{
printf ( “\nExpert C Programming”);
exit( );
main( );
}
```

```
getch();
}
```

Output:

```
Expert C Programming
```

Problem 30

Find the output of the following program?

```
#include<stdio.h>
#include<conio.h>
void main( )
{
static int i = 0;
i++;
if (i <= 5)
{
printf ("\n%d", i);
main( );
}
else
exit( );
getch();
}
```

Output:

```
1
2
3
4
5
```

Problem 31

Find the output of the following program?

```
#include<stdio.h>
#include<conio.h>
void main( )
{
printf ( “\nExpert C Programming” );
display( );
getch();
}
display( )
{
printf ( “\nSolved Programming in C” );
main( );
}
```

Output:

Both the printf() messages will get printed indefinitely.

Problem 32

Find the output of the following program?

```
#include<stdio.h>
#include<conio.h>
void main( )
{
printf ( “\nElaborate C” );
main( );
getch();
}
```

Output:

The printf() message will get printed indefinitely.

Problem 33

Find the output of the following program?

```
#include<stdio.h>
#include<conio.h>
void compare(int);
void main( )
{
int i = 5, j;
j = compare(i);
printf ( "\n%d", j);
getch();
}
void compare(int k)
{
if ( k >= 5 )
return (10);
else
return (10 * 10);
}
```

Output:

100

Problem 34

Find the output of the following program?

```
#include<stdio.h>
#include<conio.h>
void compare(int);
void main( )
{
```

```
int i = 5, j;
j = mul( i * 1000);
printf ( "\n%d", j);
getch();
}
void compare(int k)
{
if (k >= 40000)
return (k/10);
else
return (10);
}
```

Output:

```
The function mul is not defined.
```

Problem 35

Find the output of the following program?

```
#include <stdio.h>
#include <conio.h>
int f();
int i;
void main ( )
{
while (i)
{
f( );
main( );
}
printf ("Welcome");
getch();
}
```

```
f( )
{
printf ("How are you");
}
```

Output:

```
Welcome
```

Problem 36

Find the output of the following program?

```
#include <stdio.h>
#include <conio.h>
void main ( )
{
int j = 0;
j++;
if (j <= 10)
{
printf ("Khalsa College Amritsar");
exit ( );
main ( );
}
getch();
}
```

Output:

```
main( ) cannot call itself.
```

Problem 37

Write a recursive procedure recursv() that prints numbers from 10 to 1.

Output:

```
num =10;
recursv (int num)
```

```
{
if (num <1)
{
return 0;
}
else
{
printf ("%d", num);
recursv(—num);
}
}
```

Problem 38

The keyword used to transfer control from a function back to the calling function is:

Output:

```
return
```

Problem 39

Find the output of the following program?

```
#include <stdio.h>
#include <conio.h>
void main ( )
{
int i = 2, j = 5, m, n;
m = addmul(i, j);
printf ("\n%d %d", m, n);
getch();
}
int addmul(int x, int y)
```

```
{
int p, q;
p = x + y;
q = x*y;
return (p, q);
}
```

Output:

10 10

Problem 40

Find the output of the following program?

```
#include <stdio.h>
#include <conio.h>
int check (int);
void main ( )
{
int i = 56, j;
j = check (i);
printf ("\n%d", j);
getch();
}
check (int k)
{
if (k >= 56)
return (100);
else
return (10);
}
```

Output:

100

Problem 41

Find the output of the following program?

```
#include <stdio.h>
#include <conio.h>
int reverse (int);
void main ( )
{
int num = 10;
reverse (num);
getch();
}
reverse (int num)
{
if (num = = 0)
return 0;
else
printf ("%d", num);
reverse (num–);
}
```

Output:

```
Program runs in an infinite loop.
```

Problem 42

Find the output of the following program?

```
long factorial (int num)
{
int i;
long fact = 1;
for (i = 1; <= num; i++)
fact = fact * i;
```

```
return (fact);
}
```

Output:

The procedure calculates the factorial value of an integer.

Problem 43

Check the errors from the following program?

```
#include<stdio.h>
#include<conio.h>
void f(int i)
{
printf("Value of i is %d\n", i);
}
void main()
{
int i=10, j;
j=f(i);
printf("Value of j is %d", j);
getch();
}
```

Output:

Error

Problem 44

Find the output of the following program?

```
#include<stdio.h>
#include<conio.h>
f(int i)
{
printf("Value of i is %d", i);
```

```
}
void main()
{
int i=10, j;
j=f(i);
printf("Value of j is %d", j);
getch();
}
```

Output:

```
Value of i is 10
Value of j is 50
```

NOTE: No data type is specified for function f(). So for j it prints last computed result.

Problem 45

Find the output of the following program?

```
#include<stdio.h>
#include<conio.h>
f(int i)
{
printf("Value of i is %d\n", i);
i+2;
}
void main()
{
int i=5, j;
j=f(i);
printf("Value of j is %d", j);
getch();
}
```

Output:

```
Value of i is 5
Value of j is 7
```

Problem 46

Find the output of the following program?

```
#include<stdio.h>
#include<conio.h>
int add(int, int);
void main()
{
int i=10, j=20, k;
k=add(i, j);
printf("Addition is %d", k)
getch();
}
int add(int i, int j)
{
i+j;
}
```

Output:

```
Addition is 30
```

Problem 47

Find the output of the following program?

```
#include<stdio.h>
#include<conio.h>
int add(int, int);
void main()
{
```

```
int i=10, j=20, k;
k=add(i, j);
printf("Addition is %d", k)
getch();
}
int add(int i, int j)
{
i+j;
return;
}
```

Output:

Error

Problem 48

Check the errors from the following program?

```
#include<stdio.h>
#include<conio.h>
int add(int i, int j)
{
return i+j;
}
void main()
{
int k;
k=add(10);
printf("Addition is %d", k)
getch();
}
```

Output:

Error

NOTE: Too few parameter in call to add(int, int)

Problem 49

Find the output of the following program?

```
#include<stdio.h>
#include<conio.h>
int add(int i, int j=5)
{
return i+j;
}
void main()
{
int k;
k=add(10);
printf("Addition is %d", k)
getch();
}
```

Output:

Addition is 15

Problem 50

Find the output of the following program?

```
#include<stdio.h>
#include<conio.h>
int add(int i, int j=12)
{
return i+j;
}
void main()
{
int k;
k=add(10,20);
```

```
printf("Addition is %d", k)
getch();
}
```

Output:

```
Addition is 30
```

Problem 51

Check the errors from the following program?

```
#include<stdio.h>
#include<conio.h>
int add(int i=5, int j)
{
return i+j;
}
void main()
{
int k;
k=add(10, 20);
printf("Addition is %d", k)
getch();
}
```

Output:

```
Error
```

NOTE: Default value missing following parameter a.

Problem 52

Find the output of the following program?

```
#include<stdio.h>
#include<conio.h>
int add(int i, int j)
```

```
{
return i+j;
}
int sub (int i, int j)
{
return i-j;
}
int mul (int i, int j)
{
return i*j;
}
int div(int i, int j)
{
return i/j;
}
void main( )
{
int (*ptr[4]) (int, int) = {add, sub, mul, div};
int i;
for (k=0;k<4;k++)
printf("Result of called function %d is %d\n", k+1,
   ptr[k](10,5));
getch();
}
```

Output:

```
Result of called function 1 is 15
Result of called function 2 is 5
Result of called function 3 is 50
Result of called function 4 is 2
```

Problem 53

Find the output of the following program?

```
#include<stdio.h>
#include<conio.h>
int add(int, int);
int sub(int, int);
fun(int (*) (int, int));
void main( )
{
printf("%d\n", fun(add));
printf("%d", fun(sub));
getch();
}
fun (int (*i)(int, int)
{
return i(2, 3);
}
int add(int i, int j)
{
return i+j;
}
int sub (int i, int j)
{
return i-j;
}
```

Output:

```
5
-1
```

Problem 54

Find the output of the following program?

```
#include <stdio.h>
#include <conio.h>
int add (int);
void main()
{
int i, j;
i = add (123);
j = add (123);
printf ("%d %d", i, j);
getch();
}
add (int k)
{
int p, q;
if (k != 0)
{
q = k % 10;
k = k / 10;
p = q + add (k);
}
else
return (0);
return (p);
}
```

Output:

```
6 6
```

Problem 55

What will be the output of the following function?

```
fun (int i, int j)
{
int i;
i = 120;
return i;
}
```

Output:

```
Error.
```

NOTE: Redeclaration of i

Problem 56

Find the output of the following program?

```
#include <stdio.h>
#include <conio.h>
void fun (int *, int *);
void main()
{
i = 5, j = 2;
fun (&i, &i);
printf ("%d %d", i,j);
getch();
}
void fun (int *i, int *j)
{
*i = *i **i;
*j = *j **j;
}
```

Output:

```
25 4
```

Problem 57

Is there any error in the following code? Which statement will require adding to remove error?

```
#include <stdio.h>
#include <conio.h>
void main()
{
int i;
i = fun (10, 3, 14);
printf ("%d", i);
}
float fun(int ii, float jj);
}
```

Output:

```
Add the following function prototype in main( ):
float fun(int, float);
```

Problem 58

Find the output of the following program?

```
#include <stdio.h>
#include <conio.h>
void main()
{
int i = 100;
void fun( );
i = fun( );
printf ("\n%d", i);
getch();
}
void fun()
```

```
{
printf ("\nAmritsar");
}
```

Output:

Do yourself

Problem 59

Find the output of the following program?

```
#include <stdio.h>
#include <conio.h>
void main()
{
int fun (int);
int i;
i = fun (20);
printf ("%d", i);
getch();
}
int fun (int j)
{
j > 20 ? return (10); return (20);
}
```

Output:

return statement cannot be used as shown with the conditional operators. Instead the following statement can be used.

```
return (j > 20 ? 10 : 20);
```

Problem 60

Find the output of the following program?

```
#include <stdio.h>
#include <conio.h>
```

```
void main()
{
int i = 1;
if (!i)
printf ("Welcome\n");
{
i = 0;
printf ("How are you\n");
main( );
}
getch();
}
```

Output:

Infinite loop

Problem 61

Tell these functions work?

```
fun1 (int i, int j)
{
return (fun2 (2));
}
fun2 (int i)
{
return (i * i);
}
```

Output:

Yes

Problem 62

Find the output of the following program?

```
#include <stdio.h>
#include <conio.h>
```

```
void main()
{
int fun( );
int i;
i = fun( );
printf ("%d", i);
getch();
}
fun ( )
{
_AX = 2011;
}
```

Output:

2011

Problem 63

Find the output of the following program?

```
#include <stdio.h>
#include <conio.h>
void main()
{
int fun (int);
int i = fun (100);
printf ("%d\n", -i);
getch();
}
int fun (int i)
{
return (i++);
}
```

Output:

99

Problem 64

Find the output of the following program?

```
#include <stdio.h>
#include <conio.h>
void fun (int);
void main( )
{
int i;
i = 3;
fun (i);
getch();
}
void fun (int n)
{
if (n > 0)
{
fun (--n);
printf ("%d", n);
fun (--n);
}
}
```

Output:

0 1 2 0

Problem 65

Find the output of the following program?

```
#include <stdio.h>
#include <conio.h>
int f1 (int);
```

```
void main()
{
int i = 35;
i = f1 (i = f1 (i = f1 (i));
printf ("i = %d", i);
getch();
}
f1 (int i)
{
i++;
return (i);
}
```

Output:

38

Problem 66

Find the output of the following program?

```
#include <stdio.h>
#include <conio.h>
void main()
{
int incr(int);
int i = 7;
incr (i = incr(incr(i)));
printf ("%d", i);
getch();
}
incr (int i)
{
i++;
```

```
return (i);
}
```

Output:

9

Problem 67

Find the output of the following program?

```
#include <stdio.h>
#include <conio.h>
int incr(int);
void main ( )
{
float f = 5;
incr (f = incr(incr (f)));
printf ("%f", f);
}
incr (int i)
{
i++;
return i;
}
```

Output:

7.000000

Problem 68

Find the output of the following program?

```
#include <stdio.h>
#include <conio.h>
int i;
int j = 1;
```

```
int f1 (int);
int f2 (int);
void main( )
{
extern int j;
int i = 3;
f1 (i);
printf ("%d", i);
f2 (i);
printf (*%d", i);
getch();
}
f1 (int j)
{
printf ("%d", ++j);
}
f2 (int i)
{
printf ("%d", ++i);
}
```

Output:

4 3 4 3

Problem 69

Find the output of the following program?

```
#include <stdio.h>
#include <conio.h>
int fptr (int (*)());
void main ( )
{
```

```
fun (main);
printf ("Welcome");
getch();
}
fptr (int (*ptr)())
{
printf ("How are you");
}
```

Output:

```
How are you Welcome
```

Problem 70

Find the output of the following program?

```
#include<stdio.h>
#include<conio.h>
void main( )
{
int a;
a=printf("Khalsa")+printf("College");
printf("\n%d characters",a);
getch();
}
```

Output:

```
Khalsa College
13 characters printed
```

Problem 71

Check the errors from the following program?

```
#include<stdio.h>
#include<conio.h>
```

```
void main( )
{
int i=2, j=3, k;
k=add(i,j);
printf("Addition is %d", k);
getch();
}
int add(int i, int j)
{
return i+j;
}
```

Output:

Error

NOTE: Call to undefined function add

Problem 72

Find the output of the following program?

```
#include<stdio.h>
#include<conio.h>
void main( )
{
int add(int, int), i, j;
i=j=5;
printf("Addition is %d" add(i, j));
getch();
}
int add (int i, int j)
{
return i+j;
}
```

Output:

Addition is 20

Problem 73

Find the output of the following program?

```
#include<stdio.h>
#include<conio.h>
int add(int, int);
void main( )
{
int i=10, j=10, k;
k=add(i, j);
printf("Addition is %d", k);
getch();
}
int add(int i, int j)
{
return i+j;
}
```

Output:

```
Addition is 20
```

Problem 74

Check the errors from the following program?

```
#include<stdio.h>
#include<conio.h>
void main( )
{
int add(int, int),i,j,k;
i=10; j=20;
k=add(i, j);
```

```
printf("Addition is %d", add(i,j));
getch();
}
int add(int i, j)
{
return i+j;
}
```

Output:

Error

Problem 75

Check the errors from the following program?

```
#include<stdio.h>
#include<conio.h>
void main( )
{
int add(int, int),i,j,k;
i=10; j=20;
k=add(i, j);
printf("Addition is %d", k);
int add(int i, int j)
{
return i+j;
}
getch();
}
```

Output:

Error

B. FILL IN THE BLANKS

1. A function is invoked using a ....
2. The type of variable that is known only within the function in which it is defined is called a ....
3. The .... statement in a called function passes the value of an expression back to the calling function.
4. .... help in to divide large program into smaller simple programs.
5. The execution of a C program always begins with function ....
6. The expressions that appear within the parentheses of a function call are known as ....
7. The keyword void means function have to returns ....
8. The three ways to return control from a called function to a caller are .... , ... and ....
9. .... are used to communicate the values between the functions.
10. If a function returns no value, ... is specified in the place of return type.
11. A function returning a .... may be used in an expression.
12. A function assumes .... data type as return type if no return type is specified in the function header.
13. Header files include .... functions.
14. Function names starting with underscores are meant for .... function names.
15. Function declaration ends with a ....
16. Parameters can use .... storage class.
17. A function uses .... parameter passing mechanism.
18. The storage classes .... and .... are allowed in functions and .... is assumed to be the default one.
19. A .... allows the compiler to check the number, data types and order of the arguments passed to a function.

20. The two ways of passing arguments to a function are .... and ....
21. The variables declared in the parameter declaration list in the function header are known as ....
22. The return type of each math library function is ....
23. A function that calls itself either directly or indirectly (i.e., through another function) is a .... function.
24. The return type of a function cannot be ....
25. .... is a special case of recursion in which the last operation of a function is a recursive call.
26. The return type of a function is .... by default.
27. The activation records for all of the active functions are stored in the region of memory called ....
28. When function call itself again and again is known as ....
29. .... functions are predefined and supplied along with the compiler.
30. The function .... is the first calling function in any C program.
31. An identifier(other than keywords) followed by an open parenthesis is recognized as a .... by the compiler.
32. Function .... is mandatory for all functions.
33. All the string manipulation functions have been included in the header file ....
34. The function main( ) can use only .... data type as its return data type.

Answers

1. function call
2. local variable
3. return
4. Functions
5. main
6. actual arguments
7. nothing
8. return, return expression or return variable

9. parameters
10. void
11. single value
12. int
13. library
14. library
15. semicolon
16. register
17. call by value
18. extern, static, extern
19. function prototype
20. call by value, call by address/reference
21. formal parameters
22. double
23. recursive
24. an array type or a function type
25. Tail recursion
26. int
27. stack
28. recursion
29. built in functions
30. main( )
31. functions name
32. definition
33. string.h
34. int

C. TRUE OR FALSE

State whether each of the following is true or false

1. Recursion is a repetitive process in which a function calls itself.
2. The principles of top-down design and structured programming dictate that a program should be divided into a main module and its related modules.
3. The parameters in a function definition are defined in the function's body (local declaration section).
4. In C all functions except main( ) can be called recursively.
5. A function CANNOT be defined inside another function.
6. Functions can be called either by value or by reference.
7. Functions cannot return more than one value at a time.
8. main() is a library-defined function.
9. There can be only one return statement within a function body.
10. printf is an example of a variable argument function.
11. The function designator implicitly refers to the starting address of the function.

12. The return statement is used to terminate the execution of a program.
13. The address operator (&) is used to tell the compiler to store data at an address.
14. Variables defined within a block have global scope.
15. A function can be defined within the body of another function, and the function defined within another function is known as nested function.
16. Directly recursive functions are also known as mutually recursive functions.
17. A function need not be declared, if it is defined before it is called.
18. Linker converts the object code into executable code.
19. The function main( ) is a built-in function.
20. Names of functions in two different files linked together must be unique.
21. A function can return more than one value.
22. There is a limit on the number of times a function is called.
23. A function can be called from more than one place within a program.
24. The function call floor (5.9) returns 5 and floor (5.1) also returns 5.
25. The function call ceil (6.9) returns 7 and ceil (6.1) returns 6.
26. Every function must return a value.
27. Maximum number of arguments that a function can take is 12.
28. Two functions can have the same name in a single program.
29. A function with no action is an invalid function.
30. A function may have any number of return statements each returning different values.
31. The function memcpy( ) is faster than the function memmove( ).
32. One function cannot be defined within another function definition.
33. Recursive call is not allowed for main( ) function.

34. The shorthand declaration of parameters in the parameter list is not allowed.
35. One of the uses of function prototype is in type checking.
36. The function definition contains the code for a function.
37. If return type for a function is not specified, it default to int.
38. Functions cannot return a floating point number.
39. Function calls that return void may not be used as a part of an expression.
40. If the arguments are passed reference, the changes made in the values pointes to by the formal parameters in the called function are reflected to the calling function.
41. A function can return only one value.
42. Is it possible to use nested functions?

Answers

1. True	2. True	3. True	4. False
5. True	6. True	7. True	8. False
9. False	10. True	11. True	12. False
13. True	14. False	15. False	16. False
17. True	18. True	19. False	20. True
21. False	22. False	23. True	24. True
25. False	26. False	27. False	28. False
29. False	30. True	31. True	32. True
33. False	34. True	35. True	36. True
37. True	38. False	39. True	40. True
41. True	42. True		

D. OBJECTIVE TYPE QUESTIONS

1. Parameters are used
   (a) to return values from the called function

(b) to send values from the calling function

(c) options a and b

(d) to specify the data type of the return value

2. Identify the correct statement

(a) A function can be defined more than once in a program

(b) Function definition cannot appear in any order

(c) Functions cannot be distributed in many files

(d) One function cannot be defined within another function definition.

3. The default return data type in function definition is

(a) void (b) int

(c) float (d) char

4. The parameters in a function call are

(a) actual parameters (b) formal parameters

(c) dummy parameters (d) optional

5. The parameters in a function definition are

(a) actual parameters (b) formal parameters

(c) dummy parameters (d) optional

6. What function must all C programs have?

(a) start( ) (b) main( )

(c) return( ) (d) exit( )

7. In C, which of the following statement(s) is (are) TRUE about the way the arguments are passed?

1. The order of evaluation of arguments is compiler dependant.

2. Arguments are passed by reference.

(a) both options 1 and 2 (b) only option 1

(c) only option 2 (d) neither option 1 nor 2

8. Which of the following statements in C is/are TRUE?

1. Two functions can have the same name in a single program.

2. Function calls can be recursive.

(a) both options 1 and 2 (b) only option 1
(c) only option 2 (d) neither option 1 nor 2

9. Which of the following would compute the square of x in C?
(a) pow(2, x); (b) pow(x, 2)
(c) x**2 (d) power(x, 2);

10. All standard C library <math.h> functions return what data type?
(a) decimal (b) float
(c) double (d) int

11. The parameters passing mechanism used in C is
(a) call by reference (b) call by name
(c) call by value (d) options a and b

12. The storage class than can precede return data type in function declaration is
(a) extern (b) static
(c) options a and b (d) register

13. Recursive call results when
(a) a function calls itself
(b) a function 1 calls another function, which in turn calls the function 1
(c) options a and b
(d) a function calls another function

14. The main( ) function calls in a C program
(a) allows recursive call
(b) does not allow recursive call
(c) is optional
(d) is a built-in function

15. The function floor(x) in math.h
(a) returns the value rounded down to the next lower integer
(b) returns the value rounded down to the next higher integer
(c) the next higher value (d) the next lower value

16. What function must all C programs have?
    (a) start( ) (b) main( )
    (c) return( ) (d) exit( )
17. Which of the following would compute the square of x in C?
    (a) pow(2,x); (b) pow(x,2);
    (c) x* * 2; (d) power(x,2);
18. All standard C library < math.h > functions return what data type?
    (a) decimal (b) float
    (c) double (d) int
19. The program execution starts from
    (a) the function which is first defined
    (b) main( ) function
    (c) the function which is last defined
    (d) the function other than main( )
20. How many main( ) functions can be defined in a C program?
    (a) 1 (b) 2
    (c) 3 (d) any number of times
21. A function is identified by an open parenthesis following
    (a) a keyword
    (b) an identifier other than keywords
    (c) an identifier including keywords
    (d) an operator
22. A function with no action
    (a) is an invalid function
    (b) produces syntax error
    (c) is allowed and is known as dummy function
    (d) returns zero
23. Parameters are used
    (a) to return values from the called function
    (b) to send values from the calling function

(c) options a and b

(d) to specify the data type of the return value

24. Identify the correct statement

(a) a function can be defined more than once in a program

(b) function definition cannot appear in any order

(c) functions cannot be distributed in many files

(d) one function cannot be defined

25. The default return data type in function definition is

(a) void (b) int

(c) float (d) char

26. The parameters in a function call are

(a) actual parameters (b) formal parameters

(c) dummy parameters (d) optional

27. The program execution starts from

(a) the function which is first defined

(b) main( ) function

(c) the function which is last defined

(d) the function other than main( )

28. How many main( ) functions can be defined in a C program?

(a) 1 (b) 2

(c) 3 (d) any number of times

29. A function is identified by an open parenthesis following

(a) a keyword

(b) an identifier other than keywords

(c) an identifier including keywords

(d) an operator

30. What is the output generated by the following program?

```
#include <stdio.h>
#include <conio.h>
void main( )
```

```
{
int i, x;
for (i=1; i<=5; i++)
{
x = square (i);
printf ("%d", x);
}
getch();
}
square (int x)
{
return x*x;
}
```

(a) 1234567 (b) 2516941

(c) 9162514 (d) 1491625

31. What is the output of the following code?

```
int n = -24;
main( )
{
printd(n);
}
printd(int n)
{
for (n < 0)
{
printf("-");
n = -n;
}
if (n % 10) printf ("&d", n);
```

```
else printf ("%d", n/10);
printf ("%d", n);
}
```

(a) –24 (b) 24

(c) –2424 (d) –24

32. What is the output of the following code?

```
void main( )
{
int x = 80, a = -80;
void swap (int, int);
swap (x, a);
printf ("numbers are %d\t%d", a, x)
}
void swap (int y, int b)
{
int t=y;
y=b;
b=t;
}
```

(a) numbers are 80 -80 (b) numbers are 80 80

(c) numbers are -80 80 (d) numbers are -80 -80

33. A function with no action
   (a) is an invalid function
   (b) produces syntax error
   (c) is allowed and is known as dummy function
   (d) returns zero

34. C allows
   (a) only call by value
   (b) only call by reference
   (c) both
   (d) only call by value and sometimes call by reference

35. main ( )

```
{            }
 int a;
f1( ) { }
f2( ) { }
```

To which of the above functions is int a available for?

(a) All of them (b) Only f2.

(c) Only f1 (d) f1 and f2 only

36. The function main( ) is

(a) a built-in function (b) a user-defined function

(c) optional (d) all the above

37. The storage class allowed for parameters is

(a) auto (b) static

(c) extern (d) register

38. Functions are assigned by default

(a) auto storage class (b) static storage class

(c) extern storage class (d) register storage class

39. long factorial (long x)

```
{
????
return x * factorial (x -1);
}
```

What would you replace the ???? with, to make the function shown above, return the correct answer?

(a) if (x = = 0)return 0; (b) if (x = = 0) return 1;

(c) if (x < = 1) return 1; (d) return 1;

40. if (x ? y : z) do Something( );

Referring to the sample above, which statement correctly identifies when y is evaluated?

(a) y is evaluated only when x = = 1

(b) y is evaluated only when x > = 1

(c) y is evaluated only when x! = 0

(d) y is evaluated only when x = = 0

41. const in var1 = 1;

```
static int var2 = 2;
void func( )
{
int var3 = 3;
static int var4 = 4;
}
```

Which of the above variables exist after the function returns and cannot be accessed from another file?

(a) var2 only

(b) var4 only

(c) var2 and var4 only

(d) var2, var3, and v4 only

42. void func (int x)

```
{
if (x > 0) func (-x);
printf ("%d,", x);
}
int main( )
{
func (5);
return 0;
}
```

What will the above sample code produce when executed?

(a) 0,1,2,3,4,5

(b) 0,0,1,2,3,4

(c) 4,3,2,1,0

(d) 5,4,3,2,1,0

43. #include <stdio.h>

```
void show
{
```

```
printf ("Water\n");
}
/* main.c */
#include <stdio.h>
static void show( )
{
printf ("Drink\n");
}
int main( )
{
show ( );
return 0;
}
```

Referring to the program given by the 2 source files defined in the code above, what will happen when you try to build and run the program?

(a) It will print water (b) It will print Drink

(c) It will print: Drink Water (d) It will not compile

44. char var1 [10];

char var2 [5] "Angel";

strcpy (var1, var2);

What will happen when the above code is executed?

(a) The linker will reject this as an array overflow error

(b) The variable var1 and var2 will contain the string "Angel" and no problems will occur

(c) The compiler will reject it because only string pointers can be initialized this way

(d) The variable var2 will contain the word "Angel", but the behaviour of strcpy is undefined

45. void display (????)

{

```
printf ("%d\n", list [1] [0]);
}
int main( )
{
int ary [2] [2] = {1, 2, 3, 4};
display ((void *) ary);
return 0;
}
```

Which of the following when substituted for the ???? above, will NOT correctly print out the number 3?

(a) int list[][2]
(b) int list[2][2]
(c) int (*list)[2]
(d) int *list[2]

46. What does strncat append to the target string after the specified number of characters have been copied?

(a) Nothing
(b) NULL
(c) 0
(d) -0

47. int strcmp(s1, s2) compares strings s1 and s2 and

(a) returns a value less than zero if s2 is lexicographically greater than s1
(b) returns zero if s1 is lexicographically less than s2
(c) returns 1 if s1 is equal to s2
(d) returns a value less than zero if s1 is lexicographically greater than s2

48. int func (char *sv)

```
{
static char info [] = "If anything can go wrong, it will"; ????
}
```

From the sample above, which of the following could replace the ???? to correctly copy text from info the passed buffer without any illegal memory accesses?

(a) sv = info;

(b) strncpy (sv, info, sizeof (info));

(c) strncpy (sv, info, strlen (info) + 1);

(d) strncpy (sv, info, strlen (sv) + 1);

49. return (x = ((((y=2) *z) + (a | b) * (2+s)))));

Which of the following expressions use the minimum number of parentheses and is equivalent to the expression above?

(a) return (x = (y=2) *z+(a|b) * (2+2));

(b) return (x((y=2) *z+ (a|b) * (2+s)));

(c) return x = (y =2) *z+a|b* (2+s);

(d) return (x=(y=2) *z(a/b) * (2+s);

50. When a function is recursively called all automatic variable are

(a) stored in stack
(b) stored in queue
(c) stored in array
(d) stored in linked list

51. Functions have

(a) file scope
(b) local scope
(c) block scope
(d) function scope

52. The function defined in math.h file for returning the arc tangent of x is

(a) tan_1(x)
(b) atan(x)
(c) tanh(x)
(d) arctan(x)

53. The function cell(x) defined in math.h

(a) returns the value rounded down to the next lower integer

(b) returns the value rounded up to the next higher integer

(c) the next higher value

(d) the next lower value

54. The function floor(x) in math.h

(a) returns the value rounded down to the next lower integer

(b) returns the value rounded up to the next higher integer

(c) the next higher value

(d) the next lower value

55. The parameters in a function definition are
    (a) actual parameters (b) formal parameters
    (c) dummy parameters (d) Optional
56. The parameters passing mechanism used in C is
    (a) call by reference (b) call by name
    (c) call by value (d) options a and b
57. The storage class that can precede return data type in function declaration is
    (a) extern (b) static
    (c) options a and b (d) register
58. Recursive call results when
    (a) a function calls itself
    (b) a function calls another function, which in turn calls the function 1
    (c) options a and b
    (d) a function calls another function
59. The main( ) function calls in a C program
    (a) allows recursive calls (b) does not allow recursive call
    (c) is optional (d) is a built in function
60. The function main( ) is
    (a) a built-in function (b) a user defined function
    (c) optional (d) all the above
61. The function defined in math.h file for returning the arc tangent of x is
    (a) tan_1(x) (b) atan(x)
    (c) tanh(x) (d) arctan(x)
62. The function ceil(x) defined in math.h
    (a) returns the value rounded down to the next lower integer
    (b) returns the value rounded down to the next higher integer
    (c) the next higher value
    (d) the next lower value

63. void show( );

```
main( )
{
show( );
}
void show (char *s)
{
printf("%s\n", s);
}
```

What will happen hen the above code is compiled and executed using a strict ANSI C compiler?

(a) It will compile and nothing will be printed when it is executed
(b) It will compile, but not link
(c) The compiler will generate an error
(d) The compiler will generate a warning

64. void display (int x)

```
{
if (x ! = 0)
{
display (x / 16);
putchar ("0123456789ABCDEF" [x %16]);
}
else
putchar ('\n');
}
```

What will be output if the above function is called with x = 1234?

(a) 1234 (b) 4321
(c) 4D2 (d) It will not compile

65. int i=3, a=1, b=1;

```
void func( )
```

```
{
int a = 0;
static int b = 0;
a++; b++;
}
int main( )
{
for (i=0; i < 5; i++)
{
func ( );
a++; b++;
}
printf ("a=%d b=%d\n", a, b);
}
```

What will be printed from the sample code above?

(a) a=0 b=6 (b) a=5=5

(c) a=5 b=6 (d) a=6 b=6

66. main( )

```
{
int n = 10;
fun (n);
}
int fun (int n)
{
int i;
for (i=0); i<=n; i++)
fun (n-i);
printf ("Ikvinder");
}
```

How many times is the printf statement executed for n=10?

(a) 1 (b) Infinity

(c) Zero (d) 10

67. C allows

(a) only call by value

(b) only call by reference

(c) both

(d) only call by value and sometimes call by reference

68. main( )

```
{ }
int a;
f1 ( ) { };
f2 ( ) { };
```

To which of the above functions, is int a available for?

(a) all of them (b) only f2

(c) only f1 (d) f1 and f2 only

69. What will be result of the following program?

```
main( )
void f (int, int);
int i=10;
f(i, i++);
}
void f(int i, int j)
{
if (i>50)
return;
i+=j;
f(i, j);
printf ("%d, ", i);
}
```

(a) 85, 53, 32, 21 (b) 10, 11, 21, 32, 53
(c) 32, 21, 11, 10 (d) none of the above

70. What is the output of the following code?

```
main( )
{
printf (%d\n", sum(5));
}
int sum (int n)
{
if (n<1) return n;
else return (n+sum (n-1));
}
```

(a) 10 (b) 16
(c) 14 (d) 15

Answers

1. (c)	2. (d)	3. (b)	4. (a)	5. (b)
6. (b)	7. (b)	8. (c)	9. (b)	10. (d)
11. (c)	12. (c)	13. (c)	14. (a)	15. (a)
16. (b)	17. (b)	18. (c)	19. (b)	20. (a)
21. (b)	22. (c)	23. (c)	24. (d)	25. (b)
26. (a)	27. (b)	28. (a)	29. (b)	30. (d)
31. (c)	32. (c)	33. (c)	34. (a)	35. (d)
36. (b)	37. (d)	38. (c)	39. (c)	40. (c)
41. (c)	42. (b)	43. (b)	44. (d)	45. (d)
46. (c)	47. (a)	48. (c)	49. (b)	50. (a)
51. (a)	52. (b)	53. (b)	54. (a)	55. (b)
56. (c)	57. (c)	58. (c)	59. (a)	60. (b)
61. (b)	62. (b)	63. (a)	64. (c)	65. (d)
66. (c)	67. (c)	68. (d)	69. (d)	70. (d)

CHAPTER 8

Storage Classes

A. CODE SNIPPETS

Problem 1

Check the errors from the following program?

```
#include<stdio.h>
#include<conio.h>
int i=15;
int i=35;
void main( )
{
printf("Two Values");
getch();
}
```

Output:

```
Error
```

NOTE: Variable i is initialized more than once

Problem 2

Check the errors from the following program?

```
#include<stdio.h>
```

```
#include<conio.h>
auto int i=25;
void main( )
{
printf("Value of i is %d", i);
getch();
}
```

Output:

```
Error
```

NOTE: Storage class auto is not allowed here

Problem 3

Find the output of the following program?

```
#include<stdio.h>
#include<conio.h>
void main( )
{
int code=1, j=5;
switch(code)
{
case 1:
{
int j=1;
printf("Value of j is %d\n", j);
}
case 2:
printf("Value of j is %d\n, j);
}
getch();
}
```

Output:

```
Value of j is 1
Value of j is 5
```

Problem 4

Check the errors from the following program?

```
#include<stdio.h>
#include<conio.h>
void main( )
{
extern int i;
printf("Value of i is %d", i);
getch();
}
```

Output:

```
Error
```

NOTE: Undefined symbol i

Problem 5

Find the output of the following program?

```
#include<stdio.h>
#include<conio.h>
void main( )
{
extern int i;
printf("Value of i is %d", i);
getch();
}
int i=55;
```

Output:

```
Value of i is 55
```

Problem 6

Check the errors from the following program?

```
#include<stdio.h>
#include<conio.h>
void main( )
{
extern int i;
printf("Value of i is %d", i);
int i=45;
getch();
}
```

Output:

```
Error
```

NOTE: Multiple declaration for i in main().

Problem 7

Find the output of the following program?

```
#include<stdio.h>
#include<conio.h>
extern int i=25;
void main( )
{
printf("Value of i is %d", i);
getch();
}
```

Output:

```
Value of i is 25
```

Problem 8

Check the errors from the following program?

```
#include<stdio.h>
#include<conio.h>
void main( )
{
extern int i=25;
printf("Value of i is %d", i);
extern int i=25;
}
```

Output:

Error

NOTE: extern variable cannot be initialized in main().

Problem 9

Check the errors from the following program?

```
#include<stdio.h>
#include<conio.h>
display(static int p)
{
printf("Value of p is %d", p);
}
void main( )
{
int i=2;
printf("Value of i is %d",i);
display(i);
getch();
}
```

Output:

Error

NOTE: Storage class static is not allowed here.

Problem 10

Find the output of the following program?

```
#include<stdio.h>
#include<conio.h>
int i;
void main( )
{
printf("Global variable will be %d", i);
getch();
}
```

Output:

```
Global variable will be 0
```

Problem 11

Find the output of the following program?

```
#include<stdio.h>
#include<conio.h>
void main( )
{
int i;
printf("Local variable will be %d", i);
getch();
}
```

Output:

```
Local variable will be 19125
```

Problem 12

Find the output of the following program?

```
#include<stdio.h>
#include<conio.h>
void main( )
{
static int i;
printf("Static local variable will be %d", i);
getch();
}
```

Output:

```
Static local variable will be 0
```

Problem 13

Check the errors from the following program?

```
#include<stdio.h>
#include<conio.h>
void main( )
{
static extern int i;
printf("Value of i is %d", i);
getch();
}
```

Output:

```
Error
```

NOTE: Too many storage classes in declaration in main().

Problem 14

Find the output of the following program?

```
#include<stdio.h>
```

```
#include<conio.h>
int a=15;
void main( )
{
int b=35;
printf("Value in outer block are %d %d\n", a, b);

{
int a=45;
printf("Value in inner block are %d %d\n", a, b);

}
printf("Value again in outer block are %d %d\n", a,
   b);
getch();
}
```

Output:

```
Value in outer block are 15 35
Value in inner block are 45 35
Value again in outer block are 15 35
```

Problem 15

Find the output of the following program?

```
#include<stdio.h>
#include<conio.h>
display( )
{
int x = 0, y = 1;
int z;
z=x+y; x=y; y=z;
```

```
return z;
}
void main( )
{
int countr = 0, i;
printf("Fibonacci series are:\n");
for(i=0;i<5;i++)
printf("%d", display());
getch();
}
```

Output:

```
Fibonacci series are:
1 1 1 1 1
```

Problem 16

Find the output of the following program?

```
#include<stdio.h>
#include<conio.h>
display( )
{
int x = 0, y = 1;
int z;
z=x+y; x=y; y=z;
return z;
}
void main( )
{
int countr=0, i;
printf("Fibonacci series are:\n");
for(i=0;i<5;i++)
```

```
printf("%d", display());
getch();
}
```

Output:

```
Fibonacci series are:
1 2 3 5 8
```

Problem 17

Find the output of the following program?

```
#include<stdio.h>
#include<conio.h>
void main( )
{
int i=1;
printf("Value of i is %d\n", i--);
if(i)
main( );
getch();
}
```

Output:

```
Value of i is 1
Value of i is 1
..................
..................
```

NOTE: It can print the above statement till stack does not overflow.

Problem 18

Find the output of the following program?

```
#include<stdio.h>
#include<conio.h>
```

```
void main( )
{
static int i=3;
printf("Value of i is %d\n", i--);
if(i)
main( );
getch();
}
```

Output:

```
Value of i is 3
Value of i is 2
Value of i is 1
```

Problem 19

Find the output of the following program?

```
#include<stdio.h>
#include<conio.h>
void main( )
{
int i;
for (i=0; i<3; i++)
{
int x = 0;
static int y=0;
printf("x=%d, y=%d\n", x++, y++);
}
getch();
}
```

Output:

```
x=0, y=0
```

```
x=0, y=1
x=0, y=2
```

Problem 20

Find the output of the following program?

```
#include<stdio.h>
#include<conio.h>
int *j;
display()
{
static int i=12;
j=&i;
}
void main( )
{
display();
printf("Value of i is %d", *j);
getch();
}
```

Output:

```
Value of i is 12
```

Problem 21

Find the output of the following program?

```
#include<stdio.h>
#include<conio.h>
void main( )
{
int *j;
{
```

```
int i=12;
j=&i;
printf("Value of i is %d", *j);
getch();
}
```

Output:

```
Value of i is 12
```

Problem 22

Check the errors from the following program?

```
#include<stdio.h>
#include<conio.h>
void main( )
{
int *ptr;
ptr=malloc(sizeof(int));
*ptr=25;
printf("Allocated object is %d", *ptr);
getch();
}
```

Output:

```
Error
```

NOTE: Unable to convert 'void*' to 'int*'

Problem 23

Find the output of the following program?

```
#include<stdio.h>
#include<conio.h>
void main( )
{
```

```
int *ptr;
ptr=(int*)malloc(sizeof(int));
*ptr=25;
printf("Allocated object is %d", *ptr);
getch();
}
```

Output:

```
Allocated object is 25
```

Problem 24

Find the output of the following program?

```
#include<stdio.h>
#include<conio.h>
void main( )
{
int *ptr;
ptr=(int*)malloc(sizeof(int));
printf("Allocated object is %d", *ptr);
getch();
}
```

Output:

```
No error
```

Problem 25

Find the output of the following program?

```
#include<stdio.h>
#include<conio.h>
void main( )
{
int *ptr;
```

```
ptr=(int*)calloc(sizeof(int));
printf("Allocated object is %d", *ptr);
getch();
}
```

Output:

```
Allocated object is 0
```

Problem 26

Find the output of the following program?

```
#include<stdio.h>
#include<conio.h>
void main( )
{
ptr=(int*)malloc(256*256-1);
if(ptr= = NULL)
printf("Memory allocation fails");
else
printf("Memory allocation successful");
getch();
}
```

Output:

```
Memory allocation fails
```

Problem 27

Find the output of the following program?

```
#include<stdio.h>
#include<conio.h>
void main( )
{
ptr=(int*)malloc(256*256L-1);
```

```
if(ptr= = NULL)
printf("Memory allocation fails");
else
printf("Memory allocation successful");
getch();
}
```

Output:

```
Memory allocation successful
```

Problem 28

Find the output of the following program?

```
#include<stdio.h>
#include<conio.h>
void main( )
{
ptr=(int*)malloc(256*256L);
if(ptr= = NULL)
printf("Memory allocation fails");
else
printf("Memory allocation successful");
getch();
}
```

Output:

```
Memory allocation fails
```

Problem 29

Find the output of the following program?

```
#include<stdio.h>
#include<conio.h>
void main( )
```

```
{
char *ptr;
ptr=(char*)malloc(6);
strcpy(ptr, "Links");
puts(ptr);
strcat(ptr, "Written");
puts(ptr);
getch();
}
```

Output:

```
Links
LinksWritten
```

Problem 30

Find the output of the following program?

```
#include<stdio.h>
#include<conio.h>
void main( )
{
char *ptr;
ptr=(char*)malloc(6);
strcpy(ptrl, "Links");
puts(ptrl);
ptrl=(char*)realloc)ptrl,15);
strcat(ptr, "Written");
puts(ptr);
getch();
}
```

Output:

```
Links
LinksWritten
```

Problem 31

Find the output of the following program?

```
#include<stdio.h>
#include<conio.h>
void main( )
{
typedef int value;
value i = 25;
printf("Value of i is %d", i);
getch();
}
```

Output:

```
Value of i is 200
```

Problem 32

Check the errors from the following program?

```
#include<stdio.h>
#include<conio.h>
void main( )
{
typedef static int value;
value i = 25;
printf("Value of i is %d", i);
getch();
}
```

Output:

```
Error
```

NOTE: Too many storage classes in declaration in main().

Problem 33

Find the output of the following program?

```
#include<stdio.h>
#include<conio.h>
void main( )
{
typedef char* ch;
ch i, j;
printf("Size of i and j is %d %d",sizeof(i), sizeof(j));
getch();
}
```

Output:

```
Size of i and j is 2 and 2
```

Problem 34

Find the output of the following program?

```
#include<stdio.h>
#include<conio.h>
char *display()
{
char str[]= "Welcome";
puts(str);
return str;
}
void main( )
{
```

```
puts(display());
getch();
}
```

Output:

```
Welcome
```

Problem 35

Find the output of the following program?

```
#include<stdio.h>
#include<conio.h>
int i=100;
display()
{
printf("Value of i is %d\n", i);
}
void main( )
{
printf("Value of i is %d\n", i);
i = i + 50;
display();
getch();
}
```

Output:

```
Value of i is 100
Value of i is 150
```

Problem 36

Find the output of the following program?

```
#include<stdio.h>
#include<conio.h>
```

```
int i = 10;
display()
{
int i= 20;
printf("Value of i is %d\n", i);
}
void main( )
{
printf("Value of i is %d\n", i);
i=i+30;
display();
getch();
}
```

Output:

```
Value of i is 10
Value of i is 20
```

Problem 37

Check the errors from the following program?

```
#include<stdio.h>
#include<conio.h>
display()
{
int i = 5;
printf("Value of i is %d\n" i);
}
void main( )
{
printf("Value of i is %d\n", i);
i = i + 10;
```

```
display();
getch();
}
```

Output:

```
Error
```

NOTE: Undefined symbol var in main().

Problem 38

Find the output of the following program?

```
#include<stdio.h>
#include<conio.h>
display(int i)
{
printf("Value of i is %d\n", i);
}
void main( )
{
int i = 20;
printf("Value of i is %d\n", i);
display(i/2);
getch();
}
```

Output:

```
Value of i is 20
Value of i is 10
```

Problem 39

Check the errors from the following program?

```
#include<stdio.h>
#include<conio.h>
```

```
display()
{
first:
printf("Khalsa College, Amritsar");
}
void main( )
{
goto first;
getch();
}
```

Output:

```
Error
```

NOTE: Undefined label first in main().

Problem 40

Find the output of the following program?

```
#include<stdio.h>
#include<conio.h>
int i=10;
void main( )
{
extern int var;
extern int var;
printf("Value of i is %d", i);
getch();
}
```

Output:

```
Value of i is 10
```

Problem 41

Find the output of the following program?

```
#include<stdio.h>
#include<conio.h>
char *display()
{
static char str[]= "Welcome";
puts(str);
return str;
}
void main( )
{
puts(display());
getch();
}
```

Output:

```
Welcome
Welcome
```

Problem 42

Find the output of the following program?

```
#include<stdio.h>
#include<conio.h>
char *display()
{
char *str= "Welcome";
puts(str);
return str;
}
void main( )
```

```
{
puts(display());
getch();
}
```

Output:

```
Welcome
Welcome
```

B. FILL IN THE BLANKS

1. Variables declared in a block or in the parameter list of a function are assumed to be of storage class ________ unless specified otherwise.
2. The region of the program within which an identifier is visible is determined by its ....
3. .... is the only kind of identifier that always has function scope.
4. The keyword .... provides a method for declaring an identifier without defining it.
5. One definition rule states that ....
6. Storage-class specifier .... is a recommendation to the compiler to store a variable in one of the computer's registers.
7. The principle of shadowing state that ....
8. .... is a process by which a name used in an expression is associated with a declaration.
9. All the global variables and functions by default have .... linkage.
10. The linkage of an identifier can be made internal by using .... storage class specifier in the declaration statement.
11. The .... of a variable is the portion of a program in which the variable is visible.
12. A variable having file scope is known as .... variable.

13. The auto variables have .... scope.
14. If the definition of a variable does not contain an initializer, it is known as a ....
15. If the reference of a variable is done before its definition, it is known as a ....
16. A variable declared outside any block or function is a .... variable.
17. For a local variable in a function to retain its value between calls to the function, it must be declared with the .... storage-class specifier.
18. All the identifiers with block scope or function prototype scope by default have .... linkage.
19. Function can have .... or .... linkage but cannot have .... linkage.
20. The portion of program execution during which the memory space of an object is guaranteed to be reserved is known as ....
21. Objects with .... lifetime are allocated new storage each time the execution control enters the block in which their associated identifiers are defined.
22. The allocation of memory space made at the run time is known as ....
23. A variable with block scope by default has .... storage class.
24. The storage class controls the .... , ... , and ....
25. Every occurrence of a variable in a particular source file refers to the same value, if it has an ....
26. .... variable declaration does not allocate memory for the variable.
27. An external variable declaration begins with the storage class specifier ....
28. The storage class .... renames the existing data types.

Answers

1. auto
2. scope
3. label name
4. extern
5. each variable must have only one definition in a scope
6. register
7. definition of an identifier in the immediate scope shadows/ supersedes the definitions of the identifier present in the enclosing scope
8. Name resolution
9. external
10. static
11. scope
12. global variable
13. block
14. tentative definition
15. forward reference
16. extern
17. static
18. no
19. internal, external, no
20. lifetime
21. automatic
22. dynamic memory allocation
23. auto
24. lifetime, scope, linkage
25. internal linkage
26. external
27. extern
28. typedef

C. TRUE OR FALSE

State whether each of the following is true or false.

1. The scope of an identifier is determined by a position of its declaration.
2. Function scope terminates with the end of function declaration.
3. It is possible to define an identifier with a same name and type more than once in the same scope.
4. Whenever an external variable is modified in a block the effect is propagated to all places wherever it is used.
5. External variable definition allocates memory.
6. Scope of a variable refers to the duration for which the variable retains a given value during the execution of a program.

7. More than one storage class is allowed in a declaration.
8. Register storage class is applicable only to scalar data types.
9. It is possible to define an identifier with a same name more than once, if the definitions lie in different scopes.
10. It is possible to declare identifiers with a same name but different type in different scopes.
11. An external static variable is a global variable and an internal static variable is a local variable.
12. At most one storage class specifier can be specifies in a declaration statement.
13. The variables declared with auto storage class specification are implicitly initiated.
14. Variables having block scope have no linkage.
15. Definition of an external variable may appear many times.
16. Internal static variables have temporary storage.
17. Typedef is a storage class.
18. Register variables are treated as static variable if CPU registers are not free.
19. It is not possible to specify an auto storage class specifier in the declarations that are made in the global scope.
20. It is not possible to apply address-of operator to an identifier declared with register storage class specifier.
21. External variables retain their values throughout the life of a program.
22. The value of an auto variable exists though the execution leaves the block.
23. The variables declared as register type may be stored in the CPU registers instead of in the main memory.
24. The variables declared with static storage class specification are implicitly initialized to zero.
25. The values of auto variables persist between the function calls.

Answers

1. True	2. False	3. False	4. True
5. True	6. False	7. False	8. True
9. True	10. False	11. True	12. True
13. False	14. True	15. False	16. False
17. True	18. False	19. True	20. True
21. True	22. False	23. True	24. True
25. False			

D. OBJECTIVE TYPE QUESTIONS

1. Storage class controls
   (a) lifetime of a variable (b) linkage of a variable
   (c) scope of a variable (d) all the above
2. Longevity of a variable refers to
   (a) the duration for which the variable retains a given value during the execution of a program
   (b) the portion of a program in which the variable may be visible
   (c) internal linkage of a variable
   (d) external linkage of a variable
3. Scope of a variable refers to
   (a) the duration for which the variable retains a given value during the execution of a program
   (b) the portion of a program in which the variable may be visible
   (c) the value of the variable
4. A variable with external linkage refers to
   (a) the duration for which the variable retains a given value during the execution of a program
   (b) the same value for every occurrence of that variable in a particular file

(c) the same value in every source file where source program spans over multiple files

(d) block files

5. A variable with internal linkage refers to

(a) the duration for which the variable retains a given value during the execution of a program

(b) the same value for every occurrence of that variable in a particular file

(c) the same value in every source file where source program spans over multiple files

(d) block files

6. Which of the following is a key word is used for a storage class

(a) printf (b) external

(c) auto (d) scanf

7. The storage class allowed for parameters is

(a) auto (b) static

(c) extern (d) register

8. Functions are assigned by default

(a) auto storage class (b) static storage class

(c) extern storage class (d) register storage class

9. External variable declaration

(a) does not allocate memory (b) uses keyword extern

(c) cannot be initialized (d) all the above

10. The data type that cannot be renamed by typedef is

(a) function (b) pointer

(c) options a and b (d) double

11. What are the valid C scopes of identifiers?

(a) external and local (b) project, file, and block

(c) global, file, and local (d) file and block

12. How is a variable accessed from another file?
    (a) The global variable is referenced via the global specifier
    (b) The global variable is referenced via the extern specifier
    (c) The global variable is referenced via the auto specifier
    (d) The global variable is referenced via the pointer specifier
13. Which of the following is/are achieved using typedef facility?
    1. increase the portability of code
    2. write more compact code
    (a) both options 1 and 2 (b) only option 1
    (c) only option 2 (d) neither option 1 nor 2
14. Functions have
    (a) file scope (b) local scope
    (c) block scope (d) function scope
15. When a function is recursively called all automatic variables are
    (a) stored in stack
    (b) stored in queue
    (c) stored in array
    (d) stored in linked list
16. What does the "auto" specifier do?
    (a) It automatically initializes a variable to 0;.
    (b) It indicates that a variable's memory will automatically be preserved.
    (c) It automatically increments the variable when used.
    (d) It automatically initializes a variable to NULL.
17. The typedef statement does not
    (a) create new data type (b) reserve storage
    (c) options a and b (d) rename the data type
18. Which storage class specifies local variables?
    (a) auto (b) register
    (c) internal static (d) all the above

19. Which storage class specifies global variables?
    (a) extern (b) external static
    (c) options a and b (d) typedef
20. External variable declaration uses
    (a) the keyword external
    (b) the keyword extern
    (c) no keyword such as extern or external
    (d) the keyword register
21. External variable definition
    (a) is specified outside main( ) (b) reserves memory for storage
    (c) is defined only once (d) all the above
22. extern int s;

```
int t;
static int u;
main ( )
{ }
```

    Which of s, t and u are available to a function present in another file?
    (a) only s (b) s & u
    (c) s, t, u (d) none
23. What will be the output of the following code?

```
static int i = 5;
main( )
{
int sum = 0;
do
{
sum+ = (1/i);
} while (0 <i--);
printf ("sum of the series is %d", sum);
```

}

(a) It will print the sum of the series 1/5+1/4+...+1/1

(b) It will produce a compilation error

(c) It will produce a runtime error

(d) None of the above

24. External variable definition uses

(a) the keyword external (b) the keyword extern

(c) no keyword (d) the keyword auto

25. External variable requires

(a) declaration (b) definition

(c) options a and b (d) initialization only

26. If the definition of an external variable does not contain an initialiazer, it is known as

(a) forward declaration (b) tentative definition

(b) backward reference (d) backward definition

27. External variable definition

(a) creates the variable (b) allocates memory

(c) does not use extern keyword

(d) all the above

28. What does invoking the C compiler accomplish?

(a) It links together object files

(b) It creates machine code

(c) It only provides code evaluation. You must use the linker to assemble and link programs

(d) It interprets files at run-time.

29. What does extern means in a function declaration?

(a) The function has global scope

(b) The function need not be defined

(c) Nothing really

(d) The function has local scope only to the file it is defined in.

30. A variable with no linkage refers to
    (a) the duration for which the variable retains a given value during the execution of a program
    (b) the same value for every occurrence of that variable in a particular file
    (c) the same value in every source file where source program spans over multiple files
    (d) block files
31. Which is not a storage class?
    (a) auto
    (b) struct
    (c) typedef
    (d) static
32. The automatic storage class has
    (a) temporary storage
    (b) block scope
    (c) persistent storage
    (d) options a and b
33. The register storage class has
    (a) temporary storage
    (b) block scope
    (c) persistent storage
    (d) options a and b
34. The storage class type of internal static has
    (a) temporary storage
    (b) block scope
    (c) file scope
    (d) options a and b
35. The storage class type of external static has
    (a) temporary storage
    (b) block scope
    (c) file scope
    (d) options a and b
36. The storage class type of external has
    (a) temporary storage
    (b) block scope
    (c) file scope
    (d) options a and b
37. Which storage class may help in faster execution?
    (a) static
    (b) extern
    (c) register
    (d) auto

Answers

1. (d)	2. (a)	3. (b)	4. (c)	5. (b)
6. (c)	7. (d)	8. (c)	9. (d)	10. (a)
11. (d)	12. (b)	13. (a)	14. (a)	15. (a)
16. (b)	17. (c)	18. (d)	19. (c)	20. (b)
21. (d)	22. (a)	23. (c)	24. (c)	25. (c)
26. (b)	27. (d)	28. (b)	29. (c)	30. (d)
31. (b)	32. (d)	33. (d)	34. (d)	35. (d)
36. (d)	37. (c)			

CHAPTER 9

Pointers

A. CODE SNIPPETS

Problem 1

Find the output of the following program?

```
#include<stdio.h>
#include<conio.h>
void main( )
{
int a =15;
int *ptr=&a;
printf("%d%d", ++*ptr,*ptr++);
getch();
}
```

Output:

```
15 Garbage value
```

Problem 2

Find the output of the following program?

```
#include<stdio.h>
#include<conio.h>
```

```
void main( )
{
int a=15;
int *ptr=&a;
printf("%d%d",*ptr++, ++*ptr);
getch();
}
```

Output:

16 16

Problem 3

Check the errors from the following program?

```
#include<stdio.h>
#include<conio.h>
void main( )
{
int i=15;
const int *ptr=&i;
*ptr=50;
printf("Pointed object is %d", *ptr);
getch();
}
```

Output:

Error

NOTE: Cannot modify a constant pointer

Problem 4

Check the errors from the following program?

```
#include<stdio.h>
#include<conio.h>
```

```
void main( )
{
int i=10;
int* iptr=&i;
void *vptr=iptr;
*iptr++;
*vptr++;
printf("Pointers are %d%d", *iptr, *vptr);
getch();
}
```

Output:

```
Error
```

NOTE: size of type is unknown or zero

Problem 5

Find the output of the following program?

```
#include<stdio.h>
#include<conio.h>
void main( )
{
int a[]={1,2,3,4,5};
int *ptr=a;
ptr=ptr+1;
printf("Value pointed by ptr is %d", *ptr);
getch();
}
```

Output:

```
Value pointed by ptr is 2
```

Problem 6

Find the output of the following program?

```
#include<stdio.h>
#include<conio.h>
void main( )
{
int a[]={1,2,3,4,5};
int *ptr1=a;
int *ptr2=a+3;
printf("The result is %d", ptr2-ptr1);
getch();
}
```

Output:

```
The result is 3
```

Problem 7

Check the errors from the following program?

```
#include<stdio.h>
#include<conio.h>
void main( )
{
int a[]={1,2,3,4,5};
int *ptr1=a;
int *ptr2= ptr1*2;
printf("The result of ptr2 is %p", ptr2);
getch();
}
```

Output:

```
Error
```

NOTE: Illegal use of pointers

Problem 8

Check the errors from the following program?

```
#include<stdio.h>
#include<conio.h>
void main( )
{
int i=10, j=20;
int *const ptr=&i;
*ptr=20;
printf("Pointed object i is %d", *ptr);
ptr=&j;
*ptr=10;
printf("Pointed object j is %d", *ptr);
getch();
}
```

Output:

```
Error
```

NOTE: Cannot modify a constant pointer

Problem 9

Check the errors from the following program?

```
#include<stdio.h>
#include<conio.h>
void main( )
{
int i=10, j=20;
const int *const ptr=&i;
*ptr=20;
printf("Pointed object i is %d", *ptr);
ptr=&b;
```

```
*ptr=10;
printf("Pointed object j is %d", *ptr);
getch();
}
```

Output:

```
Error
```

NOTE: Cannot modify a constant pointer

Problem 10

Check the errors from the following program?

```
#include<stdio.h>
#include<conio.h>
void main( )
{
int *ptr=10;
printf("Value of pointer is %p",ptr);
getch();
}
```

Output:

```
Error
```

NOTE: Cannot convert int to int*

Problem 11

Find the output of the following program?

```
#include<stdio.h>
#include<conio.h>
void main( )
{
int *ptr=0;
printf("Value of pointer is %p",ptr);
```

```
getch();
}
```

Output:

```
The value of pointer is 0000:0000
```

Problem 12

Find the output of the following program?

```
#include<stdio.h>
#include<conio.h>
void main( )
{
int *ptr1=0;
int *ptr2=NULL;
if(ptr1= =ptr2)
printf("ptr1 is a NULL pointer");
else
printf("ptr1 is not a NULL pointer");
getch();
}
```

Output:

```
ptr1 is a NULL pointer
```

Problem 13

Find the output of the following program?

```
#include<stdio.h>
#include<conio.h>
void main( )
{
int a[]={1,2,3,4,5};
int *ptr=a;
```

```
printf("%d%d\n%p%p", *a, *ptr, a, ptr);
getch();
}
```

Output:

```
1 1
1367:21EA 1367:21EA
```

Problem 14

Check the errors from the following program?

```
#include<stdio.h>
#include<conio.h>
void main( )
{
int a[]={1,2,3,4,5,6,7,8};
printf("%p%p\n",a,&a);
printf("%p%p",++a,++&a);
getch();
}
```

Output:

```
Error
```

NOTE: L-value required

Problem 15

Find the output of the following program?

```
#include<stdio.h>
#include<conio.h>
void main( )
{
int a[]={1,2,3,4,5,6,7,8};
printf("%p%p\n",a,&a);
```

```
printf("%p%p",a+1,&a+1);
getch();
}
```

Output:

```
No error
```

Problem 16

Find the output of the following program?

```
#include <stdio.h>
#include <conio.h>
void main ( )
{
int a[] = {10, 20, 30, 40, 50};
char *p;
p = (char *) a;
printf ("\n%d", * ((int *) p + 4));
getch();
}
```

Output:

```
50
```

Problem 17

Why we use pointers?

Output:

1. Accessing array or string elements
2. Dynamic memory allocation
3. Call by reference
4. Implementing linked lists, trees, graphs, and many other data structures

Problem 18

Find the output of the following program?

```
#include <stdio.h>
#include <conio.h>
void main ( )
{
int *j;
void fun (int **);
fun (&j);
getch();
}
void fun (int **k)
{
int i = 10;
*k = &i;
}
```

Output:

```
No error.
```

Problem 19

How will you declare an array of two function pointers where each function receives two ints and returns a float value?

Output:

```
float (*arr[2]) (int, int);
```

Problem 20

Find the output of the following program?

```
#include <stdio.h>
#include <conio.h>
```

```
void main ( )
{
float i = 10, *j;
void *k;
k = &i;
j = k;
printf ("\n%f", *j);
getch();
}
```

Output:

No error.

Problem 21

Check the errors from the following program?

```
#include <stdio.h>
#include <conio.h>
void main ( )
{
int a = 10, *j;
void *k;
j = k = &a;
j++;
k++;
printf ("\n%u %u", j, k);
getch();
}
```

Output:

Error.

Problem 22

Find the output of the following program?

```
#include<stdio.h>
#include <conio.h>
void main( )
{
void f(int, int[]);
int a[]= {4, 2, 2, 4};
int i;
f(4, a);
for (i = 0; i < 4; i++)
printf("%d", a[i]);
getch();
}
void f(int n, int a[])
{
int *p = 0;
int i = 0;
while(i++ <n)
p = &a[i];
*p = 0;
}
```

Output:

4 2 2 4

Problem 23

Find the output of the following program?

```
#include <stdio.h>
#include <conio.h>
```

```
void main ( )
{
char *s;
s = "%s";
printf (s, "C");
getch();
}
```

Output:

```
C
```

Problem 24

Find the output of the following program?

```
#include <stdio.h>
#include <conio.h>
void main ( )
{
int i, *j;
i = 4;
j = &i;
printf ("%d", i**j*i*j);
getch();
}
```

Output:

```
No error.
```

Problem 25

Find the output of the following program?

```
#include <stdio.h>
#include <conio.h>
fun (int *, int);
```

```
void main ( )
{
int i, a[] = {2, 4, 6, 8, 10};
fun (a, 5);
for (i = 0; i <= 4; i++)
printf ("%d," a[i]);
getch();
}
fun (int *c, int n)
{
int i;
for (i = 0; i <n; i++)
*(c + i) = *(c + i) + 5;
}
```

Output:

7 9 11 13 15

Problem 26

Find the output of the following program?

```
#include <stdio.h>
#include <conio.h>
int *check (static int, static int);
void main ( )
{
int *c;
c = check (30, 40);
printf ("%d", *c);
getch();
}
int * check (static int i, static int j)
```

```
{
int *p, *q;
p = &i;
p = &j;
if (i >= 45)
return (p);
else
return (q);
}
```

Output:

```
30
```

Problem 27

Find the output of the following program?

```
#include <stdio.h>
#include <conio.h>
void main ( )
{
int i = 10, *j, *k;
j = &i;                    // suppose address of i is 1000
   and integer is 4 byte wide
k = j;
*j++ = *k++;
i++;
printf (*i = %d j = %d k = %d", i, j, k);
getch();
}
```

Output:

```
11 1000 1000
```

Problem 28

Find the output of the following program?

```
// array starting address is 1000: each integer take 2
   bytes
#include<stdio.h>
#include <conio.h>
void main( )
{
int a[3][4]= {
1, 2, 3, 4,
4, 3, 2, 1,
3, 1, 2, 4
};
printf("\n%u %u", a+1, &a+1);
getch();
}
```

Output:

```
1000 1016
```

Problem 29

Find the output of the following program?

```
#include<stdio.h>
#include <conio.h>
void main( )
{
static int a[2][2]= {1, 2, 3, 4};
int i, j;
static int *p[]={(int *) a, (int *) a + 1, (int *) a +
   1};
for (i = 0; i<2; i++)
```

```
{
for (j = 0; j < 2; i++)
printf("%d %d %d %d\n",
*(*(p+i) + j),
* (*(j + p)+i),
*(*(i+p) +j),
*(*(p+j) +i));
}
getch();
}
```

Output:

```
1 1 1 1
2 3 2 3
3 2 3 2
4 4 4 4
```

Problem 30

Find the function f( ) in the following program?

```
int a[r][c];
f(a);
```

Output:

```
f(int a[][c])
{ }
OR
f(int (*ptr)[c]) /* ptr is pointer to an array */
{ }
```

Problem 31

Find the output of the following program?

```
#include<stdio.h>
```

```
#include <conio.h>
void f(int **p);
void main( )
{
int a[3][4]= {
4, 1, 3, 6,
8, 3, 3, 5,
8, 4, 2, 7
};
int *ptr;
ptr = &a[0][0];
f(&ptr);
getch();
}
void f(int **p)
{
printf("\n%d", **p);
}
```

Output:

4

Problem 32

Check the errors from the following program?

```
#include <stdio.h>
#include <conio.h>
void main ( )
{
int a[] = {10, 20, 30, 40, 50};
int i;
for (i = 0; i <5; i++)
```

```
{
printf ("\n%d", *a);
a++;
}
getch();
}
```

Output:

```
Error.
```

NOTE: Lvalue required

Problem 33

Explain the statement given below:

```
char ****k;
```

Output:

Pointer to a pointer to a pointer to a pointer to a char.

Problem 34

Find the output of the following program?

```
#include <stdio.h>
#include <conio.h>
void main ( )
{
char str[] = "peace";
char *s = str;
printf ("%s", s++ +4);
getch();
}
```

Output:

```
e
```

Problem 35

Find the output of the following program?

```
#include<stdio.h>
#include <conio.h>
void main( )
{
static int a[]= {0, 1, 2, 3, 4};
int *p[]= {a, a+1, a+2, a+3, a+4};
int *ptr = p;
ptr++;
printf("\n%d %d %d" ptr -p, *ptr - a, **ptr);
*ptr++;
printf("\n%d %d %d" ptr -p, *ptr - a, **ptr);
*++ptr;
printf("\n%d %d %d" ptr -p, *ptr - a, **ptr);
++*ptr;
printf("\n%d %d %d" ptr -p, *ptr - a, **ptr);
getch();
}
```

Output:

```
1 1 1
2 2 2
3 3 3
3 4 4
```

Problem 36

Find the output of the following program?

```
#include <stdio.h>
#include <conio.h>
void main ( )
```

```
{
char str1[] = "College";
char str2[] = "School";
char *s1 = str1, *s2 = str2;
while (*s1++ = *s2++);
printf ("%s", str1);
getch();
}
```

Output:

School

Problem 37

Find the output of the following program?

```
#include <stdio.h>
#include <conio.h>
void main ( )
{
char *ptr;
ptr = "Good";
printf ("%s", *&*&ptr);
getch();
}
```

Output:

Good

Problem 38

Find the output of the following program?

```
#include <stdio.h>
#include <conio.h>
void main ( )
```

```
{
void *vptr;
char ch = 74, *cptr = "GOOD";
int j = 65;
vptr = &ch;
printf ("%c", * (char *) vptr);
vptr = &j;
printf ("%c", *(int*) vptr);
vptr = cptr;
printf ("%s", (char *) vptr +2);
getch();
}
```

Output:

GOOD

Problem 39

Find the output of the following program?

```
#include <string.h>
#include <stdio.h>
#include <conio.h>
void main ( )
{
 int i, n;
char *p = "Peace";
n = strlen (p);
*p = p[n];
for (i = 0; i <= n; i++)
{
printf ("%s", p);
```

```
p++;
}
getch();
}
```

Output:

```
eace ace ce e
```

Problem 40

Find the output of the following program, if an integer is 4 bytes long?

```
#include <stdio.h>
#include <conio.h>
void main ( )
{
int ***r, **q, *p, i = 4;
p = &i;
q = &p;
r = &q;
printf ("%d %d %d", *p, **q, ***r);
getch();
}
```

Output:

```
4 4 4
```

Problem 41

Find the output of the following program?

```
#include <stdio.h>
#include <conio.h>
f(void *p);
int i;
void main ( )
```

```
{
void *v;
v = &i;
f(v);
getch();
}
f(void *p)
{
int **q;
q = (int **) &p;
printf ("%d", **q);
}
```

Output:

```
0
```

Problem 42

Find the output of the following program?

```
#include <stdio.h>
#include <conio.h>
void main ( )
{
char *s;
s = "%d\n";
s++;
printf (s-1, 400);
getch();
}
```

Output:

```
400
```

Problem 43

Is the NULL pointer work as an uninitialized pointer?

Output:

No

Problem 44

NULL can be defined in __________.

Output:

stdio.h and stddef.h files

Problem 45

Is there any difference between the given two statements?

```
char *ptr = 0;
char *nptr = NULL;
```

Output:

No, both are null pointers.

Problem 46

What is (void *)0?

Output:

It can represents as Null Pointer.

Problem 47

Is the given way for null pointer assignment is correct?

```
int i = 0;
char *ptr = (char *) i;
```

Output:

No.

The correct representation is:

```
char *q = 0;
```

or

```
char *ptr = (char *) 0;
```

Problem 48

What is a null pointer?

Output:

C defines a special pointer value, which is guaranteed not to point to any object or function of that type. The null pointer constant used for representing a null pointer is the integer 0.

Problem 49

What's the difference between a null pointer, a NULL macro, the ASCII NUL character and a null string?

Output:

A null pointer is a pointer, which doesn't point anywhere.

A NULL macro is used to represent the null pointer in source code. It has a value 0 associated with it.

The ASCII NULL character has all its bits as 0 but doesn't have any relationship with the null pointer.

The null string is just another name for an empty string" ".

Problem 50

Find the output of the following program?

```
#include<stdio.h>
#include<conio.h>
void main( )
{
printf ("%d %d", sizeof(NULL), sizeof (""));
getch();
```

```
}
```

Output:

```
2 1
```

NOTE: size of pointer is 2 bytes

Problem 51

Is there any error in the following program?

```
#include<stdio.h>
#include<conio.h>
void main( )
{
int *x;
*x=100;
getch();
}
```

Output:

```
No error
```

Problem 52

Is there any error in the following program?

```
*p = (char *) malloc (100);
*p = 'y';
```

Output:

```
Error
```

NOTE: use malloc like p = (char *) malloc(160);

Problem 53

How many bytes are occupied by near, far and huge pointers?

Output:

```
Near pointer = 2 bytes
```

```
Far pointer = 4 bytes
Huge pointer = 4 bytes
```

Problem 54

These three declarations char **str, char *str[], and char str[][] same?

Output:

No

Problem 55

Find the ouputof the following program?

```
#include<stdio.h>
#include<conio.h>
void main( )
{
int *p1, i = 65;
void *p2;
p1=&i;
p2=&i;
p1=p2;
p2=p1;
getch();
}
```

Output:

No

Problem 56

Find the output of the following program?

```
#include<stdio.h>
#include<conio.h>
void main( )
```

```
{
char *p1, p2;
printf("%d %d", sizeof(p1), sizeof(p2));
getch();
}
```

Output:

```
4 1
```

NOTE: p2 is a character variable.

Problem 57

Find the output of the following program?

```
#include<stdio.h>
#include<conio.h>
void main( )
{
printf("%d  %d  %d", sizeof(char*), sizeof(int*),
   sizeof(float*));
getch();
}
```

Output:

```
4 4 4
```

Problem 58

Find the output of the following program?

```
#include<stdio.h>
#include<conio.h>
void main( )
{
char far *p1, ,near *p2, huge *p3;
printf("%d %d %d", sizeof(p1), sizeof(p2), sizeof(p3));
```

```
getch();
}
```

Output:

```
4 2 4
```

Problem 59

Is there any way to combine these statements?

```
char *ptr;
ptr = (char *) malloc (200);
```

Output:

```
char *ptr = (char *) malloc (200);
```

Problem 60

These two expressions are same or not

```
*ptr++ and ++ *ptr
```

Output:

```
No.
```

NOTE: *ptr++ increments the pointer and not the value pointed by it.

```
++*ptr increments the value being pointed to by ptr.
```

Problem 61

Write an another expression which can do the same job as ++*ptr?

Output:

```
(*ptr)++
```

Problem 62

Write the equivalent pointer expression for addressing the array element a[i] [j] [k] [l]?

Output:

```
*(*(*(*(a + i) + j) + k) + l)
```

Problem 63

If size of an integer is 4 bytes what will be the output of the following program?

```
#include <stdio.h>
#include <conio.h>
void main ( )
{
int a[] = {1, 2, 3, 4};
printf ("\n%d %d %d", sizeof (a), sizeof (*a), sizeof
    (a[0]));
getch();
}
```

Output:

```
16 4 4
```

Problem 64

Find the output of the following program assume that the stating location of an array is 1000 and size of an integer is 4 bytes?

```
#include <stdio.h>
#include <conio.h>
void main ( )
{
int a[3][4] = {
11, 12, 13, 14
15, 16, 17, 18,
19, 20, 21, 22
};
printf ("\n%u %u %u", a[0] + 1, * (a[0] + 1), * (*(a +
    0) + 1));
getch();
```

```
}
```

Output:

```
1004 4 4
```

Problem 65

Check the errors from the following program?

```
#include <stdio.h>
#include <conio.h>
void main ( )
{
char str[4] = "good solution";
getch();
}
```

Output:

```
No error.
```

NOTE: There is no error if array is out of index.

Problem 66

Find the output of the following program?

```
#include <stdio.h>
#include <conio.h>
void main ( )
{
int a[2][2][2] = {1, 2, 3, 4, 5, 6, 7, 8};
int *p, *q;
p = &a[1][1][1];
*q = ***a;
printf ("%d %d, *p, *q);
getch();
}
```

Output:

8 1

Problem 67

Find the output of the following program?

```
#include<stdio.h>
#include<conio.h>
void main( )
{
int a[]={1,2,3,4,5};
printf("%d%d%d%d%d", *a,*(a+0), *(0+a),a[0],0[a]);
getch();
}
```

Output:

1 1 1 1 1

Problem 68

Find the output of the following program?

```
#include<stdio.h>
#include<conio.h>
void main( )
{
int *ptr;
int a[]={1,2,3,4,5};
ptr=a;
printf("%d%d", a[2],ptr[2]);
getch();
}
```

Output:

3 3

Problem 69

Find the output of the following program?

```
#include<stdio.h>
#include<conio.h>
void main( )
{
int a[]={2.7,3.2,4.6.2,5};
int j, *ptr=a;
for (j=0;j<5;j++)
{
printf("%d", *ptr);
++ptr;
}
getch();
}
```

Output:

```
2 3 4 6 5
```

Problem 70

Find the output of the following program?

```
#include<stdio.h>
#include<conio.h>
void main( )
{
int j=20
int a[]={10,j,30,40,50},i,*ptr;
ptr=a;
for (i=0;i<5;i++)
{
```

```
printf("%d", *ptr);
ptr++;
}
getch();
}
```

Output:

```
10 20 30 40 50
```

Problem 71

Find the output of the following program?

```
#include<stdio.h>
#include<conio.h>
void main( )
{
int a[2][2]={1,2,3,4};
printf("%p%p%\n%p%p",&a[0][0],&a[0][1],&a[1][0],&a[1][1]);
getch();
}
```

Output:

```
No error
```

Problem 72

Find the output of the following program?

```
#include<stdio.h>
#include<conio.h>
void main( )
{
int a[2][3]={1,2,3,4,5,6};
printf("%d%d%d",a[1][2],1[a][2],*(*(arr+1)+2));
getch();
```

```
}
```

Output:

```
6 6 6
```

Problem 73

Check the errors from the following program?

```
#include<stdio.h>
#include<conio.h>
void main( )
{
int a[2][3]={1,2,3,4,5,6};
printf("%d%d%d",a[1][2],1[a][2],1[2][a]);
getch();
}
```

Output:

```
Error
```

NOTE: Invalid indirection

Problem 74

Find the output of the following program?

```
#include<stdio.h>
#include<conio.h>
void main( )
{
int a[] ={0,1,2,3,4};
int *p[]={a,a+1,a+2,a+3,a+4};
int **ptr=p;
printf("%d%p%p%p%p%p\n", **ptr, &ptr, *ptr, *p, p,
   a);
getch();
```

```
}
```

Output:

No error

Problem 75

Find the output of the following program?

```
#include<stdio.h>
#include<conio.h>
void main( )
{
int a[2][2][2]={1,2,3,4,5,6,7,8};
printf("%p%p%p\n:,a,a[0],a[0][0]);
printf("%p%p%p\n",a,a[1],a[1][1]);
printf("%d%d",a[0][0][0],a[1][1][1]);
getch();
}
```

Output:

No error

Problem 76

Check the errors from the following program?

```
#include<stdio.h>
#include<conio.h>
void main( )
{
void i,j;
void *ptr;
ptr=&i;
printf("ptr points to i\n");
ptr=&j;
```

```
printf("ptr now points to j");
getch();
}
```

Output:

```
Error
```

NOTE: size of i and j is unknown

Problem 77

Find the output of the following program?

```
#include<stdio.h>
#include<conio.h>
void main( )
{
char *str;
str= ("Khalsa", "College");
puts(str);
getch();
}
```

Output:

```
College
```

Problem 78

Find the output of the following program?

```
#include<stdio.h>
#include<conio.h>
void main( )
{
char str[]= "Hello Haha";
printf("%s %s %s", &str[5], &5[str], str+5);
getch();
```

```
}
```

Output:

```
Haha Haha Haha
```

Problem 79

Find the output of the following program?

```
#include<stdio.h>
#include<conio.h>
void main( )
{
char str[]= "Hello Dear!";
printf("%c %c %c", str[6], 6[str], *(str+6));
getch();
}
```

Output:

```
D D D
```

Problem 80

Find the output of the following program?

```
#include<stdio.h>
#include<conio.h>
void main( )
{
printf("Size of string is %d\n" sizeof("Hello Dear"));
printf("The string is allocated memory starting at
   %p", & "Hello Dear!");
getch();
}
```

Output:

```
The size of string is 11
The string is allocated memory starting at 2A4F: 00AD
```

Problem 81

Find the output of the following program?

```
#include<stdio.h>
#include<conio.h>
void main( )
{
char *str1 = “Ikvinderpal”;
char *str2 = “Singh”;
char *str3;
str3 = strcat ( str1, str2 );
printf ( “\n%s”, str3 );
getch();
}
```

Output:

```
No error.
```

Problem 82

Check the errors from the following program?

```
#include<stdio.h>
#include<conio.h>
void main( )
{
char a[8] = “Triangle”;
int i;
for ( i = 0 ; i <= 7 ; i++ )
printf ( “\n%d”, *a);
a++;
getch();
}
```

Output:

```
Error.
```

NOTE: Array cannot be incremented.

Problem 83

Explain the difference in the following two statements?

```
char *chr = "Lovedeep";
char chr[] = "Lovedeep";
```

Output:

```
No.
```

NOTE: In the first statement, the character pointer chr stores the address of the string "Lovedeep". The pointer chr can be made to point to some other character string.

In the second statement, memory space for 9 characters be allocated and the name of the location is chr. Thus it specifies the size as well as initial values of the characters in array chr.

Problem 84

Find the output of the following program?

```
#include<stdio.h>
#include <conio.h>
void main( )
{
char a[] = "Sukhwant";
char *p = "Lovedeep";
a = "Lovedeep";
p = "Sukhwant";
printf("\n%s %s", a, p);
getch();
}
```

Output:

```
Error
```

Problem 85

Find the output of the following program?

```
#include<stdio.h>
#include <conio.h>
void main( )
{
char *ptr[2] = {"Amritsar","Khalsa College"};
swap (ptr[0], ptr[1]);
printf("%s\n%s", ptr[0], ptr[1]);
getch();
}
swap (char *ch1, char *ch2)
{
char *ch;
ch = ch1;
ch1 = ch2;
ch2 = ch;
}
```

Output:

```
Khalsa College
Amritsar
```

Problem 86

Find the output of the following program?

```
#include<stdio.h>
#include <conio.h>
void main( )
```

```
{
char *ptr1 = "Amritsar", *ptr2;
ptr2 = ptr1;
ptr1 = "Khalsa College";
printf("%s %s", ptr1, ptr2);
getch();
}
```

Output:

```
Khalsa College Amritsar
```

Problem 87

Find the output of the following program?

```
#include<stdio.h>
#include <conio.h>
void main( )
{
printf("%u %s", &"Avtar", &"Avtar");
getch();
}
```

Output:

```
1012 Avtar
```

Problem 88

Correct the following program?

```
#include<stdio.h>
#include <conio.h>
#include<string.h>
void main( )
{
char *str1 = "Khalsa";
```

```
char *str2 = "College";
char *str3;
str3 = strcat (str1, str2);
printf("\n%s", str3);
getch();
}
```

Output:

```
#include<stdio.h>
#include <conio.h>
#include<string.h>
void main( )
{
char str1[15]= "Khalsa";
char *str2 = "College";
char *str3;
str3=strcat(str1, str2);
printf("\n%s", str3);
getch();
}
```

Problem 89

Write the code given below strcpy( ) function into one line.

```
strcpy(char *ptr, char *ptr1)
{
while (*ptr1)
{
*ptr = *ptr1;
ptr++;
ptr1++;
```

```
}
*ptr = '\0';
}
```

Output:

```
strcpy (char *ptr, char *ptr1)
{
while (*ptr++ = *ptr1++);
}
```

Problem 90

Find the output of the following program?

```
#include<stdio.h>
#include <conio.h>
void main( )
{
char *str[] = {"Sukhwant", "Baljinder", "Kawaljit",
   "Avtar", "Jagbir"};
printf("%d %d", sizeof(str), strlen(str[0]));
getch();
}
```

Output:

```
20 8
```

NOTE: Size of a pointer is 4 bytes

Problem 91

Write a C program to find the length of each string in the program above?

Output:

```
#include<stdio.h>
#include <conio.h>
```

```
#include<string.h>
void main( )
{
char *str[] = {"Sukhwant", "Baljinder", "Kawaljit",
   "Avtar", "Jagbir"};
int i;
for (i = 0; i<=4, i++)
printf("\n%s %d", str[i], strlen(str[i]));
getch();
}
```

Problem 92

What is the difference in the following declarations?

```
char str[] = "Amritsar";
char *ptr = "Amritsar";
```

Output:

Here str is an array big enough to hold the message and the '\0' following the message. Individual characters within the array can be changed but the address of the array will remain same.

On the other hand, ptr is a pointer, initialized to point to a string constant. The pointer ptr may be modified to point to another string, but if you attempt to modify the string at which ptr is pointing the result is undefined.

Problem 93

Find the output of the following program?

```
#include<stdio.h>
#include<conio.h>
void main( )
{
```

```
char str[ ] = "Well Defined";
char temp[25];
char *s, *t;
s = str;
while ( *s != '\0' )
*s++ = *t++;
printf ( "\n%s", temp );
getch();
}
```

Output:

```
Garbage string
```

Problem 94

Find the output of the following program?

```
#include<stdio.h>
#include <conio.h>
#include<string.h>
void main( )
{
static char str[] = "Welcome!";
printf("%d", *(str + strlen (str)));
getch();
}
```

Output:

```
0
```

Problem 95

Check the errors from the following program?

```
#include<stdio.h>
#include<conio.h>
```

```
void main( )
{
char str[5][20]={"Foxpro", "Java", "VB", "C", "C++"};
int i; char *ptr;
ptr=str[3];
str[3] = str[4];
str[4] = ptr;
for(i=0;i<=4;i++)
printf("%s\n", str[i]);
getch();
}
```

Output:

Error

NOTE: L-value required

Problem 96

Find the output of the following program?

```
#include<stdio.h>
#include<conio.h>
void main( )
{
char str[][]={"Foxpro", "Java", "VB", "C", "C++"};
int i; char *ptr;
ptr=str[3];
str[3] = str[4];
str[4]=ptr;
for(i=0;i<=4;i++)
printf("%s\n", str[i]);
getch();
}
```

Output:

```
Foxpro
Java
VB
C
C++
```

Problem 97

Find the output of the following program?

```
#include<stdio.h>
#include<conio.h>
void main( )
{
char str[5][20]={"Foxpro", "Java", "VB", "C", "C++");
 int i; char *ptr;
ptr=str[0];
while(*ptr++!=32);
for(i=0;i<5;i++)
{
puts (str[0]);
strcpy(ptr, str[i+1]);
}
getch();
}
```

Output:

```
Visual Foxpro
Visual Java
Visual VB
Visual C
Visual C++
```

Problem 98

Check the errors from the following program?

```
#include <stdio.h>
#include <conio.h>
void main ( )
{
int a[3][3] = {1, 2, 3, 4};
printf ("%d", *(*(*(a))));
getch();
}
```

Output:

Error.

NOTE: Invalid indirection.

Problem 99

If a variable is a pointer to a structure, then which of the following operator is used to access data members of the structure through the pointer variable?

Output:

à

Problem 100

Find the output of the following program?

```
#include <stdio.h>
#include <conio.h>
void main ( )
{
char str[20] = "Hit";
```

```
char * const p = str;
*p = 'K';
printf ("%s", str);
getch();
}
```

Output:

```
Kit
```

Problem 101

The operator used to get value at address stored in a pointer variable is

Output:

*

Problem 102

Find the output of the following program?

```
#include<stdio.h>
#include<conio.h>
void main( )
{
char str1[]= "Hello";
char *str2= "Hello";
printf("%d %d\n", sizeof(str1), sizeof(str2));
printf("%d %d", sizeof(*str1), sizeof(*str2));
getch();
}
```

Output:

```
6 2
1 1
```

Problem 103

Find the output of the following program?

```
#include<stdio.h>
#include<conio.h>
void main( )
{
char *str;
str= "Khalsa", "College";
puts(str);
getch();
}
```

Output:

```
Khalsa
```

Problem 104

A pointer is

1. A keyword used to create variables.
2. A variable that stores address of an instruction.
3. A variable that stores address of other variable.
4. All of the above.

Output:

3

Problem 105

Explain the statement `*j = &i.`

Output:

`j is a pointer to an int and stores address of i.`

Problem 106

Find the output of the following program?

```
#include <stdio.h>
#include <conio.h>
power (int **)
void main ( )
{
int i = 8, *ptr; /* suppose the address of the variable
   i is                    1000 */
ptr = &i;
i = power (&ptr);
printf ("%d", i);
getch();
}
power (int **p)
{
int q;
q = **p ***p;
return (q);
}
```

Output:

64

Problem 107

Find the output of the following program?

```
#include<stdio.h>
#include<conio.h>
void main( )
{
int i, len;
char *ptr= "College";
len=strlen(ptr);
```

```
for(i=0;i<len;i++)
{
puts(ptr);
ptr++;
}
getch();
}
```

Output:

```
College
ollege
llege
lege
ege
ge
e
```

Problem 108

Find the output of the following program?

```
#include<stdio.h>
#include<conio.h>
str(char(*)[10]);
void main( )
{
char a[][10]={"Khalsa", "College");
str(a);
printf("%s %s", a[0], a[1]);
getch();
}
str(char (*a[10])
{
```

```
strcpy(a[1], "Amritsar");
}
```

Output:

```
Khalsa Amritsar
```

Problem 109

Find the output of the following program?

```
#include<stdio.h>
#include <conio.h>
#include<string.h>
void main( )
{
char ch1[] = "Welcome";
char ch2[10];
char *p, *p1;
p1=ch1;
p=ch2;
while (*p = *p1)
*p++ = *p1++;
printf("%s", ch2);
getch();
}
```

Output:

```
Welcome
```

Problem 110

Find the output of the following program?

```
#include<stdio.h>
#include <conio.h>
void main( )
```

```
{
char str[20], *str1;
printf("Enter string");
scanf ("%s", str);
str1 = str;
while (*str1 != '\0')
{
if(*str1 >=97 && *str1 <= 122)
*str1 = *str1 - 32;
str1++;
}
getch();
}
```

Input:

```
Enter string: welcome
```

Output:

```
WELCOME
```

Problem 111

Find the output of the following program?

```
#include<stdio.h>
#include <conio.h>
void main( )
{
char *names[]={
"Sukhwant",
"Jagbir",
"Baljinder",
"Kawaljit",
"Avtar"
```

```
};
int i;
char *str;
str=names[3];
names[3] = names[4];
names[4] = str;
for (i = 0; i <= 4; i++)
printf("%s", names[i];
getch();
}
```

Output:

```
Sukhwant Jagbir Baljinder Avtar Kawaljit
```

Problem 112

Check the errors from the following program?

```
#include<stdio.h>
#include <conio.h>
void main( )
{
char *s;
char *f( );
s = f( );
printf("%s", s);
getch();
}
char *f( )
{
char buffer [30];
strcpy (buffer "RAM-Random Access Memory");
return (buffer);
```

```
}
```

Output:

```
No error
```

Problem 113

How will you dynamically allocate a 1-D array of integers?

Output:

```
#include<stdio.h>
#include <conio.h>
#include<stdlib.h>
#define I 10
void main( )
{
int *p, i;
p = (int *) malloc (I * sizeof (int));
for (i = 0; i<I; i++)
{
p[i] = i;
printf("\n%d", p[i]);
}
getch();
}
```

Problem 114

How will you dynamically allocate a 2-D array of integers?

Output:

```
#include<stdio.h>
#include <conio.h>
#include<stdlib.h>
#define ROW 3
```

```
#define COL 4
void main( )
{
int *p, i, j;
p = = (int *) malloc (ROW * COL * sizeof(int));
for (i = 0; i<ROW; i++)
{
for (j = 0; j <COL; j++)
{
p[i * COL +j] = i;
printf ("%d", p[i * COL + j]);
}
printf ("\n");
}
getch();
}
```

Problem 115

How will you dynamically allocate a 2-D array of integers such that we are able to access any element using 2 subscripts, as in a[i][j]?

Output:

```
#include<stdio.h>
#include <conio.h>
#include<stdlib.h>
#define ROW 3
#define COL 4
void main( )
{
int *p, i, j;
p = = (int *) malloc (ROW * sizeof(int));
```

```
for (i = 0; i<ROW; i++)
{
for (j = 0; j <COL; j++)
{
p[i][j] = i;
printf ("%d", p[i][j]);
}
printf ("\n");
}
getch();
}
```

Problem 116

How many bytes will be allocated by the following code?

```
#include<stdio.h>
#include <conio.h>
#include<stdlib.h>
#define ROW 3
#define COL 4
void main( )
{
int (*p) [COL];
p = (int (*) [COL]) malloc (ROW * sizeof (*p));
getch();
}
```

Output:

24 bytes

NOTE: if integer is 2 bytes wide

Problem 117

Explain the statement given below:

```
float **** fun (float ***);
```

Output:

```
A function that receives a pointer to a pointer to a
   float and returns a pointer to a pointer to a
   pointer to a pointer to a float.
```

Problem 118

Which of the following is the correct output for the code snippet given below?

```
#include<stdio.h>
#include <conio.h>
#include<stdlib.h>
#define ROW 3
#define COL 4
void main( )
{
int (*p) [COL];
p = (int (*) [COL]) malloc (ROW * sizeof (*p));
printf ("%d %d", sizeof (p), sizeof (*p));
getch();
}
```

Output:

```
2 8
```

NOTE: if integer is 2 bytes wide

Problem 119

How will you dynamically allocate a 3-D array of integers?

Output:

```
#include<stdio.h>
#include <conio.h>
#include<stdlib.h>
#define X 3
#define Y 4
#define Z 5
void main( )
{
int (*p, i, j, k;
p = (int ***) malloc [X * sizeof (int **));
for (i = 0; i <X; i++)
{
p = (int **) malloc [Y * sizeof (int **));
for (j = 0; j <X; j++)
p[i] [j] = (int *) malloc (Z * sizeof (int));
}
for (k = 0; k <Z; k++)
{
for (i = 0; i < X; i++)
{
for (j = 0; j < Y; j++)
{
p[i][j][k] = i + j + k;
printf("%d", p[i][j][k]);
}
printf ("\n");
}
printf("\n\n");
}
```

```
getch();
}
```

Problem 120

Find the output of the following program?

```
#include <stdio.h>
#include <conio.h>
#include <stdlib.h>
void main( )
{
int *p;
p = (int *) malloc (20);
printf ("%d", sizeof (p));
free (p);
getch();
}
```

Output:

2

B. FILL IN THE BLANKS

1. Pointer is called .... variable.
2. A pointer is a variable that contains as its value the .... of another variable.
3. The three values that can be used to initialize a pointer are ...., ... and ....
4. Pointer and function are related using two techniques .... and ....
5. The object pointed to by a pointer can be indirectly accessed by using .... operator.
6. Pointers allow the direct access of ....

7. A variable is used as operand for .... pointer operator.
8. A .... memory allocation is done at compilation time.
9. The number of arguments used in the function malloc( ) is ....
10. The memory allocated by calloc( ) function contains the storage initialized to ....
11. Pointer operators are .... and ....
12. Indirection operator * returns ....
13. The expression *p++ is evaluated from ....
14. The expression a[i] + j is equivalent to ....
15. The size of the array of pointers in the declaration float *x[15]; represents the number of .... in the two dimensional array x.
16. The expression equivalent to the expression a[3][2], where a is an integer array is ....
17. The comparison of two null pointers always result in ....
18. The .... operator is used with a pointer to dereference the address contained in the pointer.
19. Pointers to pointers are a term used to describe ....
20. .... is used to allocate memory in C programming language.
21. A pointer variable must be assigned a valid .... before using it.
22. C provides an operator .... to find out the required space to store the data object of a particular data type.
23. The function .... is capable of increasing the memory space already allocated.
24. A function name itself represents the .... of that function.
25. The recursive use of a pointer declaration makes it a ....

Answers

1. Memory addressable 2. address.

3. 0, NULL, an address.
4. call by value , call by reference.
5. dereference
6. memory
7. address of
8. static
9. one
10. zero
11. * and &
12. rvalue
13. right to left
14. *(a+i)+j
15. rows
16. *(*(arr+3)+2)
17. one
18. address(&)
19. pointers whose contents are the address of another pointer
20. malloc()
21. address
22. sizeof
23. realloc( )
24. address
25. complex declaration

C. TRUE OR FALSE

State whether each of the following is true or false

1. Pointer constants are drawn from the set of addresses for a computer.
2. Pointers are declared using the address operator as a token.
3. The value of a pointer type is always an address.
4. A pointer always refers to a scalar data type.
5. Using pointers as parameters allow call by reference in C.
6. The value of the memory space allocated by using the malloc function is implicitly initialized to zero.
7. An integer can be added to a pointer.
8. Pointers can be multiplied.
9. The name of an array itself is a fixed address and it is not a variable.
10. An array name can be used at the lefthand side of an assignment.
11. A two-dimensional array can be defined as a one-dimensional array of pointers.

12. In array of pointers, the rows of the array may be of different length.
13. Careless allocation of memory of the compile time leads to memory leak.
14. A function is not a variable, but it has an address.
15. The execution of programs using pointers is faster than the programs without using pointers.
16. A pointer can be used as a scalar data type as well as a derived data type.
17. Address of operator can be applied to pointer variables only.
18. If x is an int variable, sizeof x may be used to find the number of bytes used to hold an int data type.
19. Given a pointer to an array element, ptr, ptr – 5 is a pointer to the value 5 elements toward the beginning of the array.
20. Adding 1 to a pointer increases the address stored in it by 1 byte.
21. In an array of pointers, the column size is mentioned in its declaration whereas in a pointer to an array the row size is mentioned.
22. The parameter declaration int* a can be used to declare an array of integers passed to a function.
23. Dynamic memory allocation is done at execution time.
24. Adding two pointers is an invalid operation.
25. The operand of address of operator & may be a register variable.
26. An rvalue expression can be used only to supply a value.
27. Dynamically allocated memory can only be referred to through pointers.

Answers

1. True	2. False	3. True	4. False
5. False	6. False	7. True	8. False
9. True	10. False	11. True	12. True

13. True	14. True	15. True	16. True
17. False	18. True	19. False	20. False
21. False	22. True	23. True	24. True
25. False	26. True	27. True	

D. OBJECTIVE TYPE QUESTIONS

1. Identify the invalid expression for given float x = 2.14, *y = &x;
   (a) &y (b) *&x
   (c) **&y (d) (*&)x
2. The operand of the address of operator is
   (a) a constant (b) an expression
   (c) a named region of storage (d) a register variable
3. How does compiler differentiate address of operator from bitwise AND operator?
   (a) by using the number of operands and position of operands
   (b) by seeing the declarations
   (c) both a and b
   (d) by using the value of the operand
4. How does compiler differentiate indirection operator from multiplication operator?
   (a) by using the number of operands
   (b) by seeing the position of operand
   (c) both a and b
   (d) by using the value of the operand
5. The address of operator returns
   (a) the address of its operand (b) lvalue
   (b) both options a and b (d) rvalue
6. The indirection operator returns
   (a) the data object stored in the address represented by its operand
   (b) lvalue

(c) both a and b

(d) rvalue

7. Pointer variable may be assigned

(a) an address value represented in hexadecimal

(b) an address value represented in octal

(c) the address of another variable

(d) An address value represented in binary

8. A pointer value refers to

(a) an integer constant (b) a float value

(c) any valid address in memory

(d) any ordinary variable

9. Identify the correct declaration of pointer variables p1, p2.

(a) int p1, p2 (b) int *p1, p2;

(c) int p1, *p2; (d) int *p1, *p2;

10. The operators exclusively used in connection with pointers are

(a) *and/ (b) & and *

(c) & and | (d) – and >

11. The operand of indirection operator is

(a) pointer variable (b) pointer expression

(c) both a and b (d) ordinary variable

12. The operand of address of operator may be

(a) an ordinary variable (b) an array variable

(c) a pointer variable (d) Any one of the above

13. Identify the invalid lvalue given int x, *p=&x;

(a) *(p + 1) (b) *(p – 3)

(c) both a and b (d) &x

14. After the execution of the statement int x; the value of x is

(a) 0 (b) undefined

(c) 1 (d) -1

15. Pointer variable may be initialized using
    (a) static memory allocation (b) dynamic memory allocation
    (c) both a and b (d) a positive integer
16. Identify the invalid pointer operator.
    (a) & (b) *
    (c) >> (d) none of the above
17. Assume 2 bytes for int, 4 bytes for float and 8 bytes for double data types respectively, how many bytes are assigned to the following pointer variables?

int *ip; float *fp; double *dp;

    (a) 2 bytes for ip, 4 bytes for fp and 8 bytes for dp
    (b) 2 bytes for all pointer variable ip, fp and dp
    (c) one byte for ip, 2 bytes for fp and 4 bytes for dp
    (d) 2 bytes for ip and 8 bytes for each fp and dp
18. The operand of indirection operator is
    (a) pointer variable (b) pointer expression
    (c) both options a and b (d) ordinary variable
19. The operand of address of operator may be
    (a) an ordinary variable (b) an array variable
    (c) a pointer variable (d) any one of the above
20. In the expression *cp + +
    (a) * cp is evaluated first and *cp is incremented by 1
    (b) * cp is evaluated first and cp is incremented by 1
    (c) cp is incremented by 1 first and * is applied
    (d) cp is incremented by 1 first and * is applied to the previous value of cp
21. The pointers can be used to achieve
    (a) call by function (b) call by reference
    (c) call by name (d) call by procedure

22. The first argument argc in main( ) counts
    (a) the number of command line strings including the execution command
    (b) the number of command line strings excluding the execution command
    (c) the number of lines in a program
    (d) the number of characters in a program
23. The arguments in main( ) function are known as
    (a) program parameters
    (b) command line arguments
    (c) both options a and b
    (d) memory in-line format conversion
24. The invalid address arithmetic is (are)
    (a) adding two pointers (b) multiplying two pointers
    (c) dividing two pointers (d) all the above
25. The invalid pointer arithmetic is (are)
    (a) shifting pointers using shift operators
    (b) addition of float or double values to printers
    (c) both options a and b
    (d) incrementing pointers
26. What memory function should be used to allocate memory in which all bits are initialized to 0 ?
    (a) calloc (b) malloc
    (c) alloc (d) memalloc
27. The amount of memory to be allocated for the following array of pointers

```
short *p[4];
```

    (a) no memory (b) 4 bytes
    (c) 6 bytes (d) 16 bytes

28. Which are valid?

(1) pointers can be added

(2) pointers can be subtracted

(3) integers can be added to pointers

(a) all correct
(b) only options (1) and (2)
(c) only option (3)
(d) only option (2) and (3)

29. int y[4] = { 6, 7, 8, 9 };

int *ptr = y + 2;

printf("%d\n", ptr[1]);

What is printed when the sample code above is executed?

(a) 7
(b) 8
(c) 9
(d) The code will not compile

30. A pointer to a pointer in a form of

(a) multiple indirection
(b) a chain of pointers
(c) both a and b
(d) None of these

31. Pointers are of

(a) integer data type
(b) character data type
(c) unsigned integer data types
(d) None of these

32. int y[4] = {5, 6, 7, 8};

Which of the following will declare a pointer variable that points to the array in the sample code above?

(a) int *(yptr[4]) = &y;
(b) int (yptr *) [4] = &y;
(c) int (*yptr) [4] = &y;
(d) int *yptr [4] = &y;

33. int x[] = {1, 2, 3, 4, 5};

int *ptr, **ptr2;

ptr = x;

ptr2 = &ptr;

Referring to the sample code above, how would you update x[2] to 10 using ptr2?

(a) **(ptr2 + 2) = 10;

(b) *(&ptr2 + 2) = 10;

(c) *((ptr2 + 2) = 10;

(d) (**ptr2 + 2) = 10;

34. main( )

```
{
char x[25], y[25], *p = y;
strcpy [x, "BIRTHDAY");
strcpy (y, "HAPPY");
p=x;
strcpy (x, "LOVER");
*p = 'H';
printf ("p=%s\n", p);
}
```

What will be the output when the sample code above is executed?

(a) p = HOVERDAY (b) p=LOVERDAY

(c) p=HOVER (d) p=HIRTHDAY

35. int *x;

x = (int *) 15;

Is the above code legal?

(a) Yes. A new memory space will be allocated to hold the number 15

(b) No. This would assign the number 15 to an unallocated space in memory

(c) Yes. Upon initialization, the number 15 will be stored in a special pointer memory address space.

(d) Yes. The pointer x will point at the integer in memory location 15.

36. What memory function should be used to allocate memory in which all bits are initialized to 0?

(a) calloc (b) malloc

(c) alloc (d) memalloc

37. What is the difference between the malloc and calloc functions?
    (a) Memory allocated by calloc does not need to be freed and memory allocated by malloc does
    (b) calloc returns a pointer to char and malloc returns a void pointer
    (c) calloc initializes the memory returned and malloc does not
    (d) calloc can allocate memory for an array and malloc cannot
38. int *const size = 10;

    If the address of size is 3024, then size++ is
    (a) 11 (b) 3025
    (c) 3026 (d) invalid
39. int *ptr (int *) malloc (sizeof (int));

    ptr += 3;

    If ptr points to the memory location 1000 and after execution of the statement ptr += 3, ptr will point to the memory location .... (Assume 32 bits for int).
    (a) 1006 (b) 1003
    (c) 1010 (d) none
40. The amount of memory to be allocated for the following array of pointers.

    short *p[4];
    (a) no memory (b) 4 bytes
    (c) 6 bytes (d) 16 bytes
41. int x = 1;

    int *ptr = malloc (sizeof(int));

    ptr = &x;

    x = 2;

    *ptr = 3;

    Is there anything wrong with the above code?
    (a) No, x will be set to 2 (b) No, x will be set to 3

(c) Yes, There will be a memory overwrite

(d) Yes, There will be a memory leak

42. int *ptr = malloc (5 * sizeof(int));

realloc(ptr, 10 * sizeof(int));

for (i=0; i<10; i++) {ptr[i] = 0;}

Assuming realloc succeeds, what effect will the above sample have on the rest of the program?

(a) The pointer "ptr" will contain an array of 10 that is initialized to 0 with no issues

(b) This will result in a memory overwrite but no memory leak (c)This will result in both a memory overwrite

(d) This will result in both a memory leak and memory overwrite

43. int *array [3];

int (*ptr) [ ] = array;

int x = 2, y = 3, z = 4;

Referring to the sample code above, how would you assign the second pointer in the array 'ptr' to point to the value of y?

(a) (*ptr) [1]=y;
(b) (*ptr) [2] = &y;
(c) *ptr[2] = y;
(d) (*ptr) [1] = &tl

44.
```
main( )
{
int count = 0;
int matrix [5] [5];
register int *ptr;
int i, j;
for (i=0; i<5; i++)
for (j=0; j<5; j++) matrix [i] [j] = count++;
ptr = &matrix [1] [1];
printf ("&d\n", ptr[2]);
}
```

Referring to the sample above, what will be the value of ptr[2], after execution?

(a) 6 (b) 7

(c) 8 (d) 9

45. In the declaration int x[3][2][2] = {2, 3, 4, 5, 6, 7, 8, 9, 10, 11, 12, 13};

((*(x+2) + 1) + 1) represents

(a) the element 13

(b) the element 9

(c) the address of the element of 8

(d) the address of the element of 9

46. What is the result of the expression for the following declaration?

int A[ ] = {1, 2, 3, 4, 5};

*A + 1 - *A + 3

(a) 2 (b) -2

(c) 4 (d) none of the above

47. Which are valid?

(i) Pointers can be added

(ii) Pointers can be subtracted

(iii) Integers can be added to pointers

(a) all correct (b) only options (i) and (ii)

(c) only option (iii) (d) only options (ii) and (iii)

48. x = malloc (y). Which of the following statements is correct?

(a) x is the size of the memory allocated

(b) y points to the memory allocated

(c) x points to the memory allocated

(d) none of the above

49. p and q are pointers to the same type of data items. Which of these are valid?

(i) *(p+q) (ii) *(p-q) (iii) *p – *q

(a) all
(b) options (i) and (ii)
(c) options (iii) is valid sometimes
(d) none of the above

50. (i) int *i;
(ii) float *f;
(iii) char *c;
Which are the valid castings?
(a) options (i), (ii) and (iii)
(b) only options (i) and (iii)
(c) only option (iii)
(d) only options (i) and (ii)

51. Which one of the following is a true statement about pointers?
(a) They are always 32-bit values.
(b) For efficiency, pointer values are always stored in machine registers.
(c) With the exception of generic pointers, similarly typed pointers may be subtracted from each other.
(d) A pointer to one type may not be cast to a pointer to any other type.

52. Which one of the following statements allocates enough space to hold an array of 10 integers that are initialized to 0?
(a) int *ptr = (int *) malloc(10, sizeof(int));
(b) int *ptr = (int *) calloc(10, sizeof(int));
(c) int *ptr = (int *) malloc(10*sizeof(int));
(d) int *ptr = (int *) alloc(10*sizeof(int));

53. After the execution of the statement int x; the value of x is
(a) 0
(b) undefined
(c) 1
(d) -1

54. Pointer variable may be initialized using
(a) static memory allocation
(b) dynamic memory allocation
(c) both options a and b
(d) a positive integer

55. Identify the invalid pointer operator.
(a) & (b) *
(c) >> (d) none of the above
56. The number of arguments used in malloc( ) is
(a) 0 (b) 1
(c) 2 (d) 3
57. The number of arguments used in calloc( ) is
(a) 0 (b) 1
(c) 2 (d) 3
58. The number of arguments used in realloc( ) is
(a) 0 (b) 1
(c) 2 (d) 3
59. The function used for dynamic deallocation of memory is
(a) destroy( ) (b) delete( )
(c) free( ) (d) remove( )
60. The function call realloc(ptr, 0) is
(a) same as free(ptr)
(b) used to clear the values in the address represented by ptr
(c) used to set the value of ptr to be 0
(d) invalid
61. Identify the invalid expression.
(a) r = 20 (b) &r
(c) r + 15 (d) r/10
62. Identify the invalid expression.
(a) &274 (b) &(a + b)
(c) &(a*b) (d) all the above
63. Identify the wrong declaration statement.
(a) int *p, a = 10; (b) int a = 10, *p = &a;
(c) int *p = &a, a = 10 (d) options a and b

64. Identify the invalid expression given

    int num = 15, *p = #

    (a) *num (b) *(&num)

    (c) *&*num (d) **&p

65. Pointers are supported in

    (a) FORTRAN (b) PASCAL

    (c) C (d) Both options b and c

66. Pointer variable may be assigned

    (a) an address value represented in hexadecimal

    (b) an address value represented in octal

    (c) the address of another variable

    (d) an address value represented in binary

67. A pointer value refers to

    (a) an integer constant

    (b) a float value

    (c) any valid address in memory

    (d) any ordinary variable

68. Identify the correct declaration of pointer variables p1, p2.

    (a) int p1, p2; (b) int *p1, p2;

    (c) int p1, *p2; (d) int *p1, * p2;

69. The operators exclusively used in connection with pointers are

    (a) * and / (b) & and *

    (c) & and | (d) – and >

70. Identify the invalid expression for given register int r = 10;

    (a) r = 20 (b) &r

    (c) r + 15 (d) r / 10

71. Identify the invalid expression.

    (a) &274 (b) &(a + b)

    (c) &(a * b) (d) all the above

72. The operand of the address of operator is
    (a) a constant
    (b) an expression
    (c) a named region of storage
    (d) a register variable
73. The address of operator returns
    (a) the address of its operand (b) lvalue
    (c) both options a and b (d) rvalue
74. The indirection operator returns
    (a) the data object stored in the address represented by its operand
    (b) lvalue
    (c) both options a and b
    (d) rvalue
75. The number of arguments used in malloc( ) is
    (a) 0 (b) 1
    (c) 2 (d) 3
76. The number of arguments used in calloc( ) is
    (a) 0 (b) 1
    (c) 2 (d) 3
77. The number of arguments used in realloc( ) is
    (a) 0 (b) 1
    (c) 2 (d) 3
78. The function used for dynamic deallocation of memory is
    (a) destroy( ) (b) delete( )
    (c) free( ) (d) remove( )
79. The function call realloc(ptr, 0) is
    (a) same as free(ptr)
    (b) used to clear the values in the address represented by ptr
    (c) used to set the value of ptr to be 0
    (d) invalid

80. In the expression *cp++
   (a) *cp is evaluated first and *cp incremented by 1
   (b) *cp is evaluated first and cp is incremented by 1
   (c) cp is incremented by 1 first and * is applied
   (d) cp is incremented by 1 and * is applied to previous value of cp
81. The pointers can be used to achieve
   (a) call by function (b) call by reference
   (c) call by name (d) call by procedure
82. Given int *p1, **p2, ***p3, v = 25;
   p1 = &v; p2 = &p1; p3 = &p3;
   how to obtain the value of v using pointer variable?
   (a) *p1 (b) **p2
   (c) **p3 (d) all the above
83. The declaration float *a[5]; is
   (a) an ordinary array (b) a pointer to an array
   (c) an array of pointers (d) pointer to an array
84. The declaration int (*p)[8]; is
   (a) an ordinary array (b) a pointer to an array
   (c) pointer t function (d) function returning pointer
85. Array of pointers such as int *p[5]; is used for
   (a) fixed row size and varying column size
   (b) fixed row size and fixed column size
   (c) varying row size and fixed column size
   (d) varying row size and varying column size
86. Pointer to array such as int (*a)[8]; is used for
   (a) fixed row size and varying column size
   (b) fixed row size and fixed column size
   (c) varying row size and fixed column size
   (d) varying row size and varying column size

87. Given float x[5][5]; float (*y) [5]; the assignment of the array x to the pointer variable y may be done as

    (a) y = &x; (b) y = x;

    (c) y[0] = x; (d) *y=x;

88. Given float x[5][10], *y[5]; the assignment of the array x to y is done as

    (a) y = x;

    (b) y[0] = x; y[1] = x[1]; ...; y[4] = x[4];

    (c) y[10] = x[0]; y[1] = x[1]; y[4] = x[4];

    (d) both options b and c

89. Given char *p = "ANSI C"; identify the expression returning the value C.

    (a) p[5] (b) *("ANSI C" + 5)

    (c) "ANSI C"[5] (d) all the above

90. Given char *t[10]; identify the correct statement.

    (a) strcpy (t[0], "BASIC"); (b) t[0] = "JAVA";

    (c) both options a and b (d) none of the above

91. Given char (*t) [10]; t = (char *) malloc (50); identify the illegal statement.

    (a) t[0] = "BASIC"; (b) strcpy (t[4], "FORTRAN");

    (c) strcpy (t[0], "JAVA") (d) both b and c

92. Identify the arguments of main( )

    (a) int argc (b) char 8argv [ ]

    (c) both a and b (d) no arguments are allowed

93. Which is the correct function header for function main( )?

    (a) main(int argc, char *argv [])

    (b) main(int argc, char **argv)

    (c) main(int argc, char *av[])

    (d) all the above

94. The first argument argc in main( ) counts
   (a) the number of command line strings including the execution command
   (b) the number of command line strings excluding the execution command
   (c) the number of lines in a program
   (d) the number of characters in a program
95. The arguments in main( ) function are known as
   (a) program parameters
   (b) command line arguments
   (c) both a and b
   (d) memory in-line format conversion
96. The argument argc[] is used to
   (a) count the number of command line arguments
   (b) pass strings to the programs including the execution command
   (c) both a and b
   (d) pass strings to the programs excluding the execution command
97. The argc in main( ) is used to
   (a) count the number of command line arguments
   (b) pass strings to the programs
   (c) both a and b
   (d) count the number of lines in a program
98. When applied to a variable, what does the unary "&" operator yield?
   (a) the variable's value   (b) the variable's address
   (c) the variable's format   (d) the variable's right value
99. Which of the following is the most accurate statement about runtime memory?
   1. Memory is allocated by using malloc( )
   2. Memory is freed by a garbage collector

3. Allocated memory can be freed by calling free( )

(a) option 1 only (b) options 2 only

(c) both options 1 and 2 (d) both options 1 and 3

100. Which of the following is True about pointers?

1. Pointers do not require memory storage.
2. The size of a pointer depends on the type of the variable it points to.

(a) option 1 only (b) options 2 only

(c) options 1 and 2 (d) neither option 1 nor 2

101. If ptr1 and ptr2 are valid pointers in the same array, then which of the following statements is valid?

(a) ptr1 + 2 (b) ptr1 – ptr2

(c) ptr1 * ptr2 (d) both a and b

102. char *x;

x = "SHARE";

Is the above code valid?

(a) Yes. A new memory space will be allocated to hold the string "SHARE"

(b) No. It would assign the string "SHARE" to an unallocated space in memory

(c) Yes. The pointer x will point to the memory location created for the constant "SHARE"

(d) No. This syntax is not allowed

103. char *x = NULL;

printf ("%s\n", x);

What will be the behaviour of the sample code above?

(a) This will not compile. A pointer cannot be initialized to NULL

(b) The result will fall into "undefined behaviour" and be unpredictable

(c) A "0" will be printed

(d) Nothing will be printed

104. Following code in C.

```
char fruit [] = "Orange";
char *ptr;
ptr = fruit;
```

What will be the output for the following expression?

printf ("&c", *(ptr + 2));

(a) r (b) a

(c) n (d) none

105. In the given code:

```
int a[50];
int *ptr;
ptr = a;
```

To access the 7th element of the array which of the following is incorrect?

(a) *(a+6) (b) a[6]

(c) ptr[6] (d) *(*ptr+6)

106.
```
main( )
{
int a[5] = {-1, -1, 3, 4, 5};
int *b;
b = &a[2];
}
```

Then the value of b[-1] is:

(a) 4 (b) 3

(c) -1 (d) -2

107.
```
main( )
{
int a = 5, *ptr;
ptr = &a;
printf ("%d", ++*ptr);
```

}

Then output might be:

(a) 6 (b) 5

(c) 0 (d) none

108. int x, array[10];

From the sample above, which of the following is not a valid initialization for ptr?

(a) int *ptr = *array; (b) int *ptr = 9 + array;

(c) int *ptr = &x; (d) int *ptr = (int *) 0x1000;

109. In the declaration double (*pf)();

(a) pf is a pointer to a function

(b) pf is a function returning pointer

(c) pf is a pointer to array

(d) pf is an array of pointers

110. In the declaration double *f();

(a) f is a pointer to a function

(b) f is a function returning a pointer

(c) f is an array of function

(d) f is an pointer to array

111. Identify the invalid assignment, for given int *p, x;

(a) p = 0; (b) p = 255864u;

(c) p = &x;

(d) *p = 10; /* assume valid pointer is already assigned to p*/

112. The operations that can be performed on pointers are

(a) addition or subtraction of a pointer and an integer

(b) assignment of pointer using pointer expression

(c) assignment of the value 0 to a pointer

(d) all the above

113. The invalid address arithmetic is (are)

(a) adding two pointers

(b) multiplying two pointers
(c) dividing two pointers
(d) all the above

114. The invalid pointer arithmetic is (are)
(a) shifting pointers using shift operators
(b) addition of float or double values to printers
(c) both a and b
(d) incrementing pointers

115. The declaration float(*f[5])(); is
(a) an array of pointers to a function returning float
(b) pointer to an array
(c) function returning pointer to array
(d) pointer to a function returning an array of pointers to float

116. The declaration float (*fp())(); is
(a) pointer fp returning float
(b) function fp returning a pointer to a function returning float
(c) function fp returning a pointer
(d) pointer to a function

117. The operators &, *, ++ and — have
(a) same precedence level and same associativity
(b) same associativity and different precedence level
(c) different precedence level and different associativity
(d) different precedence level and same associativity

118. Identify the invalid statement for given expression
float fnum [10];
(a) fnum + 4 (b) fptr[4]
(c) fnum = ++fptr (d) &fnum[4]

119. Identify the correct statement for given expression
float num [10];
(a) fnum is a pointer variable

(b) fnum is a fixed address and not a variable
(c) fnum is an array variable
(d) fnum is an address that can be modified

120. Given the declaration double prec[5]; the address of the element prec[2] is obtained by:
(a) &prec[2] (b) prec + 2
(c) both a and b (d) *(prec + 2)

121. Given the declaration int prec[5]; the element prec[2] is accessed by
(a) prec[2] (b) prec + 2
(c) *(prec + 2) (d) both a and c

122. Given float x[5][5]; the address of the element x[2][3] is obtained by
(a) &x[2][3] (b) x[2] + 3
(c) *(x + 2) + 3 (d) all the above

123. Given char s[4][10]; the element s[2][4] is accessed by
(a) s[2][4] (b) *(s[2] + 4)
(c) *(*(s + 2) + 4) (d) all the above

124. Given int a [5] [5]; identify the correct expression, yielding the starting element.
(a) *a[0] (b) **a
(c) a[0][0] (d) all the above

125. Given int x[5][10][8]; find the address of the element x[2][3][5].
(a) x[2][3] + 5 (c) *(x[2] + 3) + 5
(c) *(*(x+2)+3)+4) (d) all the above

126. Given int x[5][5][5]; find the address of the element x[2][3][5].
(a) x[2][3] + 5 (c) *(x[2] + 3) + 5
(c) *(*(x+2)+3)+4) (d) all the above

127. Given int a[5]; how to declare array in the function definition if the function call is sort(a).
(a) sort (int *a)

(b) sort(int a[5])
(c) both a and b
(d) sort (int a)

128. Pointers are supported in
(a) FORTRAN (b) PASCAL
(c) C (d) both options b and c

Answers

1. (d)	2. (c)	3. (a)	4. (c)	5. (a)
6. (c)	7. (c)	8. (c)	9. (d)	10. (b)
11 (c)	12. (d)	13. (d)	14. (b)	15. (c)
16. (c)	17. (b)	18. (c)	19. (d)	20. (d)
21. (b)	22. (a)	23. (c)	24. (d)	25. (c)
26. (a)	27. (d)	28. (c)	29. (c)	30. (c)
31. (a)	32. (c)	33. (c)	34. (c)	35. (d)
36. (a)	37. (c)	38. (d)	39. (d)	40. (d)
41. (c)	42. (d)	43. (a)	44. (c)	45. (a)
46. (c)	47. (c)	48. (c)	49. (c)	50. (a)
51. (c)	52. (c)	53. (b)	54. (c)	55. (c)
56. (b)	57. (c)	58. (c)	59. (c)	60. (a)
61. (b)	62. (d)	63. (c)	64. (a)	65. (d)
66. (c)	67. (c)	68. (d)	69. (b)	70. (b)
71. (d)	72. (c)	73. (a)	74. (c)	75. (b)
76. (c)	77. (c)	78. (c)	79. (a)	80. (d)
81. (b)	82. (d)	83. (c)	84. (b)	85. (a)
86. (c)	87. (b)	88. (d)	89. (d)	90. (b)
91. (a)	92. (c)	93. (d)	94. (a)	95. (c)
96. (b)	97. (a)	98. (b)	99. (d)	100. (d)
101. (d)	102. (c)	103. (b)	104. (b)	105. (d)

106. (c)	107. (a)	108. (a)	109. (a)	110. (b)
111. (b)	112. (d)	113. (d)	114. (c)	115. (a)
116. (b)	117. (a)	118. (c)	119. (b)	120. (c)
121. (d)	122. (d)	123. (d)	124. (d)	125. (d)
126. (d)	127. (c)	128. (d)		

CHAPTER 10

Structure and Union

A. CODE SNIPPETS

Problem 1

Check the errors from the following program?

```
#include<stdio.h>
#include<conio.h>
struct student
{
char ch ;
int rn ;
float fees ;
} ;
void disp(struct student);
void disp1(struct student*);
void main( )
{
struct student st = { 'C', 12, 12.54};
disp(st);
disp1(&st);
getch();
```

```
}
void disp(struct student st1)
{
printf ("\n%c %d %f", st1 -> ch, st1 -> rn, st1 ->
    fees);
}
void disp1(struct student *st1)
{
printf ("\n%c %d %f", v.ch, v.rn, v.fees);
}
```

Output:

```
Error.
```

NOTE: disp() used dot operator to access structure elements and disp1() used member selection operator to access structure elements.

Problem 2

Find the output of the following program?

```
#include<stdio.h>
#include<conio.h>
struct student
{
int rn;
struct student *ptr;
};
void main( )
{
struct student st1, st2;
st1.rn = 50;
st2.rn = 51;
st1.ptr = &st2;
```

```
st2.ptr = &st1;
printf ( "\n%d %d", st1.ptr -> rn, st2.ptr -> rn);
getch();
}
```

Output:

No error.

Problem 3

Check the errors from the following program?

```
#include<stdio.h>
#include<conio.h>
struct car
{
char *name;
char *model;
};
void main( )
{
struct car c1={"Tata", "Indica"}, c2 = {"Tata",
   "Indica"};
if(c1= =c2)
printf("Cars are same");
else
printf("Cars are different");
getch();
}
```

Output:

Error

NOTE: Illegal structure operation in main().

Problem 4

Find the output of the following program?

```
#include<stdio.h>
#include<conio.h>
struct car
{
char *name;
char *model;
};
void main( )
{
struct car c1={"Tata", "Indica"}, c2 = {"Tata",
   "Indica"};
if(c1.name= =c2.name && c1.model= = c2.model)
printf("Cars are same");
else
printf("Cars are different");
getch();
}
```

Output:

```
Cars are different
```

Problem 5

Find the output of the following program?

```
#include<stdio.h>
#include<conio.h>
struct car
{
char *name;
char *model;
```

```
};
void main( )
{
struct car c1={"Tata", "Indica"}, c2 = {"Tata",
   "Indica"};
if(strcmp(c1.name, c2.name)= =0 && (c1.model, c2.model)=
   =0)
printf("Cars are same");
else
printf("Cars are different");
getch();
}
```

Output:

```
Cars are same
```

Problem 6

Check the errors from the following program?

```
#include<stdio.h>
#include<conio.h>
struct values
{
int x;
int y;
int z;
};
void main( )
{
struct values v1, v2;
v1.x=v2.x=5;
v1.y=10; v2.y=20;
```

```
printf("Points in xy plane are:\n");
printf("v1(%d%d)\n", v1.x, v1.y);
printf("v2(%d%d)\n", v2.x, v2.y);
getch();
}
```

Output:

```
Error
```

Problem 7

Find the output of the following program?

```
#include<stdio.h>
#include<conio.h>
struct values
{
int x;
int y;
};
void main( )
{
struct values v ={2,3};
int *p1=&v.x, *p2=&v.y;
if(ptr2>ptr1)
printf("Ptr2 is greater than Ptr1\n");
else if(ptr1>ptr2)
printf("Ptr1 is greater than Ptr2\n");
else
printf("Both are same\n");
getch();
}
```

Output:

```
Ptr2 is greater than Ptr1
```

Problem 8

Find the output of the following program?

```
#include<stdio.h>
#include<conio.h>
struct values
{
int i, j;
};
void main( )
{
struct values v;
printf("Values are %d,%d", v.i, v.j);
getch();
}
```

Output:

```
Values are 10987 28712
```

Problem 9

Find the output of the following program?

```
#include<stdio.h>
#include<conio.h>
struct values
{
int i, j;
};
void main( )
{
```

```
struct values v={0};
printf("Values are %d,%d", v.i, v.j);
getch();
}
```

Output:

```
Values are 0 0
```

Problem 10

Find the output of the following program?

```
#include<stdio.h>
#include<conio.h>
struct values
{
int i, j;
};
void main( )
{
static struct values;
printf("Values are %d,%d", v.i, v.j);
getch();
}
```

Output:

```
Values are 0 0
```

Problem 11

Find the output of the following program?

```
#include<stdio.h>
#include<conio.h>
#include<alloc.h>
struct node
```

```
{
int data;
struct node *link;
};
void main( )
{
struct node* ptr, *temp;
ptr=(struct node*)malloc(sizeof(struct node));
ptr-> data=100;
temp=(struct node*)malloc (sizeof(structnode));
ptr->link=temp; temp->data=200;
temp=(struct node*)malloc(sizeof(struct node));
ptr->link->=temp; temp->data=300;
temp->link=NULL;
temp=ptr;
while(temp!=NULL)
{
printf("%d\t", temp->data);
temp=temp->link;
}
getch();
}
```

Output:

100 200 300

Problem 12

Find the output of the following program?

```
#include<stdio.h>
#include <conio.h>
void main( )
```

```
{
struct student
{
int s1: 1;
int s2: 2;
int s3: 4;
}s;
printf("%d", sizeof (s));
getch();
}
```

Output:

2

Problem 13

Find the output of the following program?

```
#include<stdio.h>
#include <conio.h>
void main( )
{
struct student
{
int s1: 1;
int s2: 4;
int s3: 4;
}s; = {1, 2, 2};
printf("%d %d %d", s.s1, s.s2, s.s3);
getch();
}
```

Output:

-1 2 2

Problem 14

Find the output of the following program?

```
#include<stdio.h>
#include <conio.h>
void main( )
{
enum student {s1 = 0, s2, s3, s4, s5} s;
printf("%d", sizeof (s));
getch();
}
```

Output:

2

Problem 15

Find the output of the following program?

```
#include<stdio.h>
#include <conio.h>
void main( )
{
struct student
{
char *name;
int age;
};
struct student st1= {"Ikvinder", 25};
struct student st2 = st1;
strupr (st2.name);
printf("\n%s", st1.name);
getch();
}
```

Output:

```
IKVINDER
```

Problem 16

Is there any error, in the following code?

```
#include<stdio.h>
#include <conio.h>
void main( )
{
struct student
{
char name[20];
int rn;
};
struct student st1 = {"Jasveen", 25};
struct student st2 = st1;
if (st1 = = st2)
printf("The structures are equal");
getch();
}
```

Output:

```
Error
```

NOTE: Comparison of structure is not done using = = and != operations.

Problem 17

Is there any error, in the following code?

Output:

```
#include<stdio.h>
#include <conio.h>
```

```
struct student
{
char name[20];
int rn;
};
structcmp (struct student, struct student);
void main( )
{
struct student st1 = {"Jasjit", 12};
struct student st2;
scanf("%s %d", st2.name, &st2.rn);
if(structcmp(st1, st2) = = 0)
printf("Structures are equal");
else
printf("Structures are unequal");
getch();
}
structcmp(struct student s1, struct student s2)
{
if (strcmp (s1.name, s2.name) = = 0)
if (s1.rn = = s2.rn)
return (0);
return (1);
}
```

Output:

```
No error
```

Problem 18

Find the output of the following program?

```
#include<stdio.h>
```

```
#include<conio.h>
struct values
{
int i;
int j;
};
void main( )
{
struct values v={12,14};
struct values *vptr=&v;
printf("Values are %d and %d", (*vptr).i, (*vptr).j);
printf("Values are %d and %d", vptr->i, vptr->j);
getch();
}
```

Output:

```
Values are 12 and 14
Values are 12 and 14
```

Problem 19

Check the errors from the following program?

```
#include<stdio.h>
#include<conio.h>
union mobile
{
char m1[10];
char m2[10];
char m3[10];
};
void main( )
{
```

```
union mobile m= {"9465560001", "9501076151",
   "9915700412"};
printf("Mobile number1 of my friend is %s\n", m.m1);
printf("Mobile number2 of my friend is %s", m.m2);
getch();
}
```

Output:

Error

Problem 20

Find the output of the following program?

```
#include<stdio.h>
#include<conio.h>
union values
{
int i;
int j;
};
void main( )
{
union values v;
v.i=20;
v.j=30;
printf("Values are %d,%d", v.i, v.j);
getch();
}
```

Output:

Values are 20 30

Problem 21

Find the output of the following program?

```
#include<stdio.h>
#include<conio.h>
#define struct union
struct datatype
{
char ch;
int i;
float f;
};
void main( )
{
printf("Size of defined structure type is %d",
   sizeof(struct datatype));
getch();
}
```

Output:

```
Size of defined structure datatype is 4
```

Problem 22

Check the errors from the following program?

```
#include<stdio.h>
#include<conio.h>
typdef struct union;
struct datatype
{
char ch;
int i;
float f;
```

```
};
void main( )
{
printf("Size of defined structure datatype is %d",
   sizeof(struct datatype));
getch();
}
```

Output:

Error

Problem 23

Find the output of the following program?

```
#include<stdio.h>
#include <conio.h>
void main( )
{
enum ways {w1 = -1, w2, w3 = 3, w4, w5, w6);
printf("%d %d %d %d %d %d", w1, w2, w3, w4, w5, w6);
getch();
}
```

Output:

-1 0 3 4 5 6

Problem 24

Check the errors from the following program?

```
#include<stdio.h>
#include <conio.h>
void main( )
{
enum ways {w1 = -1, w2, w3 = 3, w4, w5, w6);
```

```
printf("%d %d %d %d %d %d", ++w1, w2, ++w3, w4-, w5,
   w6);
getch();
}
```

Output:

```
Error
```

Problem 25

Find the output of the following program?

```
#include<stdio.h>
#include <conio.h>
void main( )
{
union value
{
int i, j;
};
union value v;
v.i = 100;
v.j = 200;
printf(""%d", v.i,v.j);
getch();
}
```

Output:

```
100 200
```

Problem 26

Is there any error, in the following code?

```
#include<stdio.h>
#include <conio.h>
```

```
void main( )
{
struct student
{
float fees : 2;
}s;
printf("%d", sizeof(s));
getch();
}
```

Output:

```
Error
```

NOTE: Bit fields can be set only for a signed int or an unsigned int not for float.

Problem 27

Is there any error, in the following code?

```
#include<stdio.h>
#include <conio.h>
void main( )
{
struct student
{
int rn : 20;
}s;
printf("%d", sizeof(s));
getch();
}
```

Output:

```
Error
```

NOTE: Bit field too large(not more than 16 bits).

Problem 28

Is there any error, in the following code?

```
#include<stdio.h>
#include <conio.h>
void main( )
{
struct student
{
char name[20];
float fees;
};
struct student st[5];
int i;
for (i = 0; i <= 4; i++)
scanf("%s %f", st[i].name, &st[i].fees);
getch();
}
```

Output:

Error

NOTE: Floating point formats not linked.

Problem 29

Is there any error, in the following code?

```
#include<stdio.h>
#include <conio.h>
struct student
{
int rn;
char name[30];
float fees;
```

```
}
void main (int argc, char *argv[])
{
struct student st;
scanf ("%d %s %f", &st.rn, st.name, &st.fees);
printf("%d %s %f", st.rn, st.name, st.fees);
getch();
}
```

Output:

Error

NOTE: Semicolon missing at the end of the structure declaration.

Problem 30

Is there any error, in the following code?

```
#include<stdio.h>
#include <conio.h>
void main( )
{
struct student
{
rollno: 5;
idno: 4;
};
printf("size = %d", sizeof(struct s));
getch();
}
```

Output:

Error

NOTE: Bit fields must be of the type signed int or unsigned int. We cannot defined type of rollno and idno.

Problem 31

Find the output of the following program?

```
#include<stdio.h>
#include<conio.h>
void main( )
{
struct address
{
int n;
char str[50];
char str1[50];
} a;
a.n = 10;
strcpy ( a.str, "Hello" ) ;
strcpy ( a.str1, "How are you" ) ;
printf ( "\n%u %u %u", &a.n, a.str, a.str1 ) ;
getch();
}
```

Output:

Address of each structure element would be printed out.

Problem 32

Find the output of the following program?

```
#include<stdio.h>
#include<conio.h>
struct address
{
int n;
char str[50];
```

```
char str1[50];
} a = { 2, "God is Great", "God help those who help
   themselves"};
void main( )
{
struct address a1, a2;
a1 = a;
a2 = a1;
printf ( "\n%d %s %s", a.n, a1.str, a2.str1);
getch();
}
```

Output:

2 God is Great God help those who help themselves

Problem 33

Check the errors from the following program?

```
#include<stdio.h>
#include<conio.h>
void main( )
{
struct student
{
char name[20];
int rn;
};
struct student st;
strcpy (st.name, "Ikvinder");
rn = 12;
printf ("\n%s %d", st.name, rn);
getch();
```

```
}
```

Output:

```
Error.
```

NOTE: Access the rollno like this way st.rn = 12.

Problem 34

Find the output of the following program?

```
#include<stdio.h>
#include<conio.h>
void main( )
{
struct
{
char bookname[20];
char author[40];
};
struct book b = { "Testing", "IP" };
printf ( "\n%s %d", b.bookname, b.author);
getch();
}
```

Output:

```
Error.
```

NOTE: Undefined structure book

Problem 35

Check the errors from the following program?

```
#include<stdio.h>
#include<conio.h>
struct library
{
```

```
char book[20];
char author[40];
int page;
} b[2] = {
"Testing", "Ikvinder", 450,
"Microprocessor", "Jagbir", 355
};
void main( )
{
int i;
for ( i = 1; i <=2; i++ )
printf ( "\n%s %s", b.signature, b.status );
getch();
}
```

Output:

Error.

NOTE: b[i].signature and b[i].status

Problem 36

What's the difference between a structure and a union?

Output:

A union is essentially a structure in which all of the fields overlap each other. At a time only one field can be used.

For Example:

```
struct student
{
char grade;
int rollno;
float fees;
```

```
double marks;
} st;
```

The storage of memory locations to these member are represented by using the structure be as below:

Structure Data Type Memory Allocation

2000	2001	2003	2007	2015
I	12	4.3	442.33333367	
←a→	←b→	←c→	←d→	

Total size= char + int + float + double= 1+2+4+8=15 bytes

The storage of memory locations to these member are represented by using the union be as below:

For Example:

```
union student
{
char grade;
int rollno;
float fees;
double marks;
} st;
```

Union Data Type Memory Allocation

1000				1008
I	12	4.3	442.33333367	

←a→ (1000 to end of first cell)
←b→ (1000 to end of second cell)
←c→ (1000 to end of third cell)
←d→ (1000 to 1008)

Total size= 8 bytes (all other data types share same memory)

Problem 37

Is it necessary that the size of all elements in a union should have same number of bits?

Output:

No.

NOTE: Union elements can be of different sizes.

Problem 38

Is there an easy way to print enumeration values symbolically?

Output:

No.

Problem 39

What is the use of bit fields in a structure declaration?

Output:

Bit fields are used to save space in structures.

Problem 40

Can we have an array of bits fields?

Output:

No

Problem 41

Find the output of the following program?

```
#include<stdio.h>
#include <conio.h>
void main( )
{
struct node
{
```

```
int data;
struct node *link;
};
struct node *ptr, *q;
ptr = (struct node *) malloc (sizeof(struct node));
q = (struct node *) malloc (sizeof (struct node));
printf("%d %d", sizeof (ptr), sizeof (q));
getch();
}
```

Output:

2 2

Problem 42

Is there any error, in the following code?

```
#include<stdio.h>
#include <conio.h>
void main( )
{
struct student
{
char name[20];
int rn;
float fees;
};
struct student st[2];
int i = 0;
for (i = 0; i <2; i++)
scanf("%s %d %f", st[i].name &st[i].rn, &st[i].fees);
for (i = 0; i <2; i++)
printf("%s %d %f", st[i].name, st[i].rn, st[i].fees);
```

```
getch();
}
```

Output:

```
Error
```

NOTE: Floating-point formats not linked.

Problem 43

Explain the following statement:

```
student.result.marks = 25;
```

Output:

Structure student is nested within structure result.

Problem 44

Find the output of the following program?

```
#include<stdio.h>
#include <conio.h>
void main( )
{
struct student
{
int rn: 1;
};
struct student st = {1};
printf("%d", st.rn);
getch();
}
```

Output:

```
-1
```

Problem 45

Find the output of the following program?

```
#include<stdio.h>
#include <conio.h>
struct date
{
int date;
int month;
int year;
};
void main( )
{
struct date d;
struct date *ptr;
ptr = &d;
ptr -> month = 12·
printf("%d", ptr->month);
getch();
}
```

Output:

```
12
```

Problem 46

Find the output of the following program?

```
#include<stdio.h>
#include <conio.h>
void main( )
{
enum result{pass, fail, comp};
enum result r1, r2, r3;
```

```
r1 = pass;
r2 = comp;
r3 = fail;
printf("\n%d %d %d", r1, r2, r3);
getch();
}
```

Output:

```
0 2 1
```

Problem 47

Find the output of the following program?

```
#include<stdio.h>
#include <conio.h>
void main( )
{
int i = 4, j = 8;
printf("%d %d %d", i | j & j |i, i| j && j | i, i ^ j);
getch();
}
```

Output:

```
12 1 12
```

Problem 48

Find the output of the following program?

```
#include<stdio.h>
#include <conio.h>
void main( )
{
union value
{
```

```
int i;
char str[2];
};
union value v;
v.str[0] = 4;
v.str[1]=12;
printf("%d %d %d", v.str[0], v.str[1], v.i);
getch();
}
```

Output:

```
4 12 any value
```

Problem 49

Find the output of the following program?

```
#include<stdio.h>
#include<conio.h>
struct book
{
char title[20];
char author[20];
int pages;
float price;
};
void main( )
{
book b1;
printf("Size of variable b1 is %d bytes", sizeof(b1));
getch();
}
```

Output:

Error

NOTE: Undefined symbol book in main().

Problem 50

Check the errors from the following program?

```
#include<stdio.h>
#include<conio.h>
struct book
{
char title[20];
char author[20];
int pages;
float price;
};
void main( )
{
struct book b1;
b1.title = "Soft Computing";
b1. Author="Ikvinderpal Singh";
b1.pages = 450;
b1.price = 325.50;
printf("%s by %s is of %f rupees", b1.title, b1.author,
   b1.price);
getch();
}
```

Output:

Error

NOTE: L-value required.

Problem 51

Find the output of the following program?

```
#include<stdio.h>
#include<conio.h>
struct book
{
char *title;
char *author;
int pages;
float price;
};
void main( )
{
struct book b1;
b1.title = “Soft Computing”;
b1.Author=”Ikvinderpal Singh”;
b1.pages = 450;
b1.price = 325.50;
printf(“%s by %s is of %f rupees”, b1.title, b1.author,
   b1.price);
getch();
}
```

Output:

```
Soft Computing by Ikvinderpal Singh is of 325.500000
   rupees.
```

Problem 52

Check the errors from the following program?

```
#include<stdio.h>
#include<conio.h>
```

```
struct car
{
struct engine e;
struct chassis c;
};
struct engine
{
int hp;
int cc;
};
struct chassis
{
int len;
int w;
};
void main( )
{
struct car c1 = {{145,2500}, {2400, 2876}};
if(c1.e.cc<2500)
printf("Small Car\n");
else if(c1.e.cc>=2400 && c1.e.cc<2600)
printf("Middle Car\n");
else
printf("Big Car\n");
getch();
}
```

Output:

Error

NOTE: Undefined structure engine and chasis.

Problem 53

Find the output of the following program?

```
#include<stdio.h>
#include<conio.h>
struct car
{
struct engine {int hp; intcc;}e;
struct chassis {int length; int width;}ch;
};
void main( )
{
struct c1={{48, 2434}, {3500, 2487}}, c2={{42, 1300},
   {3300, 2500}};
if (c1.ch.length>c2.ch.length)
printf("Your Car is larger\n");
else
printf("My Car is larger\n");
getch();
}
```

Output:

```
My car is larger
```

Problem 54

Find the output of the following program?

```
#include<stdio.h>
#include<conio.h>
struct car
{
char *name;
char *model;
```

```
char *regno;
struct {int hp; int cc;} e;
struct {int len, int w; char *color”}c;
float cost;
void main( )
{
struct car c1;
printf(“Size of type struct car is %d\n”, sizeof (struct
   car));
printf(“The variables of type struct car will take %d
   bytes of memory\n”, sizeof(c1));
getch();
}
```

Output:

```
Size of type struct car is 28
The variables of type struct car will take 28 bytes of
   memory
```

Problem 55

Find the output of the following program?

```
#include<stdio.h>
#include<conio.h>
struct car
{
char *company= “Tata”;
char *name;
};
void main()
{
struct car c1, c2;
c1.name= “Indica”;
```

```
c2.name = "Indigo";
printf("We own %s and %s cars manufactured by %s",
    c1.name, c2.name, c1.company);
getch();
}
```

Output:

```
Error
```

Problem 56

Find the output of the following program?

```
#include<stdio.h>
#include<conio.h>
struct car
{
char *name;
char *model;
};
void main()
{
struct car c1 = {"Tata", "Indica"};
struct car c2 = c1;
strupr (c2.name);
strupr (c2.model);
printf("Car is %s-%s\n", c2.name, c2.model);
printf("Car is %s-%s\n", c1.name, c1.model);
getch();
}
```

Output:

```
Car is Tata Indica
Car is Tata Indica
```

Problem 57

Tell the similarity between a structure and union?

Output:

Both are used for heterogenous collection of data types.

Problem 58

Given below statement works?

```
typedef struct student
{
int rn;
float fees;
}student;
```

Output:

Yes

Problem 59

Structure can point itself using pointers?

Output:

Yes.

NOTE: Self-referential structures.

Problem 60

Find the output of the following program?

```
#include<stdio.h>
#include <conio.h>
struct student
{
char name[20];
int rn;
```

```
};
void display (struct student *);
void main( )
{
struct student s = {"Ikvinder", 12};
display (&s);
printf("\n%s %d", s.name, s.rn);
getch();
}
void display (struct student *ptr)
{
strupr (ptr -> name);
ptr -> rn = p -> rn +2;
}
```

Output:

```
IKVINDER
14
```

Problem 61

Is there any error, in the following code?

```
struct student
{
int rn;
struct student s;
};
```

Output:

```
Error.
```

NOTE: The student structure contains a member s of the same type.

Problem 62

Is there any error, in the following code?

```
struct student
{
int rn;
struct student *s;
};
```

Output:

```
No Error.
```

NOTE: This structure student *s is known as self-referential structure.

Problem 63

Is there any error, in the following code?

```
typedef struct student stud;
struct student
{
int rn;
stud *st;
};
```

Output:

```
No error.
```

NOTE: The stud is known at the point of declaring the structure, as it is already defined.

Problem 64

Find the output of the following program?

```
#include <stdio.h>
#include <conio.h>
#include <alloc.h>
```

```
struct student
{
int len;
char name[10];
};
void main( )
{
char name1[] = "Sukhwant";
struct student *s = (struct student *) malloc (sizeof
   (struct student) -1+ strlen (name1) + 1);
s->len = strlen (name1);
strcpy (s -> name, name1);
printf("\n%d%s", s ->len, s -> name);
getch();
}
```

Output:

```
8 Sukhwant
```

Problem 65

Check the errors from the following program?

```
#include<stdio.h>
#include<conio.h>
struct values
{
int i;
int j;
};
void main( )
{
struct values v={12,14};
```

```
struct values *vptr=&v;
printf("Values are %d and %d", *vptr.i, *vptr.j);
getch();
}
```

Output:

```
Error
```

NOTE: Structure required on the left side of main().

Problem 66

Find the output of the following program?

```
#include<stdio.h>
#include<conio.h>
enum color {green, pink, blue};
void main( )
{
printf("Values of enum constants are %d %d %d", green,
   pink, blue);
getch();
}
```

Output:

```
Values of enum constants are 0 1 2
```

Problem 67

Find the output of the following program?

```
#include<stdio.h>
#include<conio.h>
enum color {red, green=red, blue = green};
void main( )
{
printf("Values of enum constants are %d %d %d", red,
   green, blue);
```

```
getch();
}
```

Output:

```
Values of enum constants are 0 0 0
```

Problem 68

Check the errors from the following program?

```
#include<stdio.h>
#include<conio.h>
enum values {i, j=32767, k};
void main( )
{
printf("Values of enumeration constants are %d %d %d",
   i, j, k);
getch();
}
```

Output:

```
Error
```

NOTE: Value of c is not within the range of an int.

Problem 69

Find the output of the following program?

```
#include<stdio.h>
#include<conio.h>
enum values{i=2, j=3, k};
void main( )
{
int x=6, s1, s2;
s1= x%b;
s2= s1%s2;
```

```
printf("Values of s1 and s2 are %d and %d", s1, s2);
getch();
}
```

Output:

```
Values of s1 and s2 are 0 and 1
```

Problem 70

Find the output of the following program?

```
#include<stdio.h>
#include<conio.h>
void main( )
{
int bitfield: 2;
bitfield = 3;
printf("Value of bitfield is %d", bitfield);
getch();
}
```

Output:

```
Error
```

Problem 71

Is there any error, in the following code?

```
#include<stdio.h>
#include <conio.h>
struct student
{
char *str;
int i;
}st;
void main( )
```

```
{
scanf("%s %d", st.str, &st.i);
printf("%s", st.str);
getch();
}
```

Output:

```
Error
```

Problem 72

Find the output of the following program?

```
#include<stdio.h>
#include <conio.h>
struct student
{
int rn;
char name[20];
};
void main( )
{
struct student st[] =
{{12, "Ikvinder"},
{13, "Jagbir"},
{14, "Kawaljit"}};
getch();
}
```

Output:

```
12 Ikvinder
```

B. FILL IN THE BLANKS

1. Structures can be used for the storage of data of .... type.

2. A structure that contains a pointer to an instance of itself is known as ....
3. .... and .... are collectively known as aggregate type.
4. Like elements of an array are accessed by their indices, the elements of a structure are accessed by their ....
5. The members of a structure object can be accessed via a pointer to the structure object by using .... operator.
6. Related data items of different types are organized using ....
7. The keyword .... is used to declare union.
8. Structure declaration describes the .... of a structure.
9. A structure name is represented by its ....
10. Bit fields are declared in a ....
11. The precedence of the direct member access operator is .... than the dereference operator.
12. The memory allocated to a union object is the amount necessary to contain its .... member.
13. The .... can be used to create an alias for a previously defined type.
14. The .... of a structure not followed by a structure variable does not reserve any storage.
15. The expression (*ptr).x is equivalent to ....
16. The variables named in a structure are ....
17. Initialization of a union variable can initialize its .... only.
18. The expression ++ptr->a increments ....

Answers:

1. heterogeneous	2. self-referential structure
3. Arrays, structures	4. names 5.arrow
6. structure	7. union
8. prototype	9. tag

10. structure
11. higher
12. largest
13. typedef
14. declaration
15. ptr->x
16. members
17. first member
18. a

C. TRUE OR FALSE

State whether each of the following is the true or false

1. Unlike functions, a structure can be defined within another structure-type definition.
2. The return statement can be used within a calling function of a structure.
3. It is not possible to create an array of pointer to structures.
4. One of the elements of a structure can be a pointer to the same structure.
5. The keyword typedef is used to create a new data type.
6. Unions can be initialized in the same way as structures are initialized.
7. On declaring a structure zero bytes are reserved in memory.
8. A union cannot be nested in a structure.
9. The '->' operator can be access structure elements using a pointer to a structure variable.
10. The alignment of structure members in memory varies from one compiler to another.
11. Memory gets allocated for the members of a structure only when a structure variable is defined.
12. A structure may have date items of similar data types.
13. Structure declaration does not require a semicolon after closing brace.
14. A structure can contain similar or dissimilar elements.
15. Nested unions are not allowed.

16. The variables of the defined structure type can only be declared in the scope in which the defined structure type is visible.
17. In C language, an object of a structure type can be created by just using its tag-name.
18. The alignment of structure members in memory can be controlled using the #pragma pack preprocessor directive.
19. Bit fields CANNOT be used in a union.
20. Like an array name, the name of a structure refers to its base address.
21. The assignment operator copies all the members of a structure object to a structure variable along with the padding bytes.
22. A structure declaration-list cannot contain a member of void, function or incomplete type.
23. The elements of a union are always accessed using & operator.
24. Unions can be used as members of structures and structures can be used as members of unions.
25. The scope of a structure should be global if it is to be used in all functions in the program.
26. A structure definition does not reserve any space in the memory.
27. Structure members can be initialized during the structure definition.
28. The '.' operator can be used access structure elements using a structure variable.
29. A structure can be nested inside another structure.
30. The declaration struct first{int x;} is equivalent to struct second {int x;};
31. The declaration and definition cannot be combined.
32. Size of the union is size of the longest element in the union.
33. If we initialize one element of the union it also initializes other elements of the union.
34. A structure can be read and displayed as a whole.
35. Enumeration can have an effect local to the block, if desired.

36. Structure, unions and enumerations are collectively known as aggregate type.
37. User has to explicitly define the numeric values of enumerations.
38. The tag name of a structure can be used as an ordinary variable name or a member variable name without any conflict in a program.
39. By default a structure variable will be of auto storage class.
40. Union elements can be different sizes.
41. User has a control over the size of enumeration variables.
42. A structure cannot contain the structure itself as its member.
43. A structure that contains an instance of itself is known as a self-referential structure.
44. Enumeration has a global effect throughout the file.
45. The square brackets of an array of structures must be associated with the array name and not with any structure member name to access the members of the structure.
46. union variables can have local scope or global scope.
47. The name of a structure member can be the same as the structure tag-name.
48. A pointer to a union CANNOT be created.
49. Nested unions and self referential unions are not possible in C.
50. Structures cannot be passed to functions.
51. Structure padding can appear anywhere within a structure object.

Answers

1. True	2. True	3. False	4. True
5. False	6. False	7. True	8. False
9. True	10. True	11. True	12. True
13. False	14. True	15. False	16. True
17. False	18. True	19. True	20. False
21. False	22. True	23. False	24. True
25. True	26. True	27. False	28. True

29. True	30. False	31. False	32. True
33. True	34. False	35. True	36. False
37. False	38. True	39. True	40. True
41. False	42. True	43. False	44. False
45. True	46. True	47. True	48. False
49. False	50. False	51. False	

D. OBJECTIVE TYPE QUESTIONS

1. Structure is a
   (a) scalar data type (b) derived data type
   (c) both a and b (d) primitive data type
2. Structure is a data type in which
   (a) each element must have the same data type
   (b) each element must have pointer type only
   (c) each element may have different data type
   (d) no element is defined
3. C provides a facility for user defined data type using
   (a) pointer (b) function
   (c) structure (d) array
4. The keyword used to represent a structure data type is
   (a) structure (b) struct
   (c) struc (d) structr
5. Structure declaration
   (a) describes the prototype
   (b) creates structure variable
   (c) defines the structure function
   (d) is not necessary
6. Structure definition
   (a) describes the prototype
   (b) creates structure variable

(c) defines the structure function

(d) is not necessary

7. A structure can have

(a) pointers as its members

(b) scalar data type as its members

(c) structure as its members

(d) all the above

8. A structure

(a) allows array of structure

(b) does not allow of structure

(c) does not use array as its members

(d) is a scalar data type

9. The operator exclusively used with pointer to structure is

(a) . (b) - >

(c) [ ] (d) *

10. If one or more members of a structure are pointers to the same structure, the structure is known as

(a) nested structure (b) invalid structure

(c) self referential structure (d) structured structure

11. Identify the wrong statement.

(a) Structure variable can be passed as argument

(b) Pointer to structure can be passed as argument

(c) None of the above

12. Union is

(a) a special type of structure (b) a pointer data type

(c) a function data type (d) not a data type

13. The restriction with union is

(a) The last member can only be initialized

(b) The first member can only be initialized

(c) Any member can be initialized

(d) Union cannot be initialized

14. Union differs from structure in the following way:

(a) All members are used at a time

(b) Only one member can be used at a time

(c) Union cannot have more members

(d) Union initializes all members as structure

15. Identify the correct statement.

(a) Unions can be members of structures

(b) Structures can be members of unions

(c) Both a and b

(d) Union can contain bit field

16. What is not possible with union?

(a) Array of union (b) Pointer to union

(c) Self-referential union (d) None of the above

17. Structure is used to implement the data structure.

(a) stack (b) queue

(c) tree (d) all the above

18. The nodes in a linked list are implemented using

(a) self-referential structure (b) nested structure

(c) array of structure (d) ordinary structure

19. Identify the wrong statement.

(a) An array is a collection of data items of same data type

(b) An array declaration reserves memory space and structure declaration does not reserve memory space

(c) Array uses the keyword array in its declaration

(d) A structure is a collection of data items of different data types

20. Identify the wrong statement

(a) An array can have bit fields

(b) A structure may contains bit fields

(c) A structure has declaration and definition

(d) A structure variable can be initialized

21. A bit field is

    (a) a pointer variable in a structure

    (b) one bit or a set of adjacent bits within a word

    (c) a pointer variable in a union

    (d) not used in C

22. A bit field can be of

    (a) int (b) float

    (c) double (d) all the above

23. Structure is used to implement the data structures

    (a) stack (b) queue

    (c) tree (d) all the above

24. The nodes in a linked list are implemented using

    (a) self-referential structure (b) nested structure

    (c) array of structure (d) ordinary structure

25. Consider the following structure.

```
struct numname
{
int no;
char name [25];
};
struct numname n1[ ] =
{
{12, Raja "},
{15, "Selvan"},
{18, "Prema"}'
{21, "Naveen"}
};
```

The output for the following statement would be:

```
printf ("%d, %d", n1[2].no, (*(n1 + 2)).no);
```

(a) 18,ASCII value of p (b) 18, 18

(c) 18,ASCII valur of r (d) 18,ASCII value of e

26. struct customer *ptr = malloc (sizeof (struct customer));

    Given the sample allocation for the pointer "ptr" found above, which statement would be used to reallocate ptr to be an array of 10 elements?

    (a) ptr = realloc (ptr, 10 * sizeof (struct customer));

    (b) ptr = realloc (ptr, 9* sizeof (struct customer)) ;

    (c) realloc (ptr, 9* sizeof (struct customer));

    (d) realloc (ptr, 10 * sizeof (struct customer));

27. Which of the following will define a type NODE that is a node in a linked list.

    (a) struct node

    ```
    {
    NODE *next;
    int x;
    };
    typedef struct node NODE;
    ```

    (b) typdef struct NODE

    ```
    {
    struct NODE *next;
    int x;
    };
    ```

    (c) typedef struct node NODE;

    ```
    struct node
    {
    NODE *next;
    int x;
    ```

```
};
```

(d) typedef struct

```
{
NODE *next;
int x;
} NODE;
```

28. The size of the following union, where an int occupies 4 bytes of memory is

```
union arc
{
char x;
int y;
char ax [8];
}aha;
```

(a) 16 bytes (b) 13 bytes
(c) 8 bytes (d) 4 bytes

29. Structure is a
(a) scalar data type (b) derived data type
(c) both options a and b (d) primitive data type

30. A Structure
(a) can be read as a single entity
(b) cannot be read as a single entity
(c) can be displayed as a single entity
(d) has member variables that cannot be read individually

31. Structure is a data type in which
(a) each element must have the same data type
(b) each element must have pointer type only
(c) each element may have different data type
(d) no element is defined

32. C provides a facility for user defined data type using
   (a) pointer (b) function
   (c) structure (d) array
33. The keyword used to represent a structure data type is
   (a) structure (b) struct
   (c) struc (d) structr
34. Structure declaration
   (a) describes the prototype
   (b) creates structure variable
   (c) defines the structure function
   (d) is not necessary
35. Structure definition
   (a) describes the prototype
   (b) creates structure variable
   (c) defines the structure function
   (d) is not necessary
36. The operator used to access the structure member is
   (a) * (b) .
   (c) [ ] (d) &
37. A structure
   (a) can be read as a single entity
   (b) cannot be read as a single entity
   (c) can be displayed as a single entity
   (d) has member variables that can not be individually read
38. Identify the wrong syntax
   (a) typedef struct {member declaration;} NAME; NAME V1, V2;
   (b) typedef struct tag {member declaration;} NAME; NAME V1, V2;
   (c) typedef struct {member declaration;} NAME; NAME V1, V2;

(d) typedef struct tag {member declaration;} NAME; NAME V1, V2;

39. Identify the wrong syntax
   (a) struct tag {member declaration;};
   (b) struct tag {member declaration;} V1, V2;
   (c) struct tag {member declaration;}
   (d) struct tag {member declaration;} V1, V2;

40. The operator used to access the structure member is
   (a) * (b) .
   (c) [] (d) &

41. A structure
   (a) can be read as a single entity
   (b) cannot be read as a single entity
   (c) can be displayed as a single entity
   (d) has member variables that cannot be individually read

42. A structure can have
   (a) pointers as its members
   (b) scalar data type as its members
   (c) structure as its members
   (d) all the above

43. The structure declaration
   struct person {char name[20]; int age; struct person woman;};
   (a) is a valid nested structure
   (b) is not a valid nested structure
   (c) uses an invalid data type
   (d) is a self-referential structure

44. A structure
   (a) allows array of structure
   (b) does not allow array of structures

(c) does not use array as its members

(d) is a scalar data type

45. In a structure definition.

(a) initialization of structure members are possible

(b) initialization of array of structures are possible

(c) both a and b

(d) initialization of array of structures are not possible

46. The operator exclusively used with pointer to structure is

(a) . (b) ->

(c) [] (d) *

47. If one or more members of a structure are pointer to the same structure, the structure is known as

(a) nested structure (b) invalid structure

(c) self-referential structure (d) structured structure

48. If one or more members of a structure are other structures, the structure is known as

(a) nested structure (b) invalid structure

(c) self-referential structure (d) unstructured structure

49. What type of structure is created by the following definition?

struct first {...; struct second *s};

struct second {...; struct first *f};

(a) nested structure

(b) self-referential structure invalid structure

(c) invalid structure

(d) structured structure

50. The changes made in the members of a structure are not available in the calling function if

(a) pointer to structure is passed as argument

(b) the members other than pointer type are passed as arguments

(c) structure variable is passed as argument

(d) both b and c

51. The changes made in the members of a structure are available in the calling function if

(a) pointer to structure is passed as argument

(b) structure variable is passed

(c) the members other than pointer type are passed as argument

(d) None of the above

52. If one or more members of a structure are other structures, the structure is known as

(a) nested structure (b) invalid structure

(c) self-referential structure (d) unstructured structure

53. Union is

(a) a special type of structure (b) a pointer data type

(c) a function data type (d) not a data type

54. The restriction with union is

(a) the last member can only be initialized

(b) the first member can only be initialized

(c) any member can be initialized

(d) union cannot be initialized

55. What is not possible with union?

(a) array of union (b) pointer to union

(c) self-referential union (d) none of the above

56. Identify the wrong statement(s)

(a) Bit fields have addresses

(b) Bit fields can be read using scanf( )

(c) Bit fields can be accessed using pointer

(d) all the above

57. Identify the correct statement(s).

(a) Bit fields are not arrays

(b) Bit fields cannot hold the values beyond their limits

(c) Bit fields may be unnamed also

(d) all the above

58. About structures which of the following is true.

1. Structure members are aligned in memory depending on their data type.

2. The size of a structure may not be equal to the sum of the sizes of its members.

(a) only option 1 (b) only option 2

(c) both options 1 and 2 (d) neither option1 nor 2

59. struct date

```
{
int day;
int month;
int year;
};
main( )
{
struct date *d;
...
++d->day; /*statementN*/
...
}
```

Then the statement statementN

(a) increments the pointer to point the month

(b) increment the value of day

(c) increment d by sizeof (struct date)

(d) none

60.
```
struct cost_record
{
long cost_no;
char cost_name[31];
double current_bal;
} Crecord;
```
Is the sample code above a usable structure variable declaration?

(a) Yes. Crecord can be used to access its members with the "->" operator

(b) No. A typedef must be added before "struct"

(c) Yes. Crecord can be used to access its members with the "." Operator

(d) No. Crecord must be in lowercase letters.

61.
```
struct car
{
int speed;
char type[10];
} vehicle;
struct car *ptr;
ptr = &vehicle;
```
Referring to the sample code above, which of the following will make the speed equal to 200?

(a) (*ptr).speed = 200; (b) (*ptr)->speed = 200;

(c) *ptr.speed = 200; (d) &ptr.speed = 200;

62. A bit field can be of

(a) int (b) float

(c) double (d) all the above

63. The following statement is correct:

" The size of struct is always equal to the sum of the sizes of its members."

(a) valid (b) invalid
(c) can't say (d) insufficient information

Answers

1. (b)	2. (c)	3. (c)	4. (b)	5. (a)
6. (b)	7. (d)	8. (a)	9. (b)	10. (c)
11. (d)	12. (a)	13. (b)	14. (b)	15. (c)
16. (d)	17. (d)	18. (a)	19. (c)	20. (a)
21. (b)	22. (a)	23. (d)	24. (a)	25. (b)
26. (a)	27. (c)	28. (c)	29. (b)	30. (b)
31. (c)	32. (c)	33. (b)	34. (a)	35. (b)
36. (b)	37. (b)	38. (d)	39. (c)	40. (b)
41. (b)	42. (d)	43. (b)	44. (a)	45. (c)
46. (b)	47. (c)	48. (a)	49. (b)	50. (d)
51. (a)	52. (a)	53. (a)	54. (b)	55. (d)
56. (d)	57. (d)	58. (c)	59. (b)	60. (c)
61. (a)	62. (a)	63. (c)		

CHAPTER 11

Files

A. CODE SNIPPETS

Problem 1

Explain the following program:

```
#include<stdio.h>
#include <conio.h>
void main( )
{
FILE *fp;
fp = fopen("state", "r");
getch();
}
```

Output:

```
A structure which contains a char pointer which points
    to the first character in the file.
```

Problem 2

Is there any error, in the following code?

```
#include<stdio.h>
#include <conio.h>
```

```
void main( )
{
unsigned char ch;
FILE *fp;
fp = fpopen ("state", "r");
while ((ch = getc (fp)) != EOF)
printf("%c", ch);
fclose(fp);
getch();
}
```

Output:

```
Error
```

NOTE: Declare ch as an int.

Problem 3

Is there any error, in the following code?

```
#include<stdio.h>
#include <conio.h>
#include<stdlib.h>
void main( )
{
unsigned char ch;
FILE *fp;
fp = fpopen ("state", "r");
if (!fp)
{
printf("Unable to open file");
exit (1);
}
fclose (fp);
```

```
getch();
}
```

Output:

```
No error.
```

Problem 4

If a file contains the line "I am a killer\r\n" then on reading this line into the array str using fgets( ) what will str contain?

Output:

```
I am a killer\n\0
```

Problem 5

Is there any error, in the following code?

```
#include<stdio.h>
#include <conio.h>
void main( )
{
FILE *fp;
fp = fopen("state", "r");
fseek(fp, 20L, SEEK_SET);
fclose(fp);
getch();
}
```

Output:

```
No error
```

Problem 6

Is there any error, in the following code?

```
#include<stdio.h>
#include <conio.h>
void main( )
```

```
{
FILE *fp;
char str[80];
fp=fopen("state", "r");
while (fgets(str, 80, fp) ! NULL)
putc (str);
fclose(fp);
getch();
}
```

Output:

```
No error
```

Problem 7

Find the output of the following program?

```
#include<stdio.h>
#include <conio.h>
void main( )
{
FILE *ptr;
char ch;
ptr = fopen("state.c", "r");
while((ch = fgetc(ptr))!= NULL)
printf("%c", ch);
getch();
}
```

Output:

```
Infinite loop
```

Problem 8

Find the output of the following program?

```
#include<stdio.h>
#include <conio.h>
void main( )
{
FILE *fp1, *fp2;
fp1 = fopen ("state.c", "w");
fp2 = fopen ("state.c", "w");
fputc ('I', fp1);
fputc('J', fp2);
fclose(fp1);
fclose(fp2);
getch();
}
```

Output:

```
J
```

Problem 9

Is there any error, in the following code?

```
#include<stdio.h>
#include <conio.h>
void main( )
{
FILE *fp;
fp = fopen ("c\tc\state", "w");
if (!fp);
exit( );
fclose (fp);
getch();
}
```

Output:

```
Error
```

NOTE: Path can be given as “c\\tc\\state”.

Problem 10

Check the errors from the following progra.n?

```
#include<stdio.h>
#include<conio.h>
void main( )
{
FILE *fptr;
char names[20] ;
int i;
fptr = fopen ( “Raja.c”, “wb” ) ;
for ( i = 0 ; i <= 10 ; i++ )
{
puts ( “\nEnter name “ ) ;
gets ( name ) ;
fwrite ( name, size of ( name ), 1, fptr ) ;
}
close ( fptr ) ;
getch();
}
```

Output:

```
Error.
```

Problem 11

Check the errors from the following program?

```
#include<stdio.h>
#include<conio.h>
```

```
void main( )
{
FILE *fptr;
char name[20] = "Ikvinder";
int i;
fptr = fopen ( "sherry.c", "r" );
for ( i = 0 ; i <= 10 ; i++ )
fwrite ( name, sizeof ( name ), 1, fptr );
close (fptr);
getch();
}
```

Output:

```
Error.
```

Problem 12

Check the errors from the following program?

```
#include<stdio.h>
#include<conio.h>
void main( )
{
int fptr;
fptr = open( "Raja.c" , "r" );
if ( fptr == -1 )
puts ( "cannot open file" );
else
close ( fptr );
getch();
}
```

Output:

```
Error.
```

Problem 13

Check the errors from the following program?

```
#include<stdio.h>
#include<conio.h>
void main( )
{
int fptr;
fptr = fopen ("Raja.c", READ | BINARY);
if (fptr == -1)
puts ("cannot open file");
else
close (fptr);
getch();
}
```

Output:

Error.

Problem 14

Check the errors from the following program?

```
#include<stdio.h>
#include<conio.h>
void main( )
{
FILE *fp=fopen("raj.txt", 'r');
while (!feof(fp))
printf("%c", fgetc(fp));
getch();
}
```

Output:

Error

```
raj.txt
I am working as lecturer in khalsa college Amritsar
```

Problem 15

Find the output of the following program?

```
#include<stdio.h>
#include<conio.h>
void main( )
{
FILE *fp=fopen("raj.txt", "r");
while (!feof(fp))
{
printf("%c", fgetc(fp));
fseek(fp, -1, SEEK_CUR);
}
getch();
}
```

Output:

```
IIIIIII......infinite times
raj.txt
I am working as lecturer in khalsa college Amritsar
```

Problem 16

Find the output of the following program?

```
#include<stdio.h>
#include<conio.h>
void main( )
{
int strms;
strms=flushall();
```

```
printf("Number of streams are %d", strms);
getch();
}
```

Output:

```
Number of streams are 5
```

Problem 17

Find the output of the following program?

```
#include<stdio.h>
#include<conio.h>
void main( )
{
FILE *fp=fopen("raj.txt", "r");
printf("%d", fp->fd);
getch();
}
```

Output:

```
5
raj.txt
I am working as lecturer in khalsa college Amritsar
```

Problem 18

Find the output of the following program?

```
#include<stdio.h>
#include<conio.h>
void main( )
{
FILE *fp1, *fp2;
int count1=0, count2=0;
fp1=fopen("raj.txt", "r");
```

```
fp2=fopen("raj.txt", "rb");
while(fgetc(fp1)!=EOF)
c1++;
while (fgetc(fp2)!=EOF)
c2++;
printf("Number of characters in text stream is %d\n",
   c1);
printf("Number of characters in binary stream is %d",
   c2);
getch();
}
```

Output:

```
Number of characters in text stream is 50
Number of characters in binary stream is 53
raj.txt
I am working as lecturer in khalsa college Amritsar
```

Problem 19

Find the output of the following program?

```
#include<stdio.h>
#include<conio.h>
void main( )
{
FILE *fp;
Unsigned char ch;
fp=fopen("raj.txt", "r");
while((ch=fgetc(fp))!=EOF)
printf("%c", ch);
fclose(fp);
getch();
```

```
}
```

Output:

```
I am working as lecturer in khalsa college Amritsar
raj.txt
I am working as lecturer in khalsa college Amritsar
```

Problem 20

Check the errors from the following program?

```
#include<stdio.h>
#include<conio.h>
void main( )
{
FILE *fp1, fp2;
Unsigned char ch;
fp1=fopen("raj.txt", "r");
fp2=fopen("red.txt", "w");
while((ch=fgetc(fp))!=EOF)
fputc(ch, fp);
getch();
}
```

Output:

```
Error
raj.txt
I am working as lecturer in khalsa college Amritsar
```

Problem 21

Check the errors from the following program?

```
#include<stdio.h>
#include<conio.h>
void main( )
```

```
{
FILE *fp1, fp2;
Unsigned char ch;
fp1=fopen("raj.txt", "r");
fp2=fopen("red.txt", "w");
while((ch=fgetc(fp))!=EOF)
fputc(ch, fp2);
fclose(fp1, fp2);
getch();
}
```

Output:

```
Error
raj.txt
I am working as lecturer in khalsa college Amritsar
```

Problem 22

Find the output of the following program?

```
#include<stdio.h>
#include<conio.h>
void main( )
{
FILE *fp1, fp2;
fp1=fopen("raj.txt", "r");
fp2=fopen("red.txt", "r+b");
printf("%x %x", fp1->flags, fp2->flags);
getch();
}
```

Output:

```
No error
raj.txt
```

```
I am working as lecturer in khalsa college Amritsar
```

Problem 23

```
Out of fgets( )  and gets() which function is safe to
    use?
```

Output:

```
fgets (), because unlike fgets( ), gets ( ) cannot be
    told the size of the buffer into which the string
    supplied will be stored. As a result there is
    always a possibility of overflow of buffer.
```

Problem 24

True/False

1. A file written in text mode can be read back in binary mode. F
2. We should not read after a write to a file without an intervening call to fflush( ), fseek( ) or rewind( ). F

Problem 25

Explain the following program to copy contents of one file to another?

```
/* mycopy.c */
#include<stdio.h>
#include <conio.h>
void main( )
{
char ch, str[10];
while ((ch = getc (stdin)) !=1)
putc (ch, stdout);
getch();
}
```

Output:

```
By executing the program at the command prompt as
    shown below: mycopy <sourcefile> targetfile
```

Problem 26

Check the errors from the following program?

```
#include<stdio.h>
#include<conio.h>
void main( )
{
FILE *fptr;
char ch;
fptr = fopen ( "HER.C" ,"r") ;
if ( fptr == null )
{
puts ( "Cannot open file" ) ;
exit( );
}
while ( ( ch = getc ( fptr ) ) != EOF )
putch (ch);
fclose (fptr);
getch();
}
```

Output:

Error.

NOTE: NULL should be used instead of null.

Problem 27

Check the errors from the following program?

```
#include<stdio.h>
#include<conio.h>
void main( )
{
char filename[ ] = "c:\\student.dat" ;
```

```
FILE *fptr;
fptr = fopen ( filename, “tr” ) ;
if ( fptr == NULL )
printf ( “\nUnable to open file...” ) ;
getch();
}
```

Output:

Error.

NOTE: undefined symbol FILE.

Problem 28

Check the errors from the following program?

```
#include<stdio.h>
#include<conio.h>
void main( )
{
FILE *fptr;
char str[80] ;
fptr = fopen ( “HER.C”, “r” ) ;
while ( fgets ( str, 80, fptr ) != EOF )
fputs ( str ) ;
fclose ( fptr ) ;
getch();
}
```

Output:

Error.

Problem 29

Check the errors from the following program?

```
#include<stdio.h>
```

```
#include<conio.h>
void main( )
{
FILE *fptr;
char name[20];
int age;
fptr = fopen("COVERS", "r");
while (fscanf (fptr, "%s %d", name, &age ) != NULL)
fclose (fptr);
getch();
}
```

Output:

```
Error.
```

Problem 30

Tell the purpose of "rb" in fopen( ) function given below?

```
FILE *fp;
fp = fopen( "raja.txt", "rb")
```

Output:

Open "source.txt" in binary mode for reading.

Problem 31

Find the output of the following program?

```
#include<stdio.h>
#include <conio.h>
void main( )
{
FILE *fp;
char ch [10];
```

```
fp = fopen ("raja.txt", "r");          // file contains
   Be my friend
ch = getc (fp);
fseek (fp, 0, SEEK_END);
fseek (fp, -3L, SEEK_CUR);
fgets (ch, 5, fp);
puts (c);
getch();
}
```

Output:

```
end
```

Problem 32

Find the output of the following program?

```
#include<stdio.h>
#include <conio.h>
void main( )
{
FILE *fp, *fp1, *fp2;
fp = fopen ("RAJ.C", "r");
fp1 = fopen ("BAL.C", "r");
fp2 = fopen ("SAM.C", "r");
fclose (fp, fp1, fp2);
getch();
}
```

Output:

```
RAJ.C
```

Problem 33

Find the output of the following program?

```
#include<stdio.h>
#include <conio.h>
void main( )
{
FILE *fp;
char ch;
int i = 1;
fp = fopen ("raja.c", "r");
while ((ch = gets (fp) !=EOF)
{
if (ch = = '\n')
i++;
}
fclose (fp);
getch();
}
```

Output:

No error

Problem 34

Find the output of the following program?

```
#include<stdio.h>
#include <conio.h>
void main( )
{
FILE *fp;
char ch, str[7];
fp = fopen ("state.c", "r");          //file state.c
   contain jaipur
fseek (fp, 9L, SEEK_CUR);
```

```
fgets (str, 5, fp);
puts (str);
getch();
}
```

Output:

```
aipu
```

Problem 35

Find the output of the following program?

```
#include<stdio.h>
#include <conio.h>
void main( )
{
FILE *fptr;
char str[80];
fptr = fopen (“state.dat”, “w”);
if (fptr = = NULL)
printf(“Cannot open file”);
else
{
while (strlen (gets (str)) > 0
{
fputs (str, fptr);
fputs (“\n”, fptr);
}
fclose (fptr);
}
getch();
}
```

Output:

```
No error
```

Problem 36

Find the output of the following program?

```
#include<stdio.h>
#include<conio.h>
void openfile ( char *, FILE **)
void main( )
{
FILE *fptr;
openfile ( "raj.txt", fptr ) ;
if ( fptr == NULL )
printf ( "Unable to open file..." ) ;
getch();
}
void openfile ( char *ch, FILE **f )
{
*f = fopen ( ch, "r" ) ;
}
```

Output:

```
No error.
```

Problem 37

Find the output of the following program?

```
#include<stdio.h>
#include <conio.h>
void main( )
{
FILE *fp;
```

```
char str[11], ch;
int i = 0;
fp = fopen ("INPUT.TXT", "r");
while ((ch = getc (fp)) !=EOF)
{
if (ch = = '\n' || ch = = '')
{
str[i] = '\0';
strrev (str);
printf("%s", str);
i = 0;
}
else
str[i++] = ch;
}
fclose (fp);
getch();
}
```

Output:

No error

Problem 38

Explain the following statements?

```
FILE *fp;
fp = fopen ("raj.txt", "r+");
```

Output:

We can Read, Write and Append the file.

Problem 39

Find the output of the following program?

```
#include<stdio.h>
#include <conio.h>
void main( )
{
unsigned char ch;
FILE *fp;
fp = fopen ("abc.c", "r");
if (fp = = NULL)
printf("Unable to open the file");
exit (1);
while (ch = getc (fp) ) !=EOF)
printf("%c", ch);
fclose (fp);
getch();
}
```

Output:

Infinite loop

B. FILL IN THE BLANKS

1. The .... function reads a string from the standard input device.
2. .... is not a standard file stream.
3. If a file is opened in the r mode, C..................
4. The .... function may be used to position a file at the beginning.
5. The connection to an open file is represented either as a .... or as a ....
6. Five standard header files are ...., ..., ..., ... and ....

7. The streams stdout and stderr are associated with the .... for writing the output and the errors.
8. An object of the type .... contains all the information required to control the stream.
9. .... stream is an ordered sequence of the characters composed into lines, terminated by a new-line character.
10. If a stream is fully buffered, the characters are transmitted to the file when ....
11. A .... is a source or destination of data than may be associated with a disk or an I/O device.
12. An I/O stream may be a .... or a ....
13. The mode used for opening an existing file for reading a binary stream is ....
14. The function fopen( ) returns .... if the open operation fails.
15. The standard stream pointers are .... , ... and ....
16. The function getc(stdin) is equivalent to ....
17. The function call .... gets the current file position of the file represented by the file pointer.
18. The notation .... is called token pasting operator.
19. The mode string used to open an existing file in the text mode for update is ....
20. When the end of the file is encountered, the function fgetc returns ....
21. The current location of the file position indicator for the stream can be determined by using the functions .... and ....
22. By default, the size of a buffer for a fully buffered stream is ....
23. If the argument buf in a call to the function setbuf is a null pointer, I/O will be ....

24. Enumerations are treated as .... by the compiler.
25. The identifier .... is a predefined data type, which is a pointer to the argument list in functions with variable arguments.
26. When no value is explicitly assigned, the first identifier in an enumeration list represents .... by default.
27. The .... variable may change the value of it without the program's knowledge or action.

Answer

1. fgets()
2. stdfile
3. opens the file for reading and sets the file marker at the beginning
4. fseek()
5. stream, file descriptor
6. stdin, stdout, stderr, stdaux and stdprn
7. screen
8. File
9. Text
10. the stream buffer gets full
11. stream
12. text stream, binary stream
13. "rb"14. NULL pointer
15. stdin, stdout and stderr
16. getchar( )
17. ftell (fp)
18. # #
19. "r+" 20. EOF;
21. ftell, fgetpos
22. 512
23. unbuffered 24. integer constants
25. va _list 26. zero 27. volatile

C. TRUE OR FALSE

State whether each of the following is true or false

1. User files are created using the FILE type.
2. If a file does not exist, the append mode returns an error.
3. The space flag is used to left-justify output in the printf function.
4. Standard streams are always present and need not be opened or closed.

5. In binary streams, any carriage return character that appears before a line feed character is dropped.
6. The function call putc(c,stdout) is equivalent ot the function call putchar(c).
7. stderr, stdin and stdout are FILE pointers.
8. A text stream is a sequence of characters composed into lines, each line consisting of zero or more characters plus a terminating new-line character.
9. Declaring a structure with the qualifier const makes every element in it constant.
10. FILE is a structure data type.
11. The function main( ) may take a variable number of arguments.
12. To initialize a string when it is defined, it is necessary to put the delimiter character before the terminating double quote, as in "hello\0".
13. The EOF character can be included in a file as part of its data.
14. A file can be read only if it is in the read state.
15. A file opened in the r+b mode is a binary file operand in the read state and update mode.
16. Macros are not possible in C.
17. The notation # is known as stringing operator.
18. The names of the enumerators must different from other normal variables.
19. Declaration of const variables must have initializers.
20. Binary files are read using the block input/output function fread.
21. Using fseek to position a file beyond the current end of file places the file in an error state.
22. The standard streams stdaux and stdprn are not always defined.
23. By default, the stream stdout by default is line buffered.
24. The default buffer size for a stream is 512 and can be varied by using the function setbuf.

25. The function ftell is used to position the file position indicator within the file and to report the new location of the file position indicator.
26. A file must be opened before it is used.
27. Offset used in fseek function call can be a negative number.
28. While calling the fprintf( ) function, in the format string conversion specifier %s can be used to write a character string in capital letters.
29. It is possible to associate more than one stream with a file but not a stream with two files at a time.
30. In a call to printf( ) function the format specifier %b can be used to print binary equivalent of an integer.
31. The NULL character indicates an end of a string and a file.
32. All open streams must be explicitly closed before the successful termination of the program.
33. The mode string "rb+" is the same as the mode string "r+b".

Answers

1. True	2. True	3. True	4. True
5. False	6. True	7. True	8. True
9. True	10. True	11. False	12. True
13. False	14. False	15. True	16. False
17. True	18. True	19. False	20. True
21. False	22. True	23. False	24. True
25. False	26. True	27. True	28. False
29. True	30. False	31. False	32. False
33. True			

D. OBJECTIVE TYPE QUESTIONS

1. A stream is

(a) a library function

(b) a system call

(c) a source or destination of data that may be associated with a disk or other I/O devices

(d) a file

2. If fopen( ) fails, it returns

(a) –1 (b) NULL

(c) 1 (d) the file pointer

3. The action of connecting a program to a file is obtained by using

(a) connect( ) (b) fopen( )

(c) OPEN( ) (d) file( )

4. The action of disconnecting a program from a file is obtained by the function

(a) fclose( ) (b) delete( )

(c) fdisconnect( ) (d) clear( )

5. The value returned by fclose( ), if an error occurs is

(a) 0 (b) 1

(c) EOF (d) -1

6. The value returned by fclose( ) for successful closing of a file is

(a) 0 (b) 1

(c) EOF (d) OK

7. The function(s) used for reading a character from a file is (are)

(a) getc( ) (b) fgetc( )

(c) both options a and b (d) fgetchar( )

8. The value returned by ftell( ) if an error occur is

(a) –1 (b) 0

(c) Positive value (d) MIN_INT

9. The function used for reading binary stream is

(a) read( ) (b) fread( )

(c) fscanf( ) (d) all the above

10. The function used for writing to binary stream is
    (a) write( )   (b) fwrite( )
    (c) fprintf( )   (d) all the above
11. Identify the functions for in-memory format conversions
    (a) realloc( )   (b) sprintf( )
    (c) scanf( )   (d) both options a and b
12. Identify the stringing operator
    (a) +   (b) : :
    (c) #   (d) # #
13. Identify the token pasting operator.
    (a) +   (b) + +
    (c) #   (d) # #
14. The directives used in conditional compilation is (are)
    (a) # if   (b) # elif
    (c) #else   (d) all the above
15. The default setting of enumerator starts from
    (a) 0   (b) 1
    (c) -1   (d) any positive integer
16. va_list is
    (a) va_start   (b) va_end
    (c) va_arg   (d) all the above
    (e) None of the above
17. The function(s) used for writing a character to a file is (are)
    (a) putc( )   (b) fputc( )
    (c) both options a and b   (d) fputchar( )
18. The function used for random access of a file is
    (a) fseek( )   (b) ftell( )
    (c) search( )   (d) rewind( )

19. If an error occurs, the function fseek( ) returns
    (a) non-zero (b) zero
    (c) no value (d) –1
20. The value returned by fseek( ) o9n successful action is
    (a) non-zero (b) zero
    (c) Ok (d) READY
21. File is
    (a) a data type (b) a region of storage
    (c) both a and b (d) a variable
22. The way to access file contents from a program is
    (a) by using library functions (b) by using system calls
    (c) both a and b (d) to use a linker
23. File is
    (a) a data type (b) a region of storage
    (c) both options a and b (d) a variable
24. Stream oriented files are accessed through
    (a) system calls (b) library functions
    (c) linker (d) loader
25. Low level files are accessed through
    (a) system calls (b) library functions
    (c) linker (d) loader
26. C supports
    (a) high level files (b) low level files (c) both a and b
    (d) executable files only
27. A stream is
    (a) a library function (b) a system call
    (c) a source or destination of data that may be associated with a disk or other I/O devices
    (d) a file

28. I/O stream can be
    (a) a text stream
    (b) a binary stream
    (c) both a and b
    (d) an I/O operation
29. File opening is
    (a) a default action in file processing
    (b) an action of connecting a program to a file
    (c) not necessary
    (d) not using any library function
30. FILE defined in stdio.h is
    (a) a region of storage
    (b) a data type
    (c) not a data type
    (d) a variable
31. A file pointer is
    (a) a stream pointer
    (b) a buffer pointer
    (c) a pointer to FILE data type
    (d) all the above
32. The default stream pointers available during execution of a program is
    (a) stdin
    (b) stdout
    (c) stderr
    (d) all the above
33. The function call fopen("data", "w+b")
    (a) is invalid
    (b) returns the file pointer pointing to file named data and writing using binary stream
    (c) rturns the file pointer pointing to file named data and opens the file for reading and writing using text stream
    (d) does not return file pointer.
34. If fopen( ) fails, it returns
    (a) -1
    (b) NULL
    (c) I
    (d) the file pointer
35. The function fclose( ) is
    (a) used to disconnect a program from file

(b) used to close a file logically
(c) both a and b
(d) a mandatory function call in file handling

36. A file pointer is
(a) a stream pointer
(b) a buffer pointer
(c) a pointer to FILE data type
(d) all the above

37. The default stream pointers available during execution of a program is
(a) stdin (b) stdout
(c) stderr (d) all the above

38. Stream oriented files are accessed through
(a) system calls (b) library functions
(c) linker (d) loader

39. Identify the correct statement.
(a) #include "filename" (b) #include <filename>
(c) both a and b (d) #include filename

40. The following line in a program
```
# represents
```
(a) an invalid code (b) a null directive
(c) a comment (d) a page number

41. Macros
(a) can be recursively defined
(b) cannot be recursively defined
(c) cannot be defined
(d) are not preprocessor facility

42. Identify the stringizing operator.
(a) + (b) ::
(c) # (d) ##

43. Identify the pasting operator.
    (a) + (b) ::
    (c) # (d) ##
44. The directive(s) used in conditional compilation is (are)
    (a) # if (b) #elif
    (c) # else (d) all the above
45. The default setting of enumerator starts from
    (a) 0 (b) 1
    (c) -1 (d) any positive integer
46. The action of connecting a program to a file is obtained by using I
    (a) connect( ) (b) fopen( )
    (c) OPEN() (d) file( )
47. The action of disconnecting a program from a file is obtained by the function
    (a) fclose( ) (b) delete( )
    (c) fdisconnect( ) (d) clear( )
48. The value returned by fclose( ), if an error occurs is
    (a) 0 (b) 1
    (c) EOF (d) -1
49. The value returned by fclose( ) for successful closing of a file is
    (a) 0 (b) 1
    (c) EOF (d) OK
50. The function(s) used for writing a character to a file is (are)
    (a) getc( ) (b) fgetc( )
    (c) both a and b (d) fgetchar( )
51. The function(s) used for writing a character to a file is (are)
    (a) putc( ) (b) fputc( )
    (c) both a and b (d) fputchar( )

52. The function(s) used for reading formatted input data from a file is (are)
 (a) getchar( ) (b) fscanf( )
 (c) scanf( ) (d) gets( )
53. The function used for random access of a file is
 (a) fseek( ) (b) ftell( )
 (c) search( ) (d) rewind( )
54. What is the value of origin used in fseek(fptr, position, origin);? to represent end of file
 (a) 0 (b) 1
 (c) 2 (d) EOF
55. What is the value of origin used in fseek(fptr, position, origin);?
 (a) 0 (b) 1
 (c) 2 (d) START
56. If an error occurs, the function fseek( ) returns
 (a) non-zero (b) zero
 (c) no value (d) -1
57. The value returned by fseek( ) on successful action is
 (a) non-zero (b) zero
 (c) OK (d) READY
58. The function ftell(fptr) returns
 (a) the beginning position of the file represented by fptr
 (b) the end position of file represented by fptr
 (c) the currect position of the file represented by fptr
 (d) the middle position of the file represented by fptr
59. The value returned by successful action of ftell(fptr) is
 (a) -1 (b) 0
 (c) long int value representing the current file position
 (d) MAX_INT

60. The value returned by ftell() if an error occurs is
(a) -1 (b) 0
(c) Positive value (d) MIN_INT

61. The function call fseek (fp, 0, 0); is same as
(a) fp = fopen( ) (b) rewind (fp);
(c) fclose(fp); (d) ftell (fp);

62. The way to access file contents from a program is
(a) by using library functions (b) by using system calls
(c) both options a and b (d) to use a linker

63. I/O stream can be
(a) a text stream (b) a binary stream
(c) both options a and b (d) an I/O operation

64. File opening is
(a) a default action in file processing
(b) an action of connecting a program to a file
(c) not necessary
(d) not using any library functions

65. File defined in stdio.h is
(a) a region of storage (b) a data type
(c) not a data type (d) a variable

66. The function used for reading binary stream is
(a) read( ) (b) fread( ) (c) fscanf( ) (d) all the above

67. The function used for writing to binary streams is
(a) write( ) (b) fwrite( )
(c) fprint( ) (d) all the above

68. Identify the functions for in-memory format conversions
(a) realloc() (b) sprintf( )
(c) sscanf( ) (d) both b and c

69. The value of string after executing the following statements is
int x = 25; char string [5]; sprintf (string, "%d", x);
(a) "25"
(b) 25
(c) TWO FIVE
(d) 25000

70. The value of ch after executing the following statements is
int x; char ch; char string [20] = "100 5";
sscanf(string, "%3d%c", &x, &ch);
(a) 5
(b) blank
(c) "5"
(d) NULL

71. Identify the valid constant declaration(s).
(a) varying number of parameters
(b) fixed number of parameters
(c) no argument
(d) at most five arguments

72. va_list is
(a) a macro defined in stdarg.h
(b) a predefined data type in stdarg.h
(c) a macro defined in stdlib.h
(d) a predefined data type stdlib.h

73. Identify the macro(s) defined in stdarg.h.
(a) va_start
(b) va_end
(c) va_arg
(d) all the above

74. Identify the trigraph sequence for #.
(a) ??/
(b) ??=
(c) ??'
(d) ??!

75. Identify the trigraph sequence for \.
(a) ??/
(b) ??=
(c) ??'
(d) ??!

76. Identify the trigraph sequence for ^.

(a) ??/ (b) ??=
(c) ??’ (d) ??!

77. Which of the following is valid for opening a read-only ASCII file?

(a) fileOpen (filename, “read”);
(b) fopen (filename, “r”);
(c) fileOpen (filename, “r”);
(d) fopen (filename, “read”);

78. What are two predefined FILE pointers in C?

(a) stdout and stderr (b) console and error
(c) stdout and stdio (d) stdio and stderr

79. The function used to position the file pointer in C is

(a) seekg( ) (b) fseekg( )
(c) fseek( ) (d) fcount

80. What file I/O function is used to report the number of bytes from the beginning of the file to the file position indicator?

(a) ftell (b) freport
(c) fseek (d) fcount

81. Which standard file is to be included to use the memcpy( ) function without a warning in an ANSI C compiler?

(a) string.h (b) memory.h (c) stdlib.h
(d) stdio.h

82. If there is a need to see output as soon as possible, which function will force the output from the buffer into the output stream?

(a) write( ) (b) output( )
(c) flush( ) (d) fflush( )

83. Which of the following function does not take variable number of arguments?

(a) main( ) (b) printf( )
(c) scanf( ) (d) sprintf( )

84. Low level files are accessed through
    (a) system calls (b) library functions
    (c) linker (d) loader

85.C supports
    (a) high level files (b) low level files
    (c) both options a and b (d) executable files only

Answers

1. (c)	2. (b)	3. (b)	4. (a)	5. (c)
6. (a)	7. (c)	8. (a)	9. (b)	10. (b)
11. (d)	12. (c)	13. (d)	14. (d)	15. (a)
16. (b)	17. (c)	18. (a)	19. (a)	20. (b)
21. (b)	22. (c)	23. (b)	24. (b)	25. (a)
26. (c)	27. (c)	28. (c)	29. (b)	30. (b)
31. (d)	32. (d)	33. (b)	34. (b)	35. (c)
36. (d)	37. (d)	38. (b)	39. (c)	40. (b)
41. (b)	42. (c)	43. (d)	44. (d)	45. (a)
46. (b)	47. (a)	48. (c)	49. (a)	50. (c)
51. (c)	52. (b)	53. (a)	54. (c)	55. (a)
56. (a)	57. (b)	58. (c)	59. (c)	60. (a)
61. (b)	62. (c)	63. (c)	64. (b)	65. (b)
66. (b)	67. (b)	68. (d)	69. (a)	70. (b)
71. (d)	72. (b)	73. (d)	74. (b)	75. (a)
76. (c)	77. (b)	78. (a)	79. (c)	80. (a)
81. (a)	82. (d)	83. (a)	84. (a)	85. (c)

CHAPTER

12

C Preprocessor

A. CODE SNIPPETS

Problem 1

Check the errors from the following program?

```
#include<stdio.h>
#include<conio.h>
#define FUN(i, j) i##j
void main( )
{
int x=100, y=200, z=300;
int k;
for(k=1;k<3;k++)
printf("Values are %d\n",FUN(k,i));
getch();
}
```

Output:

Error

Problem 2

Find the output of the following program?

```
#include<stdio.h>
#include<conio.h>
#define FUN(i, j) i##j
void main( )
{
int x[]={2,4,6};
int i;
for(i=0;i<2;i++)
printf("Values are %d", FUN(x,[i]));
getch();
}
```

Output:

```
Values are 2
Values are 4
Values are 6
```

Problem 3

Check the errors from the following program?

```
#include<stdio.h>
#include<conio.h>
#define A 10
#undef A
void main( )
{
printf("Value of A is %d", A);
getch();
}
```

Output:

```
Error
```

NOTE: Undefined symbol A in main()

Problem 4

Find the output of the following program?

```
#include<stdio.h>
#include<conio.h>
#define A 10
#undef B
void main( )
{
printf("Value of A is %d", A);
getch();
}
```

Output:

```
Value of A is 10
```

Problem 5

Find the output of the following program?

```
#include<stdio.h>
#include<conio.h>
#define A 5
void main( )
{
printf("Value of A is %d", A);
#undef A
getch();
}
```

Output:

```
Value of A is 5
```

Problem 6

Find the output of the following program?

```
#include<stdio.h>
#include<conio.h>
#define A 10
void main( )
{
printf("Value of A is %d", A);
getch();
}
#undef A
```

Output:

```
Value of A is 10
```

Problem 7

Find the output of the following program?

```
#include<stdio.h>
#include<conio.h>
#define A 5
void main( )
{
#define A 5
printf("Value of A is %d", A);
getch();
}
```

Output:

```
Value of A is 5
```

Problem 8

Find the output of the following program?

```
#include<stdio.h>
#include<conio.h>
```

```
void main( )
{
printf("Welcome");
getch();
}
```

Output:

```
Welcome
```

Problem 9

Find the output of the following program?

```
#include<stdio.h>
#include<conio.h>
void main( )
{
printf("Welcome Khalsa College??\tAmritsar");
getch();
}
```

Output:

```
Welcome Khalsa College Amritsar
```

Problem 10

Check the errors from the following program?

```
#include<stdio.h>
#include<conio.h>
void main( )
{
printf("Khalsa
College");
getch();
}
```

Output:

```
Error
```

NOTE: Unterminated string or character constant

Problem 11

Find the output of the following program?

```
#include<stdio.h>
#include<conio.h>
void main( )
{
printf("Khalsa\
College");
getch();
}
```

Output:

```
Khalsa College
```

Problem 12

Find the output of the following program?

```
#include<stdio.h>
#include<conio.h>
void main( )
{
printf("Khalsa" "College");
getch();
}
```

Output:

```
Khalsa College
```

Problem 13

Find the output of the following program?

```
#include<stdio.h>
#include<conio.h>
void main( )
{
printf("Khalsa\nCollege");
getch();
}
```

Output:

```
Khalsa College
```

Problem 14

Find the output of the following program?

```
#include<stdio.h>
#include<conio.h>
#define clrscr() 12
void main()
{
printf("Display \n");
clrscr();
printf("The value is %d", clrscr());
getch();
}
```

Output:

```
Display
Value is 12
```

Problem 15

Find the output of the following program?

```
#include<stdio.h>
#include<conio.h>
#define SQUARE(a) a*a
void main( )
{
printf("Square root of 3 is %d", SQUARE(3));
getch();
}
```

Output:

```
Square root of 3 is 9
```

Problem 16

Check the errors from the following program?

```
#include<stdio.h>
#include<conio.h>
#define SQUARE (x) x*x
void main( )
{
printf("Square root of 3 is %d", SQUARE(3));
getch();
}
```

Output:

```
Error
```

NOTE: Undefined symbol x in main()

Problem 17

Find the output of the following program?

```
#include<stdio.h>
#include<conio.h>
#define SQUARE(x) x*x
```

```
void main( )
{
int i = 5, j;
j = i/SQUARE(2);
printf("Value of j is %d", j);
getch();
}
```

Output:

```
Value of j is 5
```

Problem 18

Find the output of the following program?

```
#include<stdio.h>
#include<conio.h>
#define SQUARE(x) (x*x)
void main( )
{
int i = 40, j;
j=i/SQUARE(2);
printf("Value of j is %d", j);
getch();
}
```

Output:

```
Value of j is 10
```

Problem 19

Find the output of the following program?

```
#include<stdio.h>
#include<conio.h>
#define SQUARE(x) (x*x)
```

```
void main( )
{
int i = 6, j;
j=SQUARE(i+3);
printf("Value of j is %d", j);
getch();
}
```

Output:

```
Value of j is 27
```

Problem 20

Find the output of the following program?

```
#include<stdio.h>
#include<conio.h>
#define SQUARE(x) ((x)*(x))
void main( )
{
int i = 6, j;
j=SQUARE(i+3);
printf("Value of j is %d", j);
getch();
}
```

Output:

```
Value of j is 81
```

Problem 21

Find the output of the following program?

```
#include<stdio.h>
#include<conio.h>
#define SQUARE(x) ((x)*(x))
```

```
void main( )
{
int i = 2, j;
j=SQUARE(++i);
printf("Value of j is %d", j);
getch();
}
```

Output:

```
Value of j is 16
```

Problem 22

Find the output of the following program?

```
#include<stdio.h>
#include<conio.h>
#define SQUARE(x) ((x)*(x));
void main( )
{
int i= 2, j;
if (SQUARE(i)= =j)
printf("Equal");
else
printf("Not Equal");
getch();
}
```

Output:

```
Error
```

Problem 23

Find the output of the following program?

```
#include<stdio.h>
```

```
#include<conio.h>
#define exchange(i, j) i^=j; j^=i; i^=j;
void main( )
{
int i=5, j=10;
printf("Values of i and j before changes are %d %d\n",
   i, j);
exchange(i, j);
printf("Values of i and j after changes are %d %d\n",
   i, j);
getch();
}
```

Output:

```
Values of i and j before changes are 5 10
Values of i and j after changes are 10 5
```

Problem 24

Check the errors from the following program?

```
#include<stdio.h>
#include<conio.h>
#define exchange(i, j) i^=j; j^=i; i^=j;
void main( )
{
int i=5, j=10;
printf("Exchange the values of i and j only if i is
   greater than j");
if (i>j)
exchange(i, j)
else
printf("Values are not changed");
```

```
printf("Final value of i and j are %d %d", i, j);
getch();
}
```

Output:

```
Error
```

NOTE: Misplaced else in main()

Problem 25

Find the output of the following program?

```
#include<stdio.h>
#include<conio.h>
#define exchange(i, j) i^=j, j^=i, i^=j
void main( )
{
int i=5, j=10;
printf("Exchange the values of i and j only if i is
   greater than j");
if (i>j)
exchange(i, j)
else
printf("Values are not changed");
printf("Final value of i and j are %d %d", i, j);
getch();
}
```

Output:

```
Exchange the values of i and j only if i is greater
   than j
Final value of i and j are 10 5
```

Problem 26

Find the output of the following program?

```
#include<stdio.h>
#include<conio.h>
#define exchange(i, j) i^= j^= i^=j
void main( )
{
int i=5, j=10;
printf("Exchange the values of i and j only if i is
   greater than j");
if (i>j)
exchange(i, j)
else
printf("Values are not changed");
printf("Final value of i and j are %d %d", i, j);
getch();
}
```

Output:

```
Exchange the values of i and j only if i is greater
   than j
Final value of i and j are 10 5
```

Problem 27

Find the output of the following program?

```
#include<stdio.h>
#include<conio.h>
#define A 100
void main( )
{
int Ar=500;
```

```
printf("The A is %d", Ar);
getch();
}
```

Output:

```
The A is 500
```

Problem 28

Find the output of the following program?

```
#include<stdio.h>
#include<conio.h>
#define STR(str) #str
void main( )
{
printf(STR(Khalsa College));
getch();
}
```

Output:

```
Khalsa College
```

Problem 29

Find the output of the following program?

```
#include<stdio.h>
#include<conio.h>
#define STR(str) #str
void main( )
{
printf(STR(Khalsa      College));
getch();
}
```

Output:

```
Khalsa    College
```

Problem 30

Find the output of the following program?

```
#include<stdio.h>
#include<conio.h>
#define STR(str) #str
void main( )
{
printf(STR(     Khalsa College        ));
getch();
}
```

Output:

```
Khalsa College
```

Problem 31

Find the output of the following program?

```
#include<stdio.h>
#include<conio.h>
#include<stdio.h>
#include<conio.h>
#define STR(str) #str
void main( )
{
printf(STR(Khalsa "Coll"ege));
getch();
}
```

Output:

```
Khalsa "Coll"ege
```

Problem 32

Find the output of the following program?

```
#include<stdio.h>
#include<conio.h>
#define STR(i,j,k) #i#j#k
void main( )
{
char str1[50]=STR(WELCOME, KHALSA, COLLEGE);
char str2[50]=STR(WELCOME, KHALSA, COLLEGE, AMRITSAR);
puts(str1);
puts(str2);
getch();
}
```

Output:

```
WELCOME, KHALSA, COLLEGE
WELCOME, KHALSA, COLLEGE, AMRITSAR
```

Problem 33

Find the output of the following program?

```
#include<stdio.h>
#include<conio.h>
#define STR(str) #str
#include STR(stdio.h)
void main( )
{
printf("This is include directive");
getch();
}
```

Output:

```
This is include directive
```

Problem 34

Find the output of the following program?

```
#include<stdio.h>
#include<conio.h>
#define FUN(i, j) i##j
void main( )
{
int x=4;
printf("Value of x is %d", FUN(x, 1));
getch();
}
```

Output:

```
Value of x is 4
```

Problem 35

Find the output of the following program?

```
#include<stdio.h>
#include<conio.h>
void main( )
{
int i = 5;
#ifdef DEF
i = i * i;
#else
printf ( "\n%d", i );
#endif
getch();
}
```

Output:

```
5
```

Problem 36

Find the output of the following program?

```
#include<stdio.h>
#include<conio.h>
#define multiply (m) (m * m)
void main( )
{
int i = 3, j ;
j = multiply(i + 1);
printf ( "\n%d", j ) ;
getch();
}
```

Output:

7

Problem 37

Find the output of the following program?

```
#include<stdio.h>
#include<conio.h>
#define multiply (m) (m * m)
void main( )
{
int i = 3, j, k ;
j = multiply (i++);
k = multiply (++i);
printf ( "\n%d %d", j, k ) ;
getch();
}
```

Output:

9 49

Problem 38

Find the output of the following program?

```
#include<stdio.h>
#include<conio.h>
void main( )
{
printf("Khalsa??\tCollege??\nAmritsar");
getch();
}
```

Output:

```
Khalsa          College
Amritsar
```

Problem 39

Find the output of the following program?

```
#include<stdio.h>
#include<conio.h>
#define A 10
void main( )
{
#ifdef A
printf("Value of A is 10");
#else
printf("Value of A is not 10");
#endif
getch();
}
```

Output:

```
Value of A is 10
```

Problem 40

Find the output of the following program?

```
#include<stdio.h>
#include<conio.h>
#define A 10
void main( )
{
#ifdef A
printf("Value of A is 10");
#else
Is there any error??
#endif
getch();
}
```

Output:

```
Value of A is 10
```

Problem 41

Find the output of the following program?

```
#include<stdio.h>
#include<conio.h>
#define A 10
void main( )
{
#if A= = 10
printf("Value of A is 10");
#else
printf("Value of A is not 10");
#endif
getch();
```

```
}
```

Output:

```
Value of A is 10
```

Problem 42

Check the errors from the following program?

```
#include<stdio.h>
#include<conio.h>
#define A 5
void main( )
{
#ifdef A=5
printf("Value of A is 5");
#else
printf("Value of A is not 5");
#endif
getch();
}
```

Output:

```
Error
```

NOTE: L-value required

Problem 43

Check the errors from the following program?

```
#include<stdio.h>
#include<conio.h>
#define A 10
void main( )
{
int a=10;
```

```
#if a = = A
printf("Value of A is 10");
#else
printf("Value of A is not 10");
#endif
getch();
}
```

Output:

Error

NOTE: Constant expression requoired

Problem 44

Find the output of the following program?

```
#include<stdio.h>
#include<conio.h>
#define A 10
void main( )
{
const int a=10;
#if a= = A
printf("Value of A is 10");
#else
printf("Value of A is not 10");
#endif
getch();
}
```

Output:

Value of A is 10

Problem 45

Find the output of the following program?

```
#include<stdio.h>
#include<conio.h>
void main( )
{
char *str= “Welcome”;
printf(str “Amritsar”);
getch();
}
```

Output:

Error

Problem 46

Check the errors from the following program?

```
#include<stdio.h>
#include<conio.h>
#define PI=3.14
void main( )
{
int r = 2;
printf(“Circumference of the circle is %f”, 2*PI*r);
getch();
}
```

Output:

Error

Problem 47

Find the output of the following program?

```
#include<stdio.h>
```

```
#include<conio.h>
#define PI 3.14
void main( )
{
int r = 2;
printf("Circumference of the circle is %f", 2*PI*r);
getch();
}
```

Output:

```
Circumference of the circle is 12.560000
```

Problem 48

Find the output of the following program?

```
#include<stdio.h>
#include<conio.h>
#define PI 3.14;
void main( )
{
int r = 2;
printf("Circumference of the circle is %f", 2*PI*r);
getch();
}
```

Output:

```
Error
```

Problem 49

Find the output of the following program?

```
#include<stdio.h>
#include<conio.h>
#define int char
```

```
void main( )
{
int j;
printf("Size of j is %d:, sizeof(j));
getch();
}
```

Output:

```
Size of j is 1
```

Problem 50

Find the output of the following program?

```
#include<stdio.h>
#include<conio.h>
#define + -
#define * /
void main( )
{
int sum;
sum=2+3*5;
printf("Sum is %d", sum);
getch();
}
```

Output:

```
Error
```

NOTE: Define directive needs an identifier

Problem 51

Find the output of the following program?

```
#include<stdio.h>
#include<conio.h>
```

```
void main( )
{
#ifdef WINDOWS
UNIX OPERATING SYSTEM
#elif defined (LINUX)
LINUX OPERATING SYSTEM
#else
#error OS IS NOT KNOWN
#enddif
getch();
}
```

Output:

Error

Problem 52

Find the output of the following program?

```
#include<stdio.h>
#include<conio.h>
void main( )
{
/* KHALSA COLLEGE AMRITSAR
/* C IS PROGRAMMING LANGUAGE* /
FORTRAN IS ALSO PROGRAMMING LANGUAGE*/
Printf("IKVINDERPAL SINGH");
getch();
}
```

Output:

Error

Problem 53

Find the output of the following program?

```
#include<stdio.h>
#include<conio.h>
#pragma option -C
void main( )
{
/* KHALSA COLLEGE AMRITSAR
/* C IS PROGRAMMING LANGUAGE* /
FORTRAN IS ALSO PROGRAMMING LANGUAGE*/
Printf("IKVINDERPAL SINGH");
getch();
}
```

Output:

```
IKVINDERPAL SINGH
```

Problem 54

Find the output of the following program?

```
#include<stdio.h>
#include<conio.h>
#define size_of(data) ((char *)(&data+1)-(char *)
   (&data))
void main( )
{
int INT;
char CHAR;
float FLOAT;
double DOUBLE;
printf("Size of int: %d\n", size_of(INT));
printf("Size of char: %d\n",size_of(CHAR);
```

```
printf("Size of float: %d\n",size_of(FLOAT);
printf("Size of double: %d\n",size_of(DOUBLE);
getch();
}
```

Output:

```
Size of int: 2
Size of char: 1
Size of float: 4
Size of double: 8
```

B. FILL IN THE BLANKS

1 A translator that converts a program written in a high-level language into an equivalent program in a machine-level language is known as ....
2. The set of characters available when the source program file is executing is called ....
3. The .... directive is used to configure some of the compiler options.
4. The only directive that has no effect is ....
5. .... is the smallest element of the language during the third to sixth phase of translation.
6. The input character sequence x+++++y is divided into the following stream of tokens ....
7. .... is a facility provided by a C preprocessor, by which a token can be replaced by the user-defined sequence of characters.
8. Object-like macros are also known as ....

Answers

1. compiler
2. execution character set
3. pragma
4. null directive

5. Preprocessing token
6. x ++ ++ +y
7. Macro
8. symbolic constants

C. TRUE OR FALSE

State whether each of the following is true or false

1. During the preprocessing stage, each instance of backslash character immediately followed by a new-line character is deleted.
2. ## is one taken and there should be no white-space character between two ## characters.
3. A predefined macro cannot appear immediately following a define directive.
4. A predefined macro can be undefined using an undef directive.
5. The keywords are not preprocessing tokens. Thus, it is possible to use a keyword as an identifier name in a preprocessor directive, e.g. #define int char.
6. The preprocessor directives are terminated with a semicolon.
7. If the identifier specified with the undef directive is not currently defined as a macro, there will be a compilation error.
8. The scope of a macro is the block in which it is defined.
9. Macro replacement is carried out even within a string literal constant.
10. The preprocessor directives can only appear before the function main.
11. The concatenation operator (i.e. ##) can appear at the beginning or at the end of the replacement list in a macro definition.

Answers

1. True	2. True	3. True	4. False
5. True	6. False	7. False	8. False
9. False	10. False	11. False	

D. OBJECTIVE TYPE QUESTIONS

1. What is the value of CAR in the following statement?

   enum vehicle

   {BUS, SCOOTER = 2, CAR, TRAIN = 5, AEROPLANE = 6}

   (a) 0 (b) 1

   (c) 3 (d) 4

2. Identify the correct statement(s)

   (a) the values of an enumerator need not be distinct in the same enumeration type

   (b) the names of an enumerator in different enumeration type must be distinct

   (c) the names of an enumerator must be different from other normal variables

   (d) all the above

3. The qualifier const

   (a) defines a constant name

   (b) keeps the value of a variable constant during execution of the program

   (c) both a and b

   (d) does not keep the value of a variable constant

4. What is the output of the following program?

```
#define MAX(x, y) ((x) > (y) ? (x) : (y))
main( )
{
int x=5, y=5;
printf ("maximum is %d", MAX(++x, ++Y));
}
```

   (a) maximum is 7 (b) maximum is 5

   (c) maximum is 6 (d) none of the above

5. What is the value of CAR in the following enumeration?

```
enum transport
{
SCOOTER=1, BUS=4, CAR, TRAIN=8
};
```

(a) 0 (b) 5
(c) 7 (d) 4

6. What is the value of LUTUS in the following enumeration?

```
enum symbol
{
HAND, SUN, LOTUS, UMBRELLA
};
```

(a) 0 (b) 3
(c) 2 (d) none of the above

7. What is the output of the following code?

```
enum fruits
{
APPLE=1, ORANGE=1, GRAPES=3, PINEAPPLE
};
printf ("%d", ORANGE);
```

(a) Compilation error (b) Execution error
(c) 2 (d) 1

8. The typedef statement is used to
(a) create a new data type (b) rename the existing data type
(c) to define a storage class (d) create a structure

9. Identify the correct statement.
(a) typedef int HOST (b) typedef int HOST;
(c) typedef int = HOST (d) typedef int = HOST;

10. The only directive that has no effect is ....

    (a) typedef (b) Null

    (c) const (d) enum

Answers

1. (c)	2. (d)	3. (b)	4. (a)	5. (b)
6. (c)	7. (d)	8. (b)	9. (b)	10. (b)

CHAPTER 13

C Traps

1. **main()**

```
{
int i=-1,j=-1,k=0,l=2,m;
m=i++&&j++&&k++||l++;
printf("%d %d %d %d %d",i,j,k,l,m);
}
```

Answer: 0 0 1 3 1

2. **main()**

```
{
int i=3;
switch(i)
{
default:printf("zero");
case 1: printf("one");
break;
case 2:printf("two");
break;
case 3: printf("three");
break;
}
```

```
}
```

Answer: three

3. main()

```
{
printf("%x",-1<<4);
}
```

Answer: fff0

4. main()

```
{
int c=- -2;
printf("c=%d",c);
}
```

Answer: c=2;

5. main()

```
{
int i=10;
i=!i>14;
Printf ("i=%d",i);
}
```

Answer: i=0

6. main()

```
{
printf("\nab");
printf("\bsi");
printf("\rha");
}
```

Answer: hai

7. **main()**

```
{
int i=5;
printf("%d%d%d%d%d%d",i++,i-,++i,-i,i);
}
```

Answer: 45545

8. **main()**

```
{
printf("%p",main);
}
```

Answer: Some address will be printed

9. **main()**

```
{
int i=400,j=300;
printf("%d..%d");
}
```

Answer:

```
400..300
```

10. **void main()**

```
{
int i=5;
printf("%d",i++ + ++i);
}
```

Answer:

```
Output Cannot be predicted exactly.
```

11. **void main()**

```
{
int i=5;
printf("%d",i+++++i);
```

```
}
```

Answer:

```
Compiler Error
```

12. #include<stdio.h>

```
main()
{
int i=1,j=2;
switch(i)
{
case 1: printf("GOOD");
break;
case j: printf("BAD");
break;
}
}
```

Answer:

```
Compiler Error: Constant expression required in function
   main.
```

13. main()

```
{
int i;
printf("%d",scanf("%d",&i)); // value 10 is given as
   input here
}
```

Answer:

```
1
```

14. main()

```
{
int i=0;
```

```
for(;i++;printf("%d",i)) ;
printf("%d",i);
}
```

Answer:

1

15. main()

```
{
printf("%d", out);
}
int out=100;
```

Answer:

Compiler error: undefined symbol out in function main.

16. main()

```
{
int i=-1;
+i;
printf("i = %d, +i = %d \n",i,+i);
}
```

Answer:

i = -1, +i = -1

17. main()

```
{
char not;
not=!2;
printf("%d",not);
}
```

Answer:

0

18. main()

```
{
int k=1;
printf("%d==1 is ""%s",k,k==1?"TRUE":"FALSE");
}
```

Answer:

```
1==1 is TRUE
```

19. main()

```
{
int y;
scanf("%d",&y); // input given is 2000
if( (y%4==0 && y%100 != 0) || y%100 == 0 )
printf("%d is a leap year");
else
printf("%d is not a leap year");
}
```

Answer:

```
2000 is a leap year
```

20. main()

```
{
int i=-1;
-i;
printf("i = %d, -i = %d \n",i,-i);
}
```

Answer:

```
i = -1, -i = 1
```

21. #include<stdio.h>

```
main()
{
```

```
const int i=4;
float j;
j = ++i;
printf("%d %f", i,++j);
}
```

Answer:

Compiler error

22. main()

```
{
int i=5,j=6,z;
printf("%d",i+++j);
}
```

Answer:

11

23. main()

```
{
int i =0;j=0;
if(i && j++)
printf("%d..%d",i++,j);
printf("%d..%d,i,j);
}
```

Answer:

0..0

24. int i;

```
main(){
int t;
for ( t=4;scanf("%d",&i)-t;printf("%d\n",i))
printf("%d-",t-);
}
```

```
// If the inputs are 0,1,2,3 find the o/p
```

Answer:

```
4–0
3–1
2–2
```

25. main(){

```
int a= 0;int b = 20;char x =1;char y =10;
if(a,b,x,y)
printf("hello");
}
```

Answer:

```
hello
```

26. void main()

```
{
unsigned giveit=-1;
int gotit;
printf("%u ",++giveit);
printf("%u \n",gotit=–giveit);
}
```

Answer:

```
0 65535
```

27. main()

```
{
float me = 1.1;
double you = 1.1;
if(me==you)
printf("I love U");
else
printf("I hate U");
}
```

Answer:

```
I hate U
```

28. a<<1 is equivalent to

(a) multiplying by 2 (b) dividing by 2

(c) adding 2 (d) none of the above

29. The operation of a stair case switch best explains the

(a) or operation (b) and operation (c) exclusive nor operation (d) exclusive or operation

30. Which of the following is/are syntactically correct?

(a) for(); (b) for(;);

(c) for(,); (d) for(;;);

31. The expression 4+6/3*2-2+7%3 evaluates to

(a) 3 (b) 4

(c) 6 (d) 7

32. Any C program

(a) must contain at least one function

(b) need not contain ant function

(c) needs input data

(d) none of the above

33. Using goto inside for loop is equivalent to using

(a) continue (b) break

(c) return d)none of the above

34. The program fragment inta=5,b=2; printf("%d",a+++++b);

(a) prints 7 (b) prints 8

(c) prints 9 (d) none of the above

35. printf("ab" , "cd","ef"); prints

(a) ab

(b) abcdef

(c) abcdef, followed by garbage value

(d) none of the above

36. Consider the following program segment. i=6720; j=4;

```
while((i%j)==0)
{
i=i/j;
j=j+1;
}
On termination j will have the value
```

(a) 4 (b) 8

(c) 9 (d) 6720

37. main()

```
{
char s[ ]="man";
int i;
for(i=0;s[ i ];i++)
printf("\n%c%c%c%c",s[ i ],*(s+i),*(i+s),i[s]);
}
```

Answer:

```
mmmm
aaaa
nnnn
```

38. main()

```
{
extern int i;
i=20;
printf("%d",i);
}
```

Answer:

```
Linker Error : Undefined symbol '_i'
```

39. #define int char

```
main()
{
int i=65;
printf("sizeof(i)=%d",sizeof(i));
}
```

Answer:

```
sizeof(i)=1
```

40. #define square(x) x*x

```
main()
{
int i;
i = 64/square(4);
printf("%d",i);
}
```

Answer:

```
64
```

41. #include <stdio.h>

```
#define a 10
main()
{
#define a 50
printf("%d",a);
}
```

Answer:

```
50
```

42. #define clrscr() 100

```
main()
{
clrscr();
printf("%d\n",clrscr());
}
```

Answer:

100

43. main()

```
{
clrscr();
}
clrscr();
```

Answer:

No output/error

44. main()

```
{
int i=1;
while (i<=5)
{
printf("%d",i);
if (i>2)
goto here;
i++;
}
}
fun()
{
```

```
here:
printf("PP");
}
```

Answer:

Compiler error: Undefined label 'here' in function main

45. #define f(g,g2) g##g2

```
main()
{
int var12=100;
printf("%d",f(var,12));
}
```

Answer:

100

46. main()

```
{
extern out;
printf("%d", out);
}
int out=100;
```

Answer:

100

47. main()

```
{
show();
}
void show()
{
printf("I'm the greatest");
```

```
}
```

Answer:

```
Compier error: Type mismatch in redeclaration of show.
```

48. int i,j;

```
for(i=0;i<=10;i++)
{
j+=5;
assert(i<5);
}
```

Answer:

```
Runtime error: Abnormal program termination.
assert failed (i<5), <file name>,<line number>
```

49. #define FALSE -1

```
#define TRUE 1
#define NULL 0
main() {
if(NULL)
puts("NULL");
else if(FALSE)
puts("TRUE");
else
puts("FALSE");
}
```

Answer:

```
TRUE
```

50. #define max 5

```
#define int arr1[max]
main()
{
```

```
typedef char arr2[max];
arr1 list={0,1,2,3,4};
arr2 name="name";
printf("%d %s",list[0],name);
}
```

Answer:

Compiler error (in the line arr1 list = {0,1,2,3,4})

51. int i=10;

```
main()
{
extern int i;
{
int i=20;
{
const volatile unsigned i=30;
printf("%d",i);
}
printf("%d",i);
}
printf("%d",i);
}
```

Answer:

30,20,10

52. #include<stdio.h>

```
main()
{
int a[2][2][2] = { {10,2,3,4}, {5,6,7,8} };
int *p,*q;
p=&a[2][2][2];
```

```
*q=***a;
printf("%d..%d",*p,*q);
}
```

Answer:

garbagevalue..1

53. #include<stdio.h>

```
main()
{
register i=5;
char j[]= "hello";
printf("%s %d",j,i);
}
```

Answer:

hello 5

54. main()

```
{
int i=_l_abc(10);
printf("%d\n",--i);
}
int _l_abc(int i)
{
return(i++);
}
```

Answer:

9

55. main()

```
{
char c=' ',x,convert(z);
getc(c);
```

```
if((c>='a') && (c<='z'))
x=convert(c);
printf("%c",x);
}
convert(z)
{
return z-32;
}
```

Answer:

Compiler error

```
56. main()
{
int i;
i = abc();
printf("%d",i);
}
abc()
{
_AX = 1000;
}
```

Answer:

1000

57. What are the following notations of defining functions known as?

```
i. int abc(int a,float b)
{
/* some code */
}
ii. int abc(a,b)
```

```
int a; float b;
{
/* some code*/
}
```

Answer:

i. ANSI C notation

ii. Kernighan & Ritche notation

58. void main()

```
{
static int i=5;
if(-i){
main();
printf("%d ",i);
}
}
```

Answer:

0 0 0 0

59. void main()

```
{
int k=ret(sizeof(float));
printf("\n here value is %d",++k);
}
int ret(int ret)
{
ret += 2.5;
return(ret);
}
```

Answer:

Here value is 7

60. void main()

```
{
char a[]="12345\0";
int i=strlen(a);
printf("here in 3 %d\n",++i);
}
```

Answer:

```
here in 3 6
```

61. void main()

```
{
int i;
char a[]="\0";
if(printf("%s\n",a))
printf("Ok here \n");
else
printf("Forget it\n");
}
```

Answer:

```
Ok here
```

62. main()

```
{
clrscr();
}
clrscr();
```

Answer:

```
No output/error
```

63. main()

```
{
static int var = 5;
```

```
printf("%d ",var-);
if(var)
main();
}
```

Answer:

```
5 4 3 2 1
```

64. C preprocessor

(a) tales care of conditional compilation

(b) tales care of macros

(c) tales care of include files

(d) acts before compilations

65. A preprocessor command

(a) need not start on a new line

(b) need not start on the first column

(c) has # as the first character

(d) comes before the first executable statement

66. The following program

```
main()
{
int a=4;
change(a);
printf("%d",a);
}
change(int a)
{ printf("%d",++a); } outputs a)5 5 b)4 5 c) 5 4 d)4 4
```

67. The output of the following program is

```
main()
{
static int x[]={1, 2, 3, 4, 5, 6, 7, 8};
```

```
int i;
for(i=2;i<6;i++)
x[x[i]]=x[i];
for(i=0; i<8;i++)
printf("%d",x[i]);
}
```

(a) 1 2 3 3 5 5 7 8
(b) 1 2 3 4 5 6 7 8
(c) 8 7 6 5 4 3 2 1
(d) 1 2 3 5 4 6 7 8

68. The order in which actual parameters are evaluated in a function call

(a) is from the left
(b) is from the right
(c) is compiler dependent
(d) none of the above

69. The default parameter passing mechanism is

(a) call by value
(b) call by reference
(c) call by value result
(d) none

70. C does no automatic array bound checking. This is

(a) true
(b) false
(c) C's asset
(d) C's shortcoming

71. If a two dimensional array is used as a formal parameter, then

(a) both the subscripts may be left empty
(b) the first(row) subscript may be left empty
(c) the first subscript must be left empty
(d) both the subscripts must be left empty

72. If storage class is missing in the array definition, by default it will be taken to be

(a) automatic
(b) external

(c) static

(d) either automatic or external depending on the place of occurrence

73. Consider the declaration static char hello[]="hello"; The output of printf("%s\n",hello); will be the same as that of

(a) puts("hello"); (b) puts(hello);

(c) printf("%s\n","hello"); (d) puts("hello\n");

74. The array name can be pointer to

(a) another array (b) another variable

(c) to that array only (d) none

75. Array of pointers to table of strings saves

(a) time (b) memory

(c) CPU utilization (d) none of the above

76. The following program

```
main()
{
inc(); inc(); inc();
}
inc()
{
static int x;
printf("%d",++x);
} prints
```

a)0 1 2 b) 1 2 3 c) 3 consecutive, but unpredictable numbers d) 1 1 1

77. main()

```
{
int c[ ]={2.8,3.4,4,6.7,5};
int j,*p=c,*q=c;
```

```
for(j=0;j<5;j++) {
printf(" %d ",*c);
++q; }
for(j=0;j<5;j++){
printf(" %d ",*p);
++p; }
}
```

Answer:

2 2 2 2 2 2 3 4 6 5

78. main()

```
{
char *p="hai friends",*p1;
p1=p;
while(*p!='\0') ++*p++;
printf("%s %s",p,p1);
}
```

Answer:

ibj!gsjfoet

79. void main()

```
{
char far *farther,*farthest;
printf("%d..%d",sizeof(farther),sizeof(farthest));
}
```

Answer:

4..2

80. main()

```
{
char *p;
```

```
p="Hello";
printf("%c\n",*&*p);
}
```

Answer:

H

81. main()

```
{
static char
   names[5][20]={"pascal","ada","cobol","fortran","perl"};
int i;
char *t;
t=names[3];
names[3]=names[4];
names[4]=t;
for (i=0;i<=4;i++)
printf("%s",names[i]);
}
```

Answer:

Compiler error: Lvalue required in function main

82. #include<stdio.h>

```
main()
{
char s[]={'a','b','c','\n','c','\0'};
char *p,*str,*str1;
p=&s[3];
str=p;
str1=s;
printf("%d",++*p + ++*str1-32);
}
```

Answer:

M

83. main( )

```
{
int a[2][3][2] =
   {{{2,4},{7,8},{3,4}},{{2,2},{2,3},{3,4}}};
printf("%u %u %u %d \n",a,*a,**a,***a);
printf("%u %u %u %d \n",a+1,*a+1,**a+1,***a+1);
}
```

Answer:

```
100, 100, 100, 2
114, 104, 102, 3
```

84. main( )

```
{
int a[ ] = {10,20,30,40,50},j,*p;
for(j=0; j<5; j++)
{
printf("%d" ,*a);
a++;
}
p = a;
for(j=0; j<5; j++)
{
printf("%d " ,*p);
p++;
}
}
```

Answer:

```
Compiler error: lvalue required.
```

•

85. main( )

```
{
static int a[ ] = {0,1,2,3,4};
int *p[ ] = {a,a+1,a+2,a+3,a+4};
int **ptr = p;
ptr++;
printf("\n %d %d %d", ptr-p, *ptr-a, **ptr);
*ptr++;
printf("\n %d %d %d", ptr-p, *ptr-a, **ptr);
*++ptr;
printf("\n %d %d %d", ptr-p, *ptr-a, **ptr);
++*ptr;
printf("\n %d %d %d", ptr-p, *ptr-a, **ptr);
}
```

Answer:

```
111
222
333
344
```

86. pointers are of

(a) integer data type (b) character data type

(c) unsigned integer data type (d) none of these

87. main( )

```
{
void *vp;
char ch = 'g', *cp = "goofy";
int j = 20;
vp = &ch;
printf("%c", *(char *)vp);
```

```
vp = &j;
printf("%d",*(int *)vp);
vp = cp;
printf("%s",(char *)vp + 3);
}
```

Answer:

g20fy

88. main ( )

```
{
static char *s[ ] = {"black", "white", "yellow",
   "violet"};
char **ptr[ ] = {s+3, s+2, s+1, s}, ***p;
p = ptr;
**++p;
printf("%s",*-*++p + 3);
}
```

Answer:

ck

89. main()

```
{
int i, n;
char *x = "girl";
n = strlen(x);
*x = x[n];
for(i=0; i<n; ++i)
{
printf("%s\n",x);
x++;
}
```

```
}
```

Answer:

```
(blank space)
irl
rl
l
```

90. main()

```
{
char *cptr,c;
void *vptr,v;
c=10; v=0;
cptr=&c; vptr=&v;
printf("%c%v",c,v);
}
```

Answer:

Compiler error (at line number 4): size of v is Unknown.

91. main()

```
{
char *str1="abcd";
char str2[]="abcd";
printf("%d %d
   %d",sizeof(str1),sizeof(str2),sizeof("abcd"));
}
```

Answer:

2 5 5

92. main()

```
{
int *j;
{
```

```
int i=10;
j=&i;
} printf("%d",*j);
}
```

Answer:

10

93. void main()

```
{
int const * p=5;
printf("%d",++(*p));
}
```

Answer:

Compiler error: Cannot modify a constant value.

94. main()

```
{
char *p;
int *q;
long *r;
p=q=r=0;
p++;
q++;
r++;
printf("%p...%p...%p",p,q,r);
}
```

Answer:

0001...0002...0004

95. main(int argc, char **argv)

```
{
printf("enter the character");
```

```
getchar();
sum(argv[1],argv[2]);
}
sum(num1,num2)
int num1,num2;
{
return num1+num2;
}
```

Answer:

Compiler error.

96. #include <stdio.h>

```
int one_d[]={1,2,3};
main()
{
int *ptr;
ptr=one_d;
ptr+=3;
printf("%d",*ptr);
}
19
```

Answer:

garbage value

```
97. #include<stdio.h>
aaa() { printf("hi"); }
bbb(){ printf("hello"); }
ccc(){ printf("bye"); }
main()
{
int (*ptr[3])();
```

```
ptr[0]=aaa; ptr[1]=bbb;
ptr[2]=ccc; ptr[2]();
}
```

Answer:

bye

98. In the following pgm add a stmt in the function fun such that the address of

'a' gets stored in 'j'.

```
main(){
int * j;
void fun(int **);
fun(&j);
}
void fun(int **k) {
int a =0;
/* add a stmt here*/
}
```

Answer:

*k = &a

99. main()

```
{
char *p;
p="%d\n";

p++;
p++;
printf(p-2,300);
}
```

Answer:

300

100. func(a,b)

```
int a,b;
{
return( a= (a==b) );
}
main()
{
int process(),func();
printf("The value of process is %d !\n
  ",process(func,3,6));
}
process(pf,val1,val2)
int (*pf) ();
int val1,val2;
{
return((*pf) (val1,val2));
}
```

Answer:

```
The value if process is 0 !
```

101. main()

```
{
char *p;
21
printf("%d %d ",sizeof(*p),sizeof(p));
}
```

Answer:

```
1 2
```

102. main()

```
{
```

```
char string[]="Hello World";
display(string);
}
void display(char *string)
{
printf("%s",string);
}
```

Answer:

Compiler Error : Type mismatch in redeclaration of function display

103. #include<stdio.h>

```
main()
{
char s[]={'a','b','c','\n','c','\0'};
char *p,*str,*str1;
p=&s[3];
str=p;
str1=s;
printf("%d",++*p + ++*str1-32);
}
```

Answer:

77

104. #include<stdio.h>

```
main()
{
int a[2][2][2] = { {10,2,3,4}, {5,6,7,8} };
int *p,*q;
p=&a[2][2][2];
*q=***a;
```

```
printf("%d—%d",*p,*q);
}
```

Answer:

```
SomeGarbageValue—1
```

105. puts (argv[0])prints

(a) the name of the source code file

(b) the number of command line arguments

(c) argv

(d) the name of the executable code file

106. The addressoperator & , cannot act on

(a) R-values
(b) arithmetic expressions
(c) members of a structure
(d) local variables

107. The argument used to print the number of command line arguments is

(a) printf("%d",argv);
(b) printf("%d",argv[0]);
(c) printf("%d",argc);
(d) none

108. In command line arguments main() function takes ____ number of arguments

(a) 1
(b) 2
(c) 3
(d) 4

109. #include<stdio.h>

```
main()
{
struct xx
{
int x=3;
char name[]="hello";
};
struct xx *s;
```

```
printf("%d",s->x);
printf("%s",s->name);
}
```

Answer:

Compiler Error

110. #include<stdio.h>

```
main()
{
struct xx
{
int x;
struct yy
{
char s;
struct xx *p;
};
struct yy *q;
};
}
```

Answer:

Compiler Error

111. enum colors {BLACK,BLUE,GREEN}

```
main()
{
printf("%d..%d..%d",BLACK,BLUE,GREEN);
return(1);
}
```

Answer:

0..1..2

112. #include<stdio.h>

```
main()
{
struct xx
{
int x=3;
char name[]="hello";
};
struct xx *s=malloc(sizeof(struct xx));
printf("%d",s->x);
printf("%s",s->name);
}
```

Answer:

Compiler Error

113. struct aaa{

```
struct aaa *prev;
int i;
struct aaa *next;
};
main()
{
struct aaa abc,def,ghi,jkl;
int x=100;
abc.i=0;abc.prev=&jkl;
abc.next=&def;
def.i=1;def.prev=&abc;def.next=&ghi;
ghi.i=2;ghi.prev=&def;
ghi.next=&jkl;
jkl.i=3;jkl.prev=&ghi;jkl.next=&abc;
```

```
x=abc.next->next->prev->next->i;
printf("%d",x);
}
```

Answer:

2

114. struct point

```
{
int x;
int y;
};
struct point origin,*pp;
main()
{
pp=&origin;
printf("origin is(%d%d)\n",(*pp).x,(*pp).y);
printf("origin is (%d%d)\n",pp->x,pp->y);
}
```

Answer:

```
origin is(0,0)
origin is(0,0)
```

115. What is the output for the program given below

```
typedef enum errorType{warning, error,
   exception,}error;
main()
{
error g1;
g1=1;
printf("%d",g1);
}
```

Answer:

```
Compiler error: Multiple declaration for error
```

116. typedef struct error{int warning, error, exception;}error;

```
main()
{
error g1;
g1.error =1;
printf("%d",g1.error);
}
```

Answer:

```
1
```

117. main()

```
{
struct student
{
char name[30];
struct date dob;
}stud;
struct date
{
int day,month,year;
};
scanf("%s%d%d%d",stud.rollno,&student.dob.day,&student.
   dob.month, &student.dob.year);
}
```

Answer:

```
Compiler Error: Undefined structure date
```

118. Is the following code legal?

```
struct a
```

```
{
int x;
struct a *b;
}
```

Answer:

Yes.

119. #include<stdio.h>

```
main()
{
struct xx
{
int x;
struct yy
{
char s;
struct xx *p;
};
struct yy *q;
};
}
```

Answer:

Compiler Error

120. Structures may contains

(a) multiple data items (b) single data items

(c) a only (d) a&b

121. The size of structure and union is same when they contain

(a) single member (b) any number of members

(c) a & b (d) none

122. The operator used to find the size of any variable

(a) sizeof (b) Sizeof

(c) sizeOf (d) all the above

123. The operator that is used to access the members of the structure using pointer variable

(a) . (b) ->

(c) * (d) none of the above

124. The operator used to access the member of the structure

(a) . (b) ->

(c) * (d) none of the above

125. The operator -> is same as the combination of the operators

(a) * and . (b) & and .

(c) * and & (d) none of the above

126. Bitfields areused to

(a) save time (b) save memory

(c) change order of allocation of memory

(d) none of the above

127. Union can store __________ number of values at a time

(a) all its members (b) only 1

(b) 2 (d) cannot hold value

128. what will be the position of the file marker?

```
a: fseek(ptr,0,SEEK_SET);
b: fseek(ptr,0,SEEK_CUR);
```

Answer:

a: The SEEK_SET sets the file position marker to the starting of the file.

b: The SEEK_CUR sets the file position marker to the current position of the file.

129. #include<stdio.h>

```
main()
{
FILE *ptr;
char i;
ptr=fopen("zzz.c","r");
while((i=fgetch(ptr))!=EOF)
printf("%c",i);
}
```

Answer:

contents of zzz.c followed by an infinite loop

130. There were 10 records stored in "somefile.dat" but the following program printed 11 names. What went wrong?

```
void main()
{
struct student
{
char name[30], rollno[6];
}stud;
FILE *fp = fopen("somefile.dat","r");
while(!feof(fp))
{
fread(&stud, sizeof(stud), 1 , fp);
puts(stud.name);
}
}
```

Explanation:

fread reads 10 records and prints the names successfully. It will return EOF only when fread tries to read another record and fails reading EOF (and

returning EOF). So it prints the last record again. After this only the condition feof(fp) becomes false, hence comes out of the while loop.

**131. #define assert(cond) if(!(cond)) **

```
(fprintf(stderr, "assertion failed: %s, file %s, line
   %d \n",#cond,\
__FILE__,__LINE__), abort())
void main()
{
int i = 10;
if(i==0)
assert(i < 100);
else
printf("This statement becomes else for if in assert
   macro");
}
```

Answer:

No output

132. What is the problem with the following code segment?

```
while ((fgets(receiving array,50,file_ptr)) != EOF) ;
```

Answer:

fgets returns a pointer.

133. If a file is opened in r+ mode then

(a) reading is possible (b) writing is possible
(c) it will be created if it does not exist
(d) appending is possible

134. If a file is opened in w+ mode then

(a) reading is possible (b) writing is possible
(c) it will be created if it does not exist
(d) appending is possible

135. If a file is opened in r mode then

(a) reading is possible (b) writing is possible

(c) it will be created if it does not exist

(d) appending is possible

136. If a file is opened in a mode then

(a) reading is possible (b) writing is possible

(c) it will be created if it does not exist

(d) appending is possible

137. ftell

(a) is a function

(b) gives the current file position indicator

(c) can be used to find the size of a file

(d) none of the above

138. Thefseekfunction

(a) needs 2 arguments

(b) makes rewind function unnecessary

(c) takes 3 arguments (d) none of the above

139. rewind function takes __ number of arguments

(a) 1 (b) 2

(c) 3 (d) 0

140. fseek(fptr,0,0) is equivalent to

(a) ftell (b) rewind

(c) a & b (d) none of the above

141. ferror function is used to find .... errors

(a) logical (b) file opening

(c) data (d) all the above

142. The contents of the file are lost if it is opened in .... mode

(a) a (b) w

(c) w+ (d) a+

143. The contents of the file are safe if it is opened in .... mode

(a) a (b) r

(c) a+b (d) all the above

144. The valid binary modes of operation are

(a) ab (b) rb+

(c) wb+ (d) ab+

145. rewind function is used to

(a) reset the file pointer (b) point it to the end of the file

(c) stay at current position (d) none of the above

146. feof function checks for

(a) file opening error (b) data error

(c) end of file (d) file closing error

147. The value returned by fopen() function when the file is not opened

(a) 0 (b) garbage value

(c) NULL (d) none of the above

148. The fcloseall() function performs

(a) closing of all the files

(b) closes all the files that are opened by that program

(c) closes only specified files (d) none of the above

149. The function that is not used for random access to files is

(a) rewind (b) ftell

(c) fseek (d) fprintf

150. The addressoperator & , cannot act on

(a) R-values (b) arithmetic expressions

(c) members of a structure (d) local variables

APPENDIX 1

Standard Library Functions

Following is the list of selected standard library functions. The functions have been classified into broad categories.

1. Arithmetic Functions

Function	Use
abs	Returns the absolute value of an integer
cos	Calculates cosine
cosh	Calculates hyperbolic cosine
exp	Raises the exponential e to the xth power
fabs	Finds absolute value
floor	Finds largest integer less than or equal to argument
fmod	Finds floating-point remainder
hypot	Calculates hypotenuse of right triangle
log	Calculates natural logarithm
log10	Calculates base 10 logarithm
modf	Breaks down argument into integer and fractional parts
pow	Calculates a value raised to a power
sin	Calculates sine
sinh	Calculates hyperbolic sine
sqrt	Finds square root

tan	Calculates tangent
tanh	Calculates hyperbolic tangent

2. Data Conversion Functions

Function	Use
atof	Converts string to float
atoi	Converts string to int
atol	Converts string to long
ecvt	Converts double to string
fcvt	Converts double to string
gcvt	Converts double to string
itoa	Converts int to string
ltoa	Converts long to string
strtod	Converts string to double
strtol	Converts string to long integer
strtoul	Converts string to an unsigned long integer
ultoa	Converts unsigned long to string

3. String Manipulation Functions

Function	Use
strcat	Appends one string to another
strchr	Finds first occurrence of a given character in a string
strcmp	Compares two strings
strcmpi	Compares two strings without regard to case
strcpy	Copies one string to another
strdup	Duplicates a string
stricmp	Compares two strings without regard to case (identical to strcmpi)
strlen	Finds length of a string
strlwr	Converts a string to lowercase

strncat	Appends a portion of one string to another
strncmp	Compares a portion of one string with portion of another string
strncpy	Copies a given number of characters of one string to another
strnicmp	Compares a portion of one string with a portion of another without regard to case
strrchr	Finds last occurrence of a given character in a string
strrev	Reverses a string
strset	Sets all characters in a string to a given character
strstr	Finds first occurrence of a given string in another string
strupr	Converts a string to uppercase

4. I/O Functions

Function	Use
Close	Closes a file
fclose	Closes a file
feof	Detects end-of-file
fgetc	Reads a character from a file
fgetchar	Reads a character from keyboard (function version)
fgets	Reads a string from a file
fopen	Opens a file
fprintf	Writes formatted data to a file
fputc	Writes a character to a file
fputchar	Writes a character to screen (function version)
fputs	Writes a string to a file
fscanf	Reads formatted data from a file
fseek	Repositions file pointer to given location
ftell	Gets current file pointer position
getc	Reads a character from a file (macro version)
getch	Reads a character from the keyboard

getche	Reads a character from keyboard and echoes it
getchar	Reads a character from keyboard (macro version)
gets	Reads a line from keyboard
inport	Reads a two-byte word from the specified I/O port
inportb	Reads one byte from the specified I/O port
kbhit	Checks for a keystroke at the keyboard
lseek	Repositions file pointer to a given location
open	Opens a file
outport	Writes a two-byte word to the specified I/O port
outportb	Writes one byte to the specified I/O port
printf	Writes formatted data to screen
putc	Writes a character to a file (macro version)
putch	Writes a character to the screen
putchar	Writes a character to screen (macro version)
puts	Writes a line to file
read	Reads data from a file
rewind	Repositions file pointer to beginning of a file
scanf	Reads formatted data from keyboard
sscanf	Reads formatted input from a string
sprintf	Writes formatted output to a string
tell	Gets current file pointer position
write	Writes data to a file

5. Memory Allocation Functions

Function	**Use**
calloc	Allocates a block of memory
farmalloc	Allocates memory from far heap
farfree	Frees a block from far heap
free	Frees a block allocated with *malloc*
malloc	Allocates a block of memory
realloc	Reallocates a block of memory

APPENDIX 2

List of C Library

A List of C Language Library is written as below:

- 2.1 assert.h
  - 2.1.1 assert
- 2.2 ctype.h
  - 2.2.1 is... Functions
  - 2.2.2 to... Functions
- 2.3 errno.h
  - 2.3.1 EDOM
  - 2.3.2 ERANGE
  - 2.3.3 errno
- 2.4 float.h
  - 2.4.1 Defined Values
- 2.5 limits.h
  - 2.5.1 Defined Values
- 2.6 locale.h
  - 2.6.1 Variables and Definitions
  - 2.6.2 setlocale
  - 2.6.3 localeconv
- 2.7 math.h
  - 2.7.1 Error Conditions
  - 2.7.2 Trigonometric Functions
    - 2.7.2.1 acos
    - 2.7.2.2 asin

APPENDIX 3

ASCII Character Set

□	0	1	2	3	4	5	6	7	8	9
0	nul	soh	stx	etx	eot	enq	ack	bel	bs	ht
1	nl	vt	ff	cr	so	si	dle	dc1	dc2	dc3
2	dc4	nak	syn	etb	can	em	sub	esc	fs	gs
3	rs	us	sp	!	"	#	$	%	&	'
4	(	)	*	+	,	-	.	/	0	1
5	2	3	4	5	6	7	8	9	:	;
6	<	=	>	?	@	A	B	C	D	E
7	F	G	H	I	J	K	L	M	N	O
8	P	Q	R	S	T	U	V	W	X	Y
9	Z	[	\	]	^	_	‘	a	b	c
10	d	e	f	g	h	i	j	k	l	m
11	n	o	p	q	r	s	t	u	v	w
12	x	y	z	{	|	}	~	del	□	□

The digits at the left of the table are the left digits of the decimal equivalent (0127) of the character code, and the digits at the top of the table are the right digits of the character code. For example, the character code for "R" is 82, and the character code for "0" is 48.

OTHER TITLES OF INTEREST

Expert C Programming

R Singh and I Singh

ISBN: 9789380016764
No. of Pages: 718
Price: INR 375.00

Expert C++ Programming

R Singh and I Singh

ISBN: 9789380016771
No. of Pages: 1086
Price: INR 475.00

Solved Programming in C

Rachhpal Singh and Ikvinderpal Singh

ISBN: 9789380016191
No. of Pages: 508
Price: INR 350.00

Other Books By The Same Author:

1. Solved Programming In C
2. Solved Programming In C++
3. Artificial Neural Networks
4. Digital Image Processing
5. Computer Oriented Numerical And Statistical Techniques
6. Introduction To Microprocessors: 8085 And 8086
7. Expert C Programming
8. Expert C++ Programming
9. C++ And Data Structures
10. Data Structures
11. Data Structures: An Algorithmic Approach Using C
12. Data Structures: An Algorithmic Approach Using C++
13. Electronics: Analog And Digital
14. Soft Computing
15. Fuzzy Systems
16. Test Your C Programming Skills
17. Test Your C++ Programming Skills

TEST YOUR
C
PROGRAMMING SKILLS

FOR

(All Indian Universities, Engineering and Technical Colleges and Institutions, IIT's and IT Organizations)